History of Mexico

An Enthralling Guide to Millennia of Majestic Civilizations, Conquests, and Transformations Shaping the Heart of the Americas

Table of Contents

PART 1: MEXICAN HISTORY 1
  INTRODUCTION 2
  SECTION ONE: EARLY MEXICO 500 BCE-1400 CE 4
  CHAPTER 1: MEXICO BCE 5
  CHAPTER 2: ANCIENT CIVILIZATIONS 10
  CHAPTER 3: THE AZTEC ARRIVE 19
  CHAPTER 4: THE FALL OF THE AZTEC 26
  SECTION TWO: BUILDING AN EMPIRE (1500-1880 CE) 33
  CHAPTER 5: CONQUEST AND COLONIZATION 34
  CHAPTER 6: WAR OF INDEPENDENCE AND THE FIRST EMPIRE 45
  CHAPTER 7: SANTA ANNA AND THE MEXICAN-AMERICAN WAR 53
  CHAPTER 8: LIBERAL AND CONSERVATIVE REFORMS (1850-1880 CE) 63
  SECTION THREE: REVOLUTION AND EVOLUTION (1870-PRESENT) 70
  CHAPTER 9: PORFIRIO'S MEXICO 71
  CHAPTER 10: REVOLUTION! 77
  CHAPTER 11: THE MEXICAN MIRACLE AND POST-WAR EVOLUTION 84
  CHAPTER 12: FROM CRISIS TO CONTEMPORARY: MODERN MEXICO 91
  SECTION FOUR: A THEMATIC OVERVIEW 96
  CHAPTER 13: LEGENDARY BATTLES AND EVENTS 97

CHAPTER 14: KEY FIGURES 100
CHAPTER 15: THE AMERICA QUESTION 107
CHAPTER 16: POP CULTURE AND STEREOTYPES.................................. 111
CONCLUSION.. 114
PART 2: HISTORY OF ANCIENT MEXICO 115
INTRODUCTION 116
SECTION ONE: KEY CIVILIZATIONS.. 119
CHAPTER 1: THE OLMECS 120
CHAPTER 2: THE MAYA... 128
CHAPTER 3: THE ZAPOTECS... 138
CHAPTER 4: THE MIXTECS... 146
CHAPTER 5: THE TOLTECS... 153
CHAPTER 6: THE AZTECS 162
SECTION TWO: HISTORICAL PERIODS 171
CHAPTER 7: PRECLASSIC MEXICO (1900 BCE-250 CE) 172
CHAPTER 8: MEXICO IN THE CLASSIC PERIOD (250-900 CE).............. 181
CHAPTER 9: POSTCLASSIC MEXICO (900-1521 CE) 189
SECTION THREE: THE FIGHT FOR ANCIENT MEXICO 196
CHAPTER 10: PREPARING FOR BATTLE.. 197
CHAPTER 11: THE SPANISH CONQUEST AND ITS AFTERMATH 205
SECTION FOUR: AN UNFORGETTABLE LEGACY 215
CHAPTER 12: LEGENDARY FIGURES.. 216
CHAPTER 13: ART, ARCHITECTURE, AND ARTIFACTS 225
CHAPTER 14: ANCIENT CITIES 237
CHAPTER 15: ANCIENT MYTHOLOGY AND COSMOLOGY 246
CHAPTER 16: ANCIENT MEXICAN CULTURE AND LEGACY 254
CONCLUSION.. 262
HERE'S ANOTHER BOOK BY ENTHRALLING HISTORY THAT
YOU MIGHT LIKE 266
FREE LIMITED TIME BONUS 267
WORKS CITED 268

Part 1: Mexican History

An Enthralling Guide to the History of Mexico, from Its Ancient Civilizations, the Spanish Conquest, and War of Independence to the Present

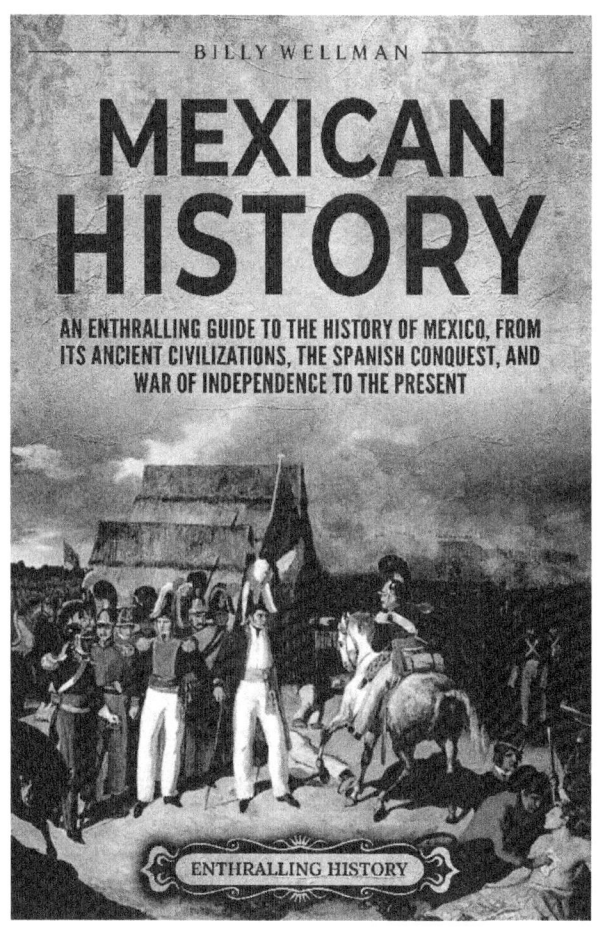

Introduction

History is, in many ways, a collection of stories. There is perhaps no more dynamic or misunderstood story than that of the people and place we call Mexico. Home to glorious ancient civilizations like the Olmec, Maya, and Aztec, it is one of a few places where the direct descendants of one of those civilizations, the Maya, still exist in large numbers and continue to practice some of their traditional culture. Huge basalt pyramids and vast cities once home to hundreds of thousands of people were swallowed by the jungles from which they were carved. The story of Mexico is the story of some of the earliest European colonization and a territory from which Spain extracted unimaginable wealth from silver mines worked by indigenous people. Mexico became the original "melting pot" where Spanish colonists married natives and descendants of African slaves and where natives, Africans, and Europeans combined cultures to form unique religious practices, dazzling works of art, and delicious cuisine.

The story of Mexico features larger-than-life characters like the Aztec Emperor Itzcóatl, conquistador **Hernán Cortés**, revolutionary Don Miguel Hidalgo, the first Mexican Emperor Agustín de Iturbide, the indomitable "Napoleon of the West" Antonio López de Santa Anna, the indigenous president and Liberal reformer **Benito Juárez**, the second Emperor Maximilian I, the dictator Porfirio Díaz, revolutionaries Emiliano Zapata and Pancho Villa, and the artist Frida Kahlo, to name just a few. The biographies of these individuals and their place in Mexican history are in the following pages, as well as the stories of the countless multitudes who have lived through times of war, disease, triumph, glory, feast, and famine and persevered through success and adversity.

The story presented here is one of diversity, clashing ideologies, invasions, battles, and assassinations but also the everyday life of farmers, ranchers, priests, teachers, lawyers, doctors, scientists, and so on. The narrative focuses on the leaders of Mexican society to show the source of decisions that rippled out into the rest of the country.

Three other countries make recurring appearances in the history of Mexico—Spain, France, and the United States. Each of these countries hoped to gain something from Mexico, and some were more successful than others. However, each has left its impression on the country in ways that even now are not fully understood. Therefore, at times, we must briefly explain what led these countries to Mexico, but these are only short asides. Overall, this book aims to provide a thorough history of the enthralling people and country that is Mexico.

Section One:
Early Mexico 500 BCE–1400 CE

Chapter 1: Mexico BCE

In the Astillero Mountains in North-Central Mexico, at an elevation of about 9,000 feet, the Chiquihuite Cave would seem an unlikely place to stir up controversy. Yet, after some initial digging indicated possible human habitation, archaeological excavations in 2016 and 2017 found evidence of human activity, mainly small stone tools. Radiocarbon dating of animal bones found near the tools indicated the site was about 16,000 years old. Conventional wisdom has long held that humans came to North America 13,000 years ago with the arrival of the Clovis Culture, known for its distinctive spearheads. The dating of artifacts in the Chiquihuite Cave contradicts this theory and indicates a much earlier arrival before or during a period known as the Last Glacial Maximum.

When this evidence was published in *Nature* in 2020, it caused a stir, and several archaeologists expressed their doubts. The rock tools could have been naturally broken rocks. The fact that the tools seemed to be only made of green and black limestone, which is not common locally, is shaky evidence, they claimed, compared to the fact that the site had no human remains, fossilized human excrement, or evidence of a fire pit. The animal bones in the cave also lacked the signs of butchering common in early human cave dwellings.

Chiquihuite Cave is not alone. Several sites around North and South America show signs of human activity before or during the Last Glacial Maximum and call into question the facts developed in the twentieth century.

There is more to the controversy of Chiquihuite Cave than simply whether an artifact was a stone tool or the exact date humans first entered the cave. The modern nation of Mexico, dynamic, vibrant, and often misunderstood, strives to define itself based on its past. The question of who the first Mexicans were and when and where Mexico began the journey to what it is today is critical in establishing a national narrative. What was prehistoric Mexico like? Who were the first people in Mexico? What were they like?

The evidence in Chiquihuite Cave provides little to answer these questions, but it might give a rough date for when the first people called Mexico home. If it was 16,000 years ago, they most likely traveled from the north in what many believe was a slow migration over thousands of years. According to the team working at Chiquihuite Cave, the first humans might have come into North America 30,000 years ago, more than twice as early as previously believed. Yet these people have left little evidence. All that can be said with any degree of certainty is that all the evidence points to a migration from Asia into North America several thousand years ago. However, even a close approximation is still being determined. From there, the first humans gradually spread south and east into the habitable regions of the Americas. The first Mexicans were among this population.

Humans first began congregating in an area known today as Mesoamerica, consisting of the modern-day nations of Costa Rica, Guatemala, Nicaragua, Honduras, El Salvador, Belize, and central and southern Mexico. Here, a distinct culture developed, defined by the cultivation of maize (corn), beans, avocado, squash, and vanilla sometime around 8000 BCE. This marks the beginning of what is known as the Mesoamerican Archaic period, which lasted until 2000 BCE. During this period, early Mexicans transitioned from a society focused on hunting to one more centered on agriculture. This is not to say that they stopped hunting but simply that farming became the primary food source. Women were responsible for much of the growing and harvesting of crops and maintained a high status in this society. Like other parts of the world at roughly the same time, the transition to agriculture is seen as a step towards a more advanced civilization.

Researchers have discovered the earliest evidence of plant cultivation in the Valley of Oaxaca in southern Mexico. During periods of abundance, Paleo-Indians, those early Mexicans, gathered in groups of twenty-five to fifty people; during lean times, the groups broke apart into nuclear families of four to six. The development of agriculture made food more abundant and food sources more reliable. This meant less frequent lean times, so the groups no longer split into smaller families. These continuously larger groups would later become sedentary and form villages. From this foundation, these natives developed more complex societies. Groups depended less and less on foraging and relied on male-led hunting parties to supplement their newly limited diet. Instead of a variety of foraged foods, these early Mexicans were now almost exclusively eating maize with a few substitutions.

The first evidence of horticulture suggests that the Paleo-Indians had small plots of land where they tried to grow food crops. Later, they expanded, and evidence of stone tools suggests they were clearing forests and digging. Then, as early as 7300 BCE, they began using slash-and-burn techniques to clear land for planting on Mexico's Caribbean coast. Domestication of plants soon followed. Plants were selected for their ability to be genetically modified. Teosinte, the wild ancestor of maize, was selectively bred to produce much larger plants with larger cobs. This new plant, maize or corn, was created in southern Mexico and spread from there. Dated to 4300 BCE, the first corn cobs had only two rows of kernels. The early Mexicans also similarly domesticated squash, beans, and chili peppers.

The Mesoamericans, Paleo-Indians who had now developed civilization, of the Archaic period used stone tools. They mostly used chert stone, often from a zone in Northern Belize. This chert was of fine quality and could be made into tools for woodcutting, scraping, digging, and as projectile points. Late in the Archaic period, Paleo-Indians in small settlements began producing Mexico's first pottery. Some examples of the earliest pieces were found in caves near Tehuacán, Mexico. The pottery was simple and monochromatic. In ceramics, this is called the Purrón period (2300–1500 BCE) after the cave where archaeologists found the first examples. The earthenware was often gourd-shaped, echoing that gourds had previously been used to store liquids. However, some earlier examples of ceramics exist, most notably at the site of Zohapilco, where 5,000-year-old human-shaped figures are believed to have been used in fertility rites.

Archaeological evidence indicates that Mesoamericans began to drift from nomadic to semi-nomadic and then semi-permanent settlements as early as 3000 BCE. This transition was not rigid but fluid. Sites on the Gulf Coast and central highlands show groups of foragers, hunters, and farmers living and working together in established permanent villages. The structures they built were perishable and not meant to last longer than a few seasons. Trade began to develop between these settlements, especially in obsidian, which has been found in villages far from its source. Villages often appeared along coasts thanks to the abundance of food and resources in sheltered lagoons. Shell mounds, large dumping sites comprised of shells, bones, and other discarded material, can be found at many of these locations. Many villages were only occupied seasonally, while some were active year-round. Resources were the first draw to many village sites, but as village populations grew and groups expanded, semi-arid areas also began to have settlements.

The late Archaic period from 2500 BCE to 1000 BCE blends into the Preclassic period when more permanent settlements were established and ceramics began to take on more pronounced styles. During this period, there was a general decline in burgeoning civilizations and a consolidation of cultures. From this, more identifiable cultures emerged. Most notable are the Olmec, discussed in the next chapter, and the Tlatilco culture, which developed in 1250 BCE in the Valley of Mexico.

The Tlatilco culture had permanent settlements. A chiefdom arose in the village of Tlatilco on Lake Texcoco. They made excellent pottery both for practical and ceremonial purposes. Tlatilco pottery is very fine, with iconography borrowed from the Olmec. It includes "baby-face figurines," statues no more than ten inches tall with cream or burnished white "slips" or coatings. The bodies are typically chubby and indistinct, while the faces are more detailed. These figures are abundant in the archaeological record. However, their purpose remains unknown. A pottery figure found at Tlatilco called the "Acrobat" shows a man resting on his elbows with his legs and back bending up behind him so that his feet rest on the top of his head. One of the knees has an opening that indicates this figure was used as a vessel for liquid.

The human remains of high-status individuals at Tlatilco show signs of artificial cranial deformation. Later civilizations continued this practice. From their records, modern researchers have learned that there were various methods for flattening and elongating a child's head that, once done, would remain into adulthood. The Tlatilco appear to have practiced these methods, as did the Olmec. This would remain a distinct part of Mesoamerican culture, along with the cultivation of maize and, eventually, human sacrifice. Much about artificial cranial deformation remains a mystery, which is today unhelpfully filled with various conspiracy theories.

The site of Tlatilco had many ceramic figures with deformities, including two-headed female figures. This has led some historians to suggest that the village might have been a cluster site for conjoined twins.

Still, the Tlatilco were a relatively small group. Central and Southern Mexico would produce much more prominent and advanced civilizations in the following 2,500 years. They would build huge, beautiful metropolitan centers with massive stone temples and large courts to play their dangerous sports. They created languages and religions with powerful kings and priests. They waged wars and conquered vast empires. Extensive trade networks spread like tendrils connecting cities to villages to coastlines. The most remarkable were the Olmec, Maya, Toltec, and Aztec.

Chapter 2: Ancient Civilizations

The Olmec

Tres Zapotes Head One.
HJPD, CC BY-SA 3.0 <https://creativecommons.org/licenses/by-sa/3.0>, via Wikimedia Commons; https://commons.wikimedia.org/wiki/File:Tres_Zapotes_Monument_A.jpg

Contemporary with the Tlatilco was a much larger and perhaps more sophisticated culture—the Olmec. Like the Tlatilco, the Olmec are an "archeological culture." This simply means that since they left no written records, they are defined solely by the artifacts that bear their hallmark. Therefore, we do not know what the Olmec called themselves. The name "Olmec" comes from later Spanish writings of a term in Nahuatl, an Aztec language. This term means "people of the rubber country," primarily in the northern part of the Isthmus of Tehuantepec. These "Olmec" lived near the southern Mexican Gulf Coast, where Olmec artifacts are found, so the name was applied to the ancient civilization. No Aztec ever met an Olmec.

Radiocarbon dating shows that the Olmec civilization existed from 1150 to 400 BCE, predating every other civilization in Mexico. The rise of the Olmec civilization coincides with what historians call the Formative period of Mesoamerica. At that time, many distinctive elements of Mesoamerican civilization were first found. Olmec sites contain skilled stone carvings, mostly of human figures with detailed expressions. Many of the Olmec cities feature earthen pyramids. The colossal heads, thrones, and statues of birds, cats, and monsters demonstrated the power of the Olmec leaders. The ability to organize the removal of stone from the Tuxtla Mountains, the delivery of the stone to the city, and the completion of the sculptures showed just how influential the leaders were. Some scholars believe each head represents a particular ruler.

The Olmec culture is perhaps best known for these colossal stone head carvings. It was just such a head that led archaeologists to suspect the existence of the Olmec. Noted by a farmer in the late 1800s and then mentioned in a book by American researchers in the 1920s, the Tres Zapotes Colossal Head One was excavated in 1938 by Smithsonian archaeologist Matthew Stirling. Once uncovered, the head was revealed to be four feet ten inches tall and appeared masculine, wearing some type of helmet. Weighing eight tons, it is made of a kind of stone not found in the region and must have been brought there over several miles of swamp land. How the Olmec managed this feat remains unknown.

The Tres Zapotes Colossal Head One might have been the first artifact to demonstrate the existence of the Olmec to the world, but the site at Tres Zapotes was far from the only Olmec site. Permanent city-temple complexes have also been found at San Lorenzo Tenochtitlan, La Venta, Laguna de los Cerros, and many smaller sites. The tallest Olmec head is eleven feet tall and is found at La Cobata in Veracruz. The La Cobata

Head is also the heaviest, weighing forty tons. Some scholars believe the La Cobata Head is actually unfinished because it lacks the rounded details of the other heads. It is also the only head found at La Cobata. The sixteen other heads can all be found at San Lorenzo, La Venta, and Tres Zapotes. There is also a possible colossal head at the site of Takalik Abaj in southwest Guatemala, dating to about 400 BCE. This is one of the first sites identified with the Maya culture. All the sites are in the Mexican states of Veracruz and Tabasco, often called Olman.

From the beginning of the Olmec period until about 900 BCE, San Lorenzo was the center of Olmec culture. More colossal heads have been found here than at any other site, the largest of which weighs twenty-eight tons. The heads are made from basalt from the mountains to the north of San Lorenzo.

After the decline of San Lorenzo in 900 BCE, the site of La Venta became the new center of Olmec power. La Venta is situated on an island in a coastal swamp closer to the Gulf of Mexico. Unlike the stonework found at San Lorenzo, La Venta's surviving structures are primarily made of clay, as stone was not abundant in the area. The city is oriented north-south along twelve miles and features a great pyramid (Complex C), four stone heads, and a plaza oriented to the star Polaris. This last feature shows that the Olmec had some understanding of astronomy. The largest of the four heads is 7.9 feet tall and weighs twenty-four tons. There are also seven basalt altars, five formal tombs, and many other monuments, sculptures, and large pavements made of jadeite.

Olmec carved jadeite with extreme skill. Starting in 900 BCE, Olmec artists began to carve life-sized jade masks that looked almost like molded plastic, showing their ability to sculpt and polish this hard stone. Their art always served a purpose, representing a living person or a religious entity. They believed the Earth was a living creature and depicted it as a monster with a huge mouth.

The Olmec worshiped the gods of wind, rain, and maize. Much of the Olmec prosperity and stability seems to have come from maize, which they harvested in large amounts and traded with outside villages. The maize god is often shown with an ear of corn protruding from his cleft head.

The Olmec spread their religion to other areas. Their empire, if it can be called that, was not one of domination but of the abundance of agriculture and the importance of maintaining good harvests. The Olmec sacrificed treasured objects to their gods at sacred mountain sites, including rubber balls and jade axes. The Olmec also worshiped at sacred caves, often with underground water features. Priests would collect the sacred water that ran into pools for various rites. These elements—corn god, rain god, sacred mountains, and caves—would appear in later Mesoamerican civilizations. The Olmec's high regard for the jaguar as a spiritual animal would also carry into later nations.

The Olmec were the first civilization to domesticate the cacao plant. Cacao beverages were a staple of many religious ceremonies, and the remains of the drinks can still be found inside pottery discovered in excavations. These very early chocolate drinks bear little resemblance to what we consume today. For one thing, the fruit pulp was left in the drink. The cacao tree was considered the "World Tree" and a conduit to the gods. The cacao beans were left to ferment and mixed with water, vanilla, cinnamon, and sometimes red chili. The drink was poured carefully into a pot to create a large amount of foam, which was believed to represent the wind god. The beverage was used in ceremonies or prescribed to cure ailments like skin conditions, fever, and seizures. It was believed that cocoa could drive the illness out of the body. Later civilizations believed humans were made from sweet things like corn and cacao. The Olmec likely believed this, as well. They did not consume it regularly like the Maya and Aztec; instead, it remained an item of religious and medicinal use.

The Maya

The Maya developed during the Archaic and Pre-Classical periods. However, their greatest impact came when they began to build cities around 750 BCE. The Maya civilization was not a true empire but comprised of loosely allied city-states. These cities featured monumental stone buildings like the temple pyramids that would become famous symbols of their achievements. Their greatest city was Tikal, in modern-day Guatemala, which had a population of over 100,000. The city of Coba held an estimated 50,000 people and reached its peaks from 500 to 900 CE. The tallest pyramid found at Coba, in the Quintana Roo state of Mexico, is Ixmoja, which stands at 138 feet. It was one of the biggest and most powerful cities in Yucatán in its day. Coba retained close contact with Tikal and arranged alliances with local cities. It also had competition from the massive central Mexican city of Teotihuacán. The Maya maintained long-distance trade between the lowlands in Mexico's Yucatán and the highlands of Guatemala.

The Maya also developed a sophisticated glyph language that was not deciphered by modern scholars until 1973. Like other Mesoamericans, they cultivated and mainly ate maize, beans, squash, and chili peppers.

The Olmec clearly influenced the Maya. Like the Olmec, they played sports with rubber balls in large courts. Most large cities had a king-priest and a noble class that married within their caste. The king or queen was the Tree of Life; through them, the city could have contact with the gods. Part of the religious rites for the Maya civilization was blood-letting and sometimes human sacrifice. Most of their religious rituals were conducted on the tops of their temple pyramids, which were made of stone and often the city's focal point.

The Maya developed an incredibly accurate calendar system, the greatest calendar of all ancient peoples. One of their calendars, the Haab cycle, is 365 days long and thus corresponds to the solar year. It also has nineteen months; eighteen are made of twenty days, and one month is just five days long. The sacred calendar, Tzolk'in, has a cycle of 260 days that corresponds with both the lunar cycle and the gestation period for human pregnancies. The calendar round is made by combining the Haab and Tzolk'in calendars. This calendar does not repeat itself until fifty-two cycles of 365 days have passed, meaning fifty-two years, the age at which a Maya could be considered an elder.

Anything over fifty-two years required a special calendar known as the Long Count. This was often used for mythical or ancient historical events. Their creation date is thus the equivalent of August 11, 3114 BCE. This calendar system is still used by Maya people who live in Mesoamerica, where their ancestors lived thousands of years ago. A misunderstanding of the Long Count led many to believe that a disaster would occur on December 21, 2012, the winter solstice that ended one part of the Long Count. For the Maya, the truth was that this simply meant the passing of a new time period, like the changing of a century or millennium.

The Classic Maya period was from 250 to 900 CE, which is sometimes broken up into the Early (250-600), Late (600-800), and Terminal (800-900). The city of Tikal constructed its huge monumental structures primarily during the Late Maya period. At Tikal, archaeologists discovered the tomb of one Maya ruler, or more accurately *ajaw*, Jasaw Chan K'awill I, also called "Ah Cacao" and "Sky Rain." He ruled Tikal from 682 until his death in 734. He notably defeated a rival Maya city of Calakmul, a powerful city in the Mexican lowlands. It was the seat of the so-called "Kingdom of the Snake" because the *ajaws* of Calakmul called themselves the Lords of the Snake.

During the Terminal period of the Classic Maya timeline, many sites, including Calakmul, Tikal, and other great cities like Copán and Palenque, began a rapid decline and were eventually abandoned. In many places, the forests reclaimed the sites, and it would be centuries before they would be uncovered. Theories for the collapse are plentiful. Some scholars suggest climate change, deforestation, warfare, disease, or foreign invasion, but no one theory seems to answer the mystery of the decline of the Maya. While their ancestors still lived in parts of Mexico, Guatemala, and elsewhere, the construction of stone structures and massive metropolitan areas ceased by 900 CE.

One theory for the decline is the collapse of Maya's intricate trade routes, which included Teotihuacán. This huge city of almost 200,000 residents began its swift decline around 750 or as early as 600 CE. Teotihuacán was not the original name of the city. This was an Aztec term meaning "Place of the Gods." This site in Central Mexico, first inhabited by humans around 600 BCE, was really a collection of a few scattered villages. In 200 BCE, Teotihuacán took on a more urban format. The site featured springs that drew farmers together. From about 1 CE, the city grew explosively. While the citizens lived in what were essentially apartment complexes, not all apartments were made the same. There is evidence of at least three different classes of dwellings due to the material used, size of rooms, and distance from the city center.

From 1 to 300 CE, Teotihuacán built many of its most notable structures, including the Pyramid of the Sun, the Pyramid of the Moon, the Temple of the Feathered Serpent, and the Avenue of the Dead. During the period from 300 to 600 CE, the city's population reached its maximum, making it the sixth-largest city in the world at the time. Half of the entire population of the Valley of Mexico lived in the sprawling city of Teotihuacán.

Teotihuacán peaked in 450, and its influence spread across Mesoamerica. However, it is unclear if this influence was direct, through militarism, or indirect, through trade and culture. The city remains mysterious because there is nothing to indicate the presence of a king or leader of the city. Unlike the cities of the Zapotec, Maya, and Olmec, there is no evidence of ball courts or even depictions of warfare.

Despite obvious contact with the literate Maya culture, there is no evidence of any writing in Teotihuacán. Their religion was complex. They practiced human sacrifice and had many gods, primarily the Great Goddess of Teotihuacán and the Feathered Serpent. The Feathered Serpent, called Quetzalcoatl by the Aztec and Kukulkan by the Yucatec Maya, was a deity thought to have originated with the Olmec. The people of Teotihuacán certainly worshiped this god as they built the Temple of the Feathered Serpent. However, there is evidence that, at some point, the cult of the Feathered Serpent went out of favor, and some religious leaders were forced to leave the city.

Some of the apartment complexes of the nobles have burn marks that most likely coincide with the city's decline. Many scholars believe internal strife led to the end of Teotihuacán. The city's population dropped dramatically. Though it was still inhabited, it never regained anything close to its size and power during its peak. The Maya cities then began their rapid decline.

Some scholars alternatively theorize that the decline of both Teotihuacan and the Maya can be ultimately traced back to climate changes due to the eruption of Ilopango Volcano in El Salvador, which is today a crater lake. This eruption could have led to poor crop yields and widespread famine in Mesoamerica. The famine led to the decline and breakup of the cities and caused the Maya to stop building monumental architecture.

The Toltec

After the decline of the Maya and Teotihuacán, the city of Tula became the center of what would become known as the Toltec Empire. While this nation was powerful and its influence spread far and wide, certain aspects remain unclear. For instance, the name "Tula" is derived from a phrase that means "near the reeds," but the later Aztec used it to mean any large urban area, perhaps indicating that the people were as thick as a bundle of reeds. For example, Teotihuacán, Cholula, and Tenochtitlan were all referred to as Tula. Thus, it is unclear if this was truly the name of the city or simply the name of cities in general. At the site of Tula is the Temple of Quetzalcoatl (Feathered Serpent Pyramid), which is topped with four massive basalt columns of warrior figures. The site features ball courts and images of jaguars and eagles similar to those of Maya sites. The city rose to prominence in the current state of Hidalgo, Mexico, in 900 CE. At its height, it had a population of 60,000. Tula was close to valuable obsidian sources used to make Mesoamerican tools. Its inhabitants traded as far away as Guatemala and Costa Rica. Today, the land around Tula is semi-arid; however, it is believed that the Tula Valley received more rainfall during the Classic period so that agriculture could support the population.

Traditionally, the first Toltec king or *tlatoani* was Mimixcoamazatzin, crowned in 700 CE. This has been disputed, with some believing the Toltec did not form a monarchy until 752. The first *tlatoani*, then, might have been Chalchiuhtlanetzin or even the mythological figure Cē Ācatl Topiltzin, who, legend says, was the son of the god of war, fire, and the hunt—Cloud Serpent. The stories claim that Cē Ācatl led the Toltec to Tula and convinced them to give up human sacrifice. He was said to have formed the cult of the serpent. When he turned fifty-three, one year after he had reached the age of an elder, he burned himself alive in a canoe. Cē Ācatl was so beloved by his people that many Toltec leaders after him claimed to be directly descended from him. Even the later Mexica people adopted his name to better rule over the Toltec.

In Tula, the secular warrior caste rose against the priest class, and the cult of Quetzalcoatl was overthrown. The warriors put Tezcatlipoca, the god of life and death, in the Feathered Serpent's place. This led to a marked increase in human sacrifices. According to the legends, Quetzalcoatl was not destroyed but had transcended to heaven as the Morningstar or the planet Venus in the night sky. Before going to heaven, it was said, he created the people of the Age of the Fifth Sun—the Nahua. These people would become the Aztec, Mexica, and other groups that speak the Nahuatl language. Tula continued to thrive until 1170, when it is believed the Chichimeca, a semi-nomadic Nahua people, destroyed the city.

However, this was not the end of the Toltec culture, which combined with elements of Maya culture in various sites in the Yucatan, especially Chichén Itzá, where the cult of Quetzalcoatl, called Kukulan there, flourished. Chichén Itzá became the most powerful city in the region for a hundred years before being overthrown by people from Mayapan. This city became the Yucatan dominant power 100 kilometers west of Chichén Itzá from 1220 to 1440.

However, the buildings at Mayapan appear to be inferior copies of what is found at other, earlier Maya sites. Like other Maya and Toltec cities, Mayapan was ruled by a dynastic monarchy drawn from a single, powerful family. In this case, it was the Cocom family, who were Maya. The ruling family of Chichén Itzá, called the Itzá, were, in fact, Toltec.

However, most of this information is based on legends, and the timing of events is not certain. For example, the Cocom family was supposed to have been led by a man named Hunac Ceel, who had been thrown into the *cenote* (sinkhole) near Chichén Itzá as a sacrifice after the Itzá had defeated him in battle. However, he climbed out of the watery pit and claimed divine protection. Most of this story, which also includes star-crossed lovers and rain god prophecies, is from the Books of Chilam Balam from the seventeenth and eighteenth centuries. The author of these books, Chilam Balam (which roughly means "Jaguar Prophet") is a legendary figure in his own right. These books are lore, not without merit, but lacking the kind of fact-based analytics scholars desire.

For students of ancient history, this is nothing new. The best evidence is in archaeological research, but much still needs to be done at Maya and Toltec sites in Mesoamerica. Perhaps somewhere in the jungles of southern Mexico are the answers to why so many Maya sites declined so rapidly. Perhaps there is a key piece of evidence to unlock the mysteries of Teotihuacán.

Chapter 3: The Aztec Arrive

The Mexica, as the Aztec called themselves, were believed to have been a semi-nomadic people. They claimed a homeland called Aztlán, which has so far not been located. They worshiped a supreme god of war, Huitzilopochtli, who led them to form a new city where they found an eagle eating a snake while perched on a cactus. They found the site on an island in the western part of Lake Texcoco in the Valley of Mexico. In 1325, they founded the city of Tenochtitlan there. Eventually, they adopted the *tlatoani* system of government in which the city was governed primarily by a spiritual and civil leader. This eventually became a single dynastic king in 1426. From 1428, the Aztec began an imperial expansion that rivaled the Inca in South America. Its rulers identified themselves with the Toltec.

Itzcóatl (1380-1440) was the fourth king of Tenochtitlan and the founder of the Aztec Empire. He led the Aztec to overthrow the Tepanec, another Nahua people, in 1428. Under his leadership, they formed the Triple Alliance between Tenochtitlan, Texcoco, and Tlacopan. This was the basis for the empire. However, the exact nature of the Aztec Empire remains unclear. It is not completely clear that anyone in the Mexico Basin regarded the political situation around Lake Texcoco as a triple alliance. It appears that Tenochtitlan was the chief city, and the ruler of Tenochtitlan was similar to the emperors of Europe. It was followed closely by Texcoco and then Tlacopan. Each of those cities represented the center for certain ethnic groups. Texcoco was the center of the Acolhuaque people, Tlacopan belonged to the Tepanec, and Tenochtitlan was the capital of the Mexica. Yet, much of the information about the Aztec comes from Spanish sources after the arrival of the conquistadors.

Part of the desire for more territory was to expand the agricultural system to feed a growing population. The Aztec had invented the *chinampas* system, which relied on "floating gardens" built up from shallow lake beds to create rectangular fields that could produce a large yield. They first built fences with interwoven branches and then filled the space within the fence with soil and other materials, where they planted crops. The *chinampas* needed water to replenish what was lost by evaporation, so the Aztec built complicated canals and irrigation systems to direct water into their fields.

The empire's primary sources of income were taxes and tribute. Unconquered city-states of strategic importance would be required to hand over periodic tributes to the Triple Alliance and the emperor in the form of luxury items, practical goods, or money, which came in the form of bolts of cloth called cotton mantas. Conquered cities provided regular taxes through a complicated system in which goods went to Tenochtitlan, but people also worked for the government and palaces for a portion of the time. In this way, the Aztec could complete large structures and monuments. All young males owed military service, but the details of these requirements are not clear. They also collected a portion of all the goods brought to market.

The Aztec system of taxation was complicated and extended far into their empire. Each city had two tax officials, one in the city and the other in Tenochtitlan. In this way, the Mexica commanded a true empire and not simply a collection of allied city-states. Some cities paid their tribute to Tenochtitlan, Texcoco, and Tlacopan, and it was split into fifths, with the first two cities getting two-fifths each and Tlacopan receiving one-fifth. Some cities gave tribute or taxes to only one of the members of the Triple Alliance.

As the first emperor, Itzcóatl took the title *Culhua teuctli* or "Lord of the Culhua-Mexica." Itzcóatl ordered the historical codices of the Valley of Mexico to be burned and allowed the Aztec to write their own version of history, which prominently featured the god of war, Huitzilopochtli. Itzcóatl continued building projects, including causeways and temples in Tenochtitlan. When he died, power passed to his nephew, Moctezuma I, in 1440. Moctezuma ruled over a period of peace and the expansion of Tenochtitlan power. His name means "he is angry like a lord." On his coronation, many prisoners were sacrificed, and the ruler of Texcoco crowned him with a turquoise crown called the "fire crown." It was under Moctezuma that the Triple Alliance was officially solidified. Moctezuma built a two-piped aqueduct system with the ruler of Texcoco, Nezahualcoyotl, to supply fresh water to both of their cities. The empire expanded beyond the Valley of Mexico and into the Gulf Coast, where Tenochtitlan gained access to cocoa, shells, cotton, and fruits.

After a series of natural disasters—namely, swarms of locusts, famine, crop destruction, and floods—Moctezuma ordered increased human sacrifice to appease the gods. This led to what has become known as a "flower war" or "flowery war." Beginning sometime in the mid-1450s, these were a series of ritual wars with neighboring populations. Some believe they were meant to gather prisoners to meet the higher demand for sacrifices. A flower war was not like a typical war. The battles were fought at predetermined places and predetermined times. The battle began with the burning of a pyre of paper and incense. No range weapons were used in a flower war. Instead, the Aztec used weapons like the *macuahuitl*.

Warriors brandishing macuahuitl.
https://commons.wikimedia.org/wiki/File:Historia_general_de_las_cosas_de_Nueva_Espa%C3%B1a_vol._1_folio_74v.png

The flower wars were chiefly between the Aztec and the Tlaxcala, Huejotzingo, and Chola of the Puebla-Tlaxcala Valley of Central Mexico. Flower wars could last a long time, though they were typically less lethal than traditional wars. Each side was equal in number, allowing the Aztec to show off their fighting prowess. To die in a flower war was considered more noble than dying in a typical war. The name for death in a flower war was *xochi miquiztli*, which means "flowery or blissful death." Another possible reason for the flower wars was to train warriors in combat.

What began as a flower war with the city of Chalco erupted into a full-blown war in 1446. This was partly because Chalco refused to provide materials to build a new Great Temple for the god of war. Moctezuma conquered Chalco in 1465, and the kings of Chalco were sent into exile.

It is believed that Moctezuma's half-brother, Tlacaelel, was the true power behind the throne and, therefore, the chief architect of the Triple Alliance and the Aztec Empire's expansion. Under Itzcóatl and Moctezuma, he held the role of first adviser to the ruler. Tlacaelel promoted the idea that the Aztec were a chosen people and strengthened laws pertaining to the different classes of Aztec society. Only nobles could build houses with more than one story, and they could build towers only by the gods' direction. Commoners could not have lip plugs or golden armbands and were prohibited from wearing certain materials. Mixing between classes could be punished with death. He is said to have established a policy that all newly conquered people's books should be burned to promote pro-Aztec history. Tlacaelel dedicated the newest Great Temple, or Templo Mayor, in the center of Tenochtitlan in 1484. The structure measured 328 by 262 feet at the base and would later be dismantled to build the Mexico City Metropolitan Cathedral. Some believe this period marked the peak of Aztec civilization.

Moctezuma died in 1469. The throne was then passed to his daughter, Atotoztli II. She married Tezozomoc, the son of Itzcóatl, and had three sons: Axayacatl, Tizoc, and Ahuitzotl. Some sources show her as the ruler of the Triple Alliance on her own, while others omit her, perhaps indicating that she acted as regent while her son, Axayacatl, was still a child. If this is the case, Axayacatl came to the throne upon the death of his grandfather in 1469. Being a new and young ruler, the kings of other cities saw Axayacatl's accession as an opportunity to challenge Tenochtitlan's primacy in the Valley of Mexico. Moquihuix, the leader of Tlatelolco and Axayacatl's brother-in-law, decided to end Mexica dominance.

Moquihuix was the fourth *tlatoani* of Tlatelolco. While he had a child with Axayacatl's younger sister, Chalchiuhnenetzin, it was said he neglected his wife and preferred the company of other women. The rumors of the time said she was forced to wear coarse clothing and sleep in a corner and that Moquihuix beat her. More outlandish legends concerning Chalchiuhnenetzin said she had many lovers while she was married but had her lovers killed and turned into statues so that she wouldn't be discovered. However, she eventually kept three lovers alive. When her husband discovered her with all three, he had the lovers and her entire household put to death. It was said that this and the queen's treatment led Axayacatl to attack Tlatelolco.

This is just one version of the events leading to the war between Tenochtitlan and Tlatelolco. Another version claims that the Aztec emperor got wind of Tlatelolco's plans to challenge his authority and attacked the other city before it formed a larger alliance. Many years after the event, a story was told that problems between the two cities began in the fifth year of Axayacatl's reign when some young Tenochca men attacked Tlatelolco young women in a market. Then, later, a Tlatelolco canal was found destroyed, and the Tenochca were also blamed for this.

Regardless of what led to the war, the Battle of Tlatelolco occurred around 1473. There may have been an initial battle in which the Tlatelolco attacked Tenochtitlan and were beaten back. Then, Axayacatl led an attack on the city of Tlatelolco. Moquihuix, the leader of Tlatelolco, and a trusted advisor, Teconal, had been outmaneuvered by Axayacatl. The hope of removing Tenochtitlan dominance had turned into a fight to preserve their city and their lives.

Axayacatl and his adviser wished to avoid more bloodshed and sent a messenger to reason with Moquihuix. The messenger returned with a message from Tlatelolco telling Axayactl to prepare for the people of Tlatelolco to avenge the deaths of their fellow countrymen. The messenger was sent back, and this time, Teconal beheaded the messenger. Axayacatl responded with action. The Tenochca were fierce in battle and quickly overwhelmed the Tlatelolco. Moquihuix and Teconal, seeing that the battle was lost, fled up the steps of Tlatelolco's pyramid temple. Axayacatl climbed the pyramid after them and found both men clinging to the altar. He killed them both and dragged their bodies out so that everyone could see the result of the rebellion. After this point, Tlatelolco was no longer considered a partner in the Triple Alliance but had to pay tribute to Tenochtitlan the same as any other conquered city.

The following year, Axayacatl invaded the Matlatzinca people's land in the rich Toluca Valley. He had previously fought these people and lost. He was personally hit by a sling and suffered a serious injury. However, when the Aztec returned to the Toluca Valley, they captured over 11,000 prisoners, who were sacrificed to the gods. They conquered the city of Calixtlahuaca and settled Nahua families there to discourage rebellion.

In the 1470s, Axayacatl faced off against the Purépecha Empire, which existed mainly in the region that is now the Mexican state of Michoacán. The Purépecha people were great metallurgists and worshipped Kurikaweri, the sun god. The Aztec first captured frontier towns. They captured many prisoners, who were quickly sacrificed.

In some instances, it is claimed that 80,000 prisoners were sacrificed during a celebration. However, the true number of human sacrifices during the height of Aztec power must be viewed with some skepticism. It should be remembered that these totals come to modern scholars through the filter of Spanish conquerors who wished to present Mesoamericans as inhumane and thus worthy of being subjugated. Accounts from Aztec during this period, mainly found in carved stelae found at archaeological sites, show the human sacrifice of enemy leaders but no large-scale executions. There is considerable logic to this. An empire that survived on tribute and taxes would not last long if it killed many people it had recently conquered. The "sacrifice" might have been a ceremony in which large numbers of people gave themselves to the authority of the Aztec. Also, the sheer physical task of systematically sacrificing tens of thousands of people in prescribed rituals makes this skepticism reasonable. It warrants a closer inspection of historical and archaeological evidence on mass human sacrifice.

One of the best sources for this period is Friar Diego Durán's writings. Durán was born and raised in Mexico and learned the Aztec language, Nahuatl, at an early age. He retrieved the stories of the late Aztec Empire through Aztec and was criticized in his own time for being biased towards the Aztec people. However, the stories he was told were about events many decades before he wrote them down, and the Aztec's own codices do not give the details provided in Duran's writing. His account of the Battle of Tlatelolco, in which Axayacatl defeats Moquihuix by killing him at the top of the temple, is the most detailed account of this battle, though it took place a hundred years before he recorded the story. Thus, the reader must retain a healthy skepticism about any accounts of the Aztec and their empire.

In 1476, Axayacatl faced off once again against the Purépecha Empire. He was soundly defeated. This defeat was significant because it was the only large-scale defeat for the Aztec up to that point. Axayacatl spent the rest of his life defending himself against critics, like his two brothers. In response, he is known to have written two poems. "Song of Axayacatl" is a rebuke of his critics, and "Song of the Ancients" is a lament of his defeat by the Purépecha. While still young, Axayacatl fell ill in 1480 and died the next year. He was succeeded by his brother Tizoc, who was the first leader of Tenochtitlan to take the title *huey tlatoani*, which means "supreme ruler." Tizoc was emperor for only five years, but he expanded the empire.

When Tizoc died, some suspected he was poisoned, and his younger brother Ahuitzotl became emperor. Ahuitzotl came to power in 1486 and quickly proved himself a great military leader. He doubled the size of the lands under Aztec control. He conquered the Mixtec, Zapotec, and people on the western coast of Mexico. He died in 1502 and was succeeded by his nephew, Moctezuma II, the great-grandson of the first Moctezuma and son of the emperor Axayacatl. He was already esteemed for his military prowess and his abilities as a priest when he came to power. He had no way of knowing that during his reign, the world would change completely for the people of Mexico.

Chapter 4: The Fall of the Aztec

Born in 1485, Hernando Cortés belonged to a lesser noble family in the town of Medellín, which was then part of the Kingdom of Castile in what is today the country of Spain. His family had hoped he'd pursue a legal career, but instead, he went to the "New World" recently discovered by Christopher Columbus. Hernando, whose name would later be shortened to Hernán, arrived on the island of Hispaniola in 1504. He was just eighteen years old. His relative, Nicolás de Ovando, was the island's governor, and he awarded Cortés an encomienda. This meant he was granted a certain number of indigenous laborers who worked on the property he had been given. Under this system, the laborers were supposed to have benefits, but in practice, it amounted to communal slavery.

Cortés took part in the conquests of Cuba and part of Hispaniola. He was awarded more lands and more slaves for his efforts. He aided Diego Velázquez de Cuéllar in the conquest of Cuba, and when Velázquez was made governor of New Spain, Cortés eventually became secretary to the governor. However, fifteen years after arriving in New Spain, he began to harbor ambitions to lead his own conquest.

By that time, relations between Cortés and Velázquez had become strained. Juan de Grijalva had led an expedition onto the mainland of Mexico and was said to have established a colony. Velázquez appointed Cortés as captain of an expedition to go further into the mainland. In 1518, Cortés gathered men and three ships in a month's time. Velázquez changed his mind and rescinded his order, but Cortés ignored this and left in February of 1519. Disobeying a direct order and sailing to the mainland was a daring risk. However, Cortés was shrewd and understood that his mutinous behavior might be overlooked if he could convince the Crown back in Spain that he had done something great. There had been rumors that the land that would one day be called Mexico was rich in precious metals. On these rumors, Cortés and his men set off across the Gulf of Mexico to make their fortunes or die in the attempt.

Moctezuma II might not have heard of the strange people coming to the eastern shore in his new palace in Tenochtitlan, but he would learn of them soon enough. Both sides were completely ignorant of the other and felt secure in their own superiority over anyone else they might meet.

Cortés commanded a small army of 500 men, including slaves, horses, and cannons. They landed in the Yucatan and met Geronimo Aguilar, a Franciscan friar who had survived a shipwreck but was a captive of the local Maya people. He had learned the Chontal Mayan language and acted as an interpreter for Cortés. While the conquistador had no real military experience, he proved to be a steadfast leader. He won several battles against the local people and, in one instance, was given twenty young indigenous women, whom he converted to Christianity. He took one of the young women, known today as La Malinche, as his mistress. She acted as an interpreter, advisor, and intermediary to Cortés. She knew the language of the Aztec as well as Chontal Mayan. The Aztec could speak to her, and she would translate to Aguilar, who would then translate to Cortés. To dispel any notions of retreat, Cortés had his eleven ships sunk.

Meanwhile, Moctezuma had undoubtedly heard of newcomers conquering the Yucatan Maya with strange beasts and weapons. He sent emissaries to meet with these people once they reached Aztec land. Still, the empire needed to function, and Tenochtitlan needed to continue. He had recently built a zoo called the *Totocalli*, or "House of Birds," which held a wide array of birds, as well as wolves, jaguars, and snakes that were sometimes fed deer, turkeys, or sacrificial victims. It was the fall of 1519, and no one living in Tenochtitlan could have guessed that the mighty Aztec Empire would fall apart in two years. The Mexica were in a strong position. Moctezuma had conquered several neighboring cities. Still, there were constant threats.

In 1516, the leader of Texcoco died suddenly. It has been suggested he died under suspicious circumstances that might have involved

Moctezuma. He had not declared an heir, and since he had many sons, there was a vote to decide who would be the next king. Moctezuma made it known that he favored the election of Cacamatzin out of the six sons because he was the emperor's nephew. The vote went Moctezuma's way, and Cacamatzin became the new king of Texcoco. However, another son, Ixtlilxochitl, disagreed with the decision because he felt Moctezuma had put Cacamatin on the throne to manipulate him. The timing of events is unclear, but Ixtlilxochitl went to Metztitlán to raise an army to defeat his brother. The new king asked for assistance from his uncle, Moctezuma. Ixtlilxochitl gathered an army of 100,000 men and began to march on Texcoco, which he placed under siege, and occupied several surrounding cities. This resulted in a stalemate. Eventually, the brothers agreed to a peaceful settlement in which they split up the region between them, with Cacamatin remaining in control of Texcoco. This was how the matter stood when Cortés and his army continued their journey inland, where they had heard of grand cities and great wealth.

Later portrait of Moctezuma (Xocoyotzin) II.
https://en.wikipedia.org/wiki/File:Moctezuma_Xocoyotzin_Newberry.jpg

As Cortés continued his march, he allied with indigenous people in Cempoala and Tlaxcala. He fought with the Otomis and Tlaxcalans, as well. However, he won many to his side by demonstrating that the Spanish were enemies of the Aztec. Cortés was, by this time, beyond the authority of the governor of Cuba and instead decided to report directly to the Spanish king. This was Carlos I, more commonly known as Charles V, the newly crowned Holy Roman Emperor. Besides being the king of Spain, he was the Archduke of Austria, Duke of Burgundy, and head of the incredibly powerful Hapsburg family. As Holy Roman Emperor, he ruled parts of Germany and Italy and colonies all over the globe. His possessions in the "new" world would make him the first ruler of an empire where the sun never sets. Despite being from a low noble family, Cortés was not intimidated by the prospect of writing directly to the king, and his series of letters remain some of the best records of the early Spanish conquest of Mexico. However, Cortés was not a historian and had his own motives for presenting events in Mexico in a certain light to his king. First, he wanted to make himself look good. Secondly, he wanted to justify his actions, especially since his expedition was illegal. Lastly, he wanted to make sure he gave the impression that he acted only as a servant of Charles V and the Roman Catholic Church.

In October 1519, Cortés and his small army marched on Cholula, the second-largest city in central Mexico. The Great Pyramid of Cholula, which the Spanish called a tower, was then the largest temple pyramid in the Americas. In fact, Cholula was much older than Tenochtitlan and had grown into a large city around the same time as Teotihuacan. However, it was not abandoned like many Mesoamerican Classic period sites. Cholula had once been allied with Tlaxcala but, in 1517, had allied with the more powerful Aztec. The king of Tlaxcala had allied with Cortés and led him to Cholula, presumably in an act of retribution. Cholula was not, in fact, on the way to Tenochtitlan, so it gives credence to the idea that the Tlaxcalans orchestrated the trip.

The Spanish were welcomed into Cholula and gathered for a feast with the city's nobles. According to Cortés and other Spanish, they became suspicious of the Cholulans' intentions. The Spanish reacted violently and put the unarmed crowd gathered in the city's plaza to the sword. Cortés later explained to Charles V that he had become convinced the Cholulans were planning to betray them, but scholars continue to debate the subject. Cortés might have simply wanted to instill fear into the rest of the Aztec, or the Tlaxcalans might have persuaded Cortés that the Cholulans meant the Spanish harm and used him for their own ends.

The Spaniards and Tlaxcalans then marched to Tenochtitlan crossing one of the wide causeways that connected the city to the mainland. Cortés would later note that the road could have fit eight horses abreast. Curious Aztec ventured out to see the strange sight. The city the Spaniards now approached was twice the size of the Spanish capital, Seville, and contained massive pyramids, sculptures, and well-built structures for homes, warehouses, and public spaces. It was also an island city with a complex system of canals and aqueducts, unlike anything seen in Europe save Venice or ancient Rome. The city gave the impression that it was floating in the middle of a beautiful lake. One of those present, Bernal Díaz, later wrote that the Spanish were uncertain of what they saw. Some wondered if it were a dream. Cortés wrote to Charles that the city was "so wondrous as not to be believed."

A thousand nobles came out to greet the army peacefully, though the Spanish continually suspected a trap. Then, Moctezuma came forward with Cacamatzin of Texcoco on one side and the emperor's brother, Cuitláhuac, on the other. There was a brief awkward moment when Cortés was stopped so that Moctezuma could perform a ritual, and then they greeted each other and exchanged gifts. Cortés gave the emperor a necklace of pearls and "glass diamonds," and Moctezuma gave the conquistador two necklaces of gold fashioned into shrimp. According to Cortés, Moctezuma brought him into the palace and put him on a throne. Then, the Aztec ruler was seated on a throne next to him. Then, as Cortés continued to say in his letters, Moctezuma gave an amazing speech in which he pledged his loyalty to Cortés and the Spanish Crown, giving Cortés exactly what he had wanted. The Aztec showered the Spanish with more gifts, perhaps hoping to appease them and send them back the way they came, but this only proved to heighten the desire for riches within the army.

One story claims that Cortés came to think that the Aztec believed him to be the returning god Quetzalcoatl, and this was why they seemed to offer no resistance to the Spanish. Still, there is no evidence showing that Cortés believed this and nothing to support the idea that the Aztec thought anything of the kind.

The Spanish continued to justify their own brutality and the eventual conquest of Mexico. They were aware of human sacrifice, and Cortés was sure to exaggerate this in his letters back to Spain. Also, almost every European in the New World agreed that the "Indians," as they were being called, were cannibals. This was significant because it was gruesome, and specific laws stated that cannibals could be rightfully enslaved. If the Aztec, for example, could be identified as cannibals, any action taken against them, including subjecting them to slavery, was justified. Cannibalism was always presented in conjunction with human sacrifice, but there is no evidence of it among the Aztec or any other Mesoamerican culture.

While Cortés and the Spanish stayed in Tenochtitlan, word came that Aztec had killed some Spaniards on the coast. Cortés used this as an excuse to capture Moctezuma and put him under house arrest in his own palace. With the emperor as a hostage, Cortés ruled Tenochtitlan through Moctezuma.

At the same time, Governor Veláquez had sent another army after Cortés. Cortés responded by taking many of his men and heading for the coast to fight off this second wave of Spanish invaders. Cortés defeated the other party despite being numerically inferior, but tragedy struck while he was gone. Cortés had left Pedro de Alvarado in charge of the Aztec city. Moctezuma had asked Alvarado if the Aztec could perform a religious ceremony. Alvarado gave his permission. However, during the ritual, Alvarado blocked the exits of the Great Temple and slaughtered the Aztec inside. Alvarado later claimed this was because the Aztec planned to make a human sacrifice. The Aztec admitted that they would sacrifice someone during the ritual. Still, Alvarado's motive seems questionable: to save one life, he killed several more when he could have simply ordered the ritual stopped.

Cortés returned to find that not only did he no longer control Tenochtitlan but Moctezuma II had been stoned to death by his own people. The Alvarado Massacre led to a revolt from the Aztec, and the Spanish were forced to flee Tenochtitlan in what was called *La Noche Triste* (The Sad Night). During their retreat, the Spanish and their allies suffered numerous casualties. Of Cortés' 1,300 men, only 500 remained.

The Spanish and their allies headed to the city of Tlaxcala, and on their way, they arrived at the plain of Otumba. Here, they met a large Aztec army led by General Matlatzincátzin consisting of about 8,000 to 10,000 warriors. Cortés had about 600 men, including the Mesoamerican allies. However, Cortés' men had the benefit of artillery and cavalry. According to the conquistador Bernal Diaz, the Castilian cavalry proved decisive in the Battle of Otumba. The Aztec wanted to capture the Spanish alive and sacrifice them to the gods, but this caused them to avoid death-dealing force. The Spanish had no such motives and were desperately fighting for their lives. Cortés also focused his army's attention on defeating the Aztec leaders and captains. He led an attack on Matlatzincátzin, who was slain, and the Aztec battle standard was taken. This led the Aztec force to retreat in a disorderly fashion, and the Spanish picked off any remaining soldiers.

This victory was crucial to Cortés' plans for the immediate future. The Spanish returned to Tlaxcala but did not have the numbers to mount another attack on Tenochtitlan. However, Cortés' army was soon repopulated with reinforcements from Cuba. By this time, Governor Diego Velázquez seemed to have given up on trying to stop or replace Cortés, who was changing his strategy for defeating the Aztec. He began to attack Aztec allied cities and cut off supplies to the city of Tenochtitlan. He constructed ships that he sailed in Lake Texcoco and used to destroy parts of the city. It was now the summer of 1520, and Cortés was determined to destroy the Aztec.

After Moctezuma's death, Tenochtitlan's new king was Cuitláhuac, an advisor and brother to Moctezuma who had led the revolt against the Spanish. However, Cuitláhuac only ruled for eighty days and died of smallpox after the Spanish had left the city. He was succeeded by Cuauhtémoc, who took power in 1520. His name meant "Descending Eagle." Cuauhtémoc was a cousin to the late Emperor Moctezuma II and the eldest legitimate son of Emperor Ahuitzotl. He also married one of Moctezuma's daughters, who was later called Isabel Moctezuma. Under his rule, Tenochtitlan suffered a terrible smallpox epidemic that the Spanish had brought to the New World.

Cuauhtémoc soon found that Tenochtitlan was quickly becoming isolated as Cortés captured city-states. Other city-states abandoned the Aztec Empire and allied themselves with Cortés and the Tlaxcalans. The only Nahua city that remained loyal to Tenochtitlan was the Tlatelolco, and many Tenocha refugees wound up in Tlatelolco. Cuauhtémoc tried to rally a defense against the Spanish, but by then, it was too late. Tenochtitlan became too dangerous. Cuauhtémoc was captured on August 13, 1521, while crossing Lake Texcoco with his family. His surrender to Cortés a short time later marked the end of the Aztec Empire. Cuauhtémoc remained in Spanish custody and was tortured by fire when the Spanish thought he was hiding the whereabouts of some of the Aztec gold. He was taken by Cortés on his expedition into Honduras. Then, in 1525, Cortés had the last Aztec emperor executed for supposedly planning to kill him.

Section Two:
Building an Empire (1500–1880 CE)

Chapter 5: Conquest and Colonization

From the fall of the Aztec Empire, much of the history of Mexico for the next several years was dictated by a monarch on the other side of the Atlantic Ocean. From 1521 to 1524, Cortés ruled much of what would become Mexico. He captured Tenochtitlan and officially named it Mexico City, claiming the whole region for King Charles V of Spain. The newly conquered land was dubbed "New Spain of the Ocean Sea." Charles made Cortés governor, captain-general, and chief justice. Cortés began constructing Mexico City, tearing down temples and buildings and using the stone to rebuild to a more European taste. It was soon the most important European settlement in the Americas. The encomienda system continued as more Spanish cities were founded, and New Spain began to sprawl across much of Mesoamerica. The translator and guide, La Malinche, had born Cortés a son he named Martín, who would become known as "El Mestizo" for his mixed-race background. Since Cortés had been unable to father any children with his wife, Martín, though illegitimate, became his only heir.

From 1524 to 1526, Cortés was in Honduras fighting Cristóbal de Olid, who had claimed the land for himself. Olid, another adventurer and conquistador, had grown up in the household of Cortés' old enemy, Diego Velázquez, and Cortés suspected that Velázquez was behind Olid's expedition. While Cortés was away from Mexico, Velázquez and an archbishop named Juan Rodríguez de Fonseca convinced the acting regent of Spain to appoint a new governor of New Spain—Luis Ponce de León (not to be confused with Juan Ponce de León, governor of Puerto Rico).

León arrived in Mexico City after Cortés had returned from Honduras, carrying orders appointing him governor. Cortés recognized the authority of the orders and stepped aside. However, León was gravely ill and handed over his powers to an assistant named Marcos de Aguilar. León died just four days later. Aguilar only lasted seven and a half months as governor before he, too, died. He named Alonso de Estrada to the governorship. This also only lasted a short time before King Charles decided to dissolve the military government of New Spain and institute a more orderly form of government. In this spirit, he created the Real Audiencia of Mexico.

In the meantime, Cortés had traveled to Spain to defend himself before Emperor Charles V. In 1528, Cortés appeared before his king. Charles honored Cortés by giving him the Marquessate of the Valley of Oaxaca, thus making Cortés a high-ranking noble. However, he did not reinstate him as viceroy of New Spain.

Since Cortés' first wife had died under mysterious circumstances, Cortés married again, this time to a Spanish noblewoman named Doña Juana de Zúñiga. She would bear him three children, including a son named Martín. This Martín, being legitimate, became Cortés' rightful heir. In 1530, Cortés returned to Mexico, but he never again held an important position in the politics of New Spain.

In 1535, Antonio de Mendoza became the first viceroy of New Spain. Mendoza's appointment did not sit well with Cortés, who retired to his palace and began to buy silver mines. By the early 1540s, he owned thirty-five silver mines. He also explored the Pacific coast of Mexico and discovered the Baja Peninsula. He returned to Spain and tried to secure repayment with the treasury but was ignored. He decided to go back to Mexico in 1547 but died in Seville.

Antonio de Mendoza found New Spain to be in almost anarchy when he arrived in 1535. After dissolving the military government and several years of shifting alliances, Mendoza worked to bring order to the colony. He was faced with indigenous unrest and squabbling among the Spanish officials. The title of viceroy (vice king) was the first of its kind in the Americas and meant that Mendoza was the living image of King Charles in Mexico. Mendoza held the office for fifteen years, longer than any of his predecessors. With this time, he managed to stabilize New Spain. He helped build the first and second universities on the mainland in the Americas and brought the first printing press to the New World. He minted the first coins and promoted improvements in agriculture, mining, and ranching. When Spain established new laws concerning the rewards of conquistadors, Mendoza limited their implementation and thus avoided rebellion. The new viceroy of Peru had not done likewise and had lost his life to angry settlers.

From 1540 to 1542, Mendoza was engaged in the Mixtón War. This was when the Caxcan people, who lived in western and central Mexico, rebelled against Spanish rule, unprovoked killings, and the practice of taking slaves. The final straw seems to have been when eighteen indigenous leaders were captured and nine of them were hanged. Natives then captured, killed, and ate a slave catcher. The Caxcanes also killed two Catholic priests. Fearing Spanish retaliation, they left their villages and hid in the nearby mountains, specifically in a hill fortress known as Mixtón. The chief leader among the Caxcan was Francisco Tenamaztle.

Viceroy Mendoza called on the conquistador Pedro de Alvarado, who had been responsible for the massacre at the temple in Tenochtitlan, to help quell this rebellion. He took 400 Spaniards and an unknown number of native allies and stormed Mixtón. Their first attempt was repelled. During a later attack, a horse fell on Alvarado, and he died just days later. Mendoza formed a larger army of 450 Spaniards and as many as 60,000 native allies. With this force, he invaded the Caxcan homeland and eventually captured Mixtón. He was brutal in the aftermath, ordering men, women, and children killed—some of them shot with a cannon and others torn apart by dogs. He sent those still living to work as slaves in the Spanish mines or fields. Francisco Tenamaztle, however, managed to escape capture for many more years before he voluntarily surrendered in 1551. He was sent to Spain to stand trial, but his fate remains unknown. The Spanish victory secured their control over Guadalajara, the second-largest city in Mexico at the time.

In 1549, Emperor Charles named Mendoza the viceroy of Peru. Mendoza left New Spain and traveled to Peru but died in 1552 and was buried at the Cathedral of Lima. Mendoza's successor was Luis de Velasco, who had impressed Emperor Charles V as the viceroy of the Kingdom of Navarre. He replaced Mendoza in 1550 and held the office until 1564.

From Cortés' appearance onward, a constant issue for the Spanish was the ever-diminishing labor force. They had hoped to exploit the indigenous people as laborers in mines and fields, but a series of epidemics saw an estimated 80 to 90 percent decrease in the native population. Perhaps more than anything else, the Spanish managed to conquer Mexico at the microscopic level. For the natives, this was a unique horror unlike anything they had experienced before. Towns, cities, and whole regions were almost totally depopulated. The Spanish might have had some idea of the toll they were taking on these people. Still, they had no better idea of how to stop it than the "Indians" who died continually of smallpox, cholera, malaria, and other waves of disease.

This extreme population decrease certainly helped the Spanish in their further expeditions in Mexico. The conquest of the Maya peoples of the Yucatan followed the same pattern used previously by Cortés and the Spanish in the Caribbean—that is, ally with those natives who would most benefit from the fall of the major power in the area.

The Spanish conquest of Mesoamerica was not just about taking land and subjugating people but was seen as a means of spreading Roman Catholicism to other areas of the world. The Catholic Church was essentially another arm of the Spanish government. Initially, the conversion of natives had been rapid. Mesoamericans simply added the Christian God to their pantheon. However, later missionaries strove to destroy the indigenous religions, especially any rituals associated with human sacrifice, and impose Catholicism. Many native codices were burned by the Spanish.

Some missionaries came to feel a connection with the native peoples they were trying to convert and strove to protect them from the cruelty of the colonists. The most famous example of this was Bartolomé de las Casas, a Dominican friar who became an activist defending the indigenous people in New Spain.

Las Casas had originally been a conquistador with land and slaves in Hispaniola. However, when he participated in the brutal conquest of Cuba, he became disgusted with the treatment of native people. He returned to Spain in 1515 and began to petition the king to outlaw indigenous slavery and end the cruel treatment of the natives of the New World. He first suggested that Africans be used as slaves instead of natives but later argued that all slavery should be abolished. The Spanish concept of slavery had been similar to that of the Moors, whom they had recently pushed out of Spain. This concept was that slavery was alright as long as it was enemies captured in war and that those enemies were not, for the Spanish, Catholic. Las Casas' initial arguments for using Africans were based on a flawed idea that Africans were better suited to labor because they were resistant to European diseases. Las Casas' argument might have encouraged a shift in the philosophy of enslaving conquered enemies to slavery based on race.

Regardless, the Crown paid no attention to Las Casas' petitions. The Dominican also went on to suggest that the native people of the New World be allowed to self-govern. The Spanish government's only concession was to allow natives to use the court system as long as they had an appointed advocate known as a "protector." Las Casas became the first protector.

In 1536, Las Casas arrived in Oaxaca, Mexico, where he debated with Franciscan monks on the appropriate method of conversion. The Franciscans held mass conversions of as many as a thousand natives at a time. Las Casas said this was pointless, as conversion without understanding meant nothing. Las Casas thought natives should be treated as rational equals who should convert of their own free will. He traveled to Guatemala to practice his theory.

Then, in 1542, Las Casas returned to Spain and once again petitioned the king. The result of his arguments was a book entitled *A Short Account of the Destruction of the Indies* and Charles V's instituting the "New Laws" that abolished the encomiendas. The abolishment was gradual, but the New Laws made it illegal to enslave any other natives. These laws were the ones viceroy Mendoza had ignored and had led to the death of the viceroy of Peru. The New Laws were repealed in 1545. Las Casas returned to the New World, where he angered more colonists, and then traveled to Spain, where he continued arguing for better treatment of the natives. He helped the hero of the Mixtón War, Francisco Tenamaztle, when he was brought to Spain as a prisoner. Las Casas died in 1566 in Madrid.

Though abuses against natives continued and indigenous people were expected to accept Catholicism and learn the Spanish language, many natives retained parts of their culture that did not conflict with Spanish society. Thus, a new culture emerged among natives, colonists, and mixed children that combined elements of Mesoamerican and Spanish culture.

Many Spanish-founded cities became the most important in New Spain, including Mexico City, Veracruz, Puebla de los Ángeles, and Antequera (now Oaxaca City). The last city was close to the site of Monte Albán, one of the first Mesoamerican cities.

From Mexico, conquistadors set out to conquer new lands. Coronado explored much of the southwest United States, and Pedro Menéndez de Avilés founded the city of St. Augustine in what would become Florida. Any places conquered in this way were under the authority of the viceroy of New Spain, thus creating an empire within an empire. Spanish explorers also left Mexican shores and reached the Philippines, where a trade route was established from Mexico to China. Silver, gold, silk, spices, and porcelain traveled along this route, enriching both sides. China needed Mexican and Peruvian silver for currency, and Spain needed Chinese luxury goods. Yet, the precious metals were also sent to Spain, which soon became the wealthiest nation on Earth.

For Spain to continue its supply of gold and goods, it needed to maintain a strong hold on New Spain. This required continual efforts to put down indigenous rebellions whenever they cropped up. The Chichimeca War lasted from 1550 to 1590, not long after the Mixtón War. The fighting was centered around the El Bajío, or lowland region of the Central Mexican Plateau, and was between the Spanish and the Chichimeca coalition. (The name "Chichimeca" was not what they called themselves but the Aztec name for these nomadic people. They called themselves the "Children of the Wind.")

Silver was discovered in this area, which caused a flood of Spanish to begin mining operations there. The Chichimecas did not like the arrival of the Spanish in their ancestral lands. The coalition was made up of four main nations: Guachichiles, Pames, Guamares, and Zacatecos. Due to their tenacity and nomadic lifestyle, the Chichimecas could maintain a long war against the Spanish. They were not tied to the earth and could remain mobile. Over the course of the war, the Chichimecas learned to use stealth to kill the Spanish horses and thus turn cavalry into foot soldiers.

The war proved much longer and more difficult than the Spanish had anticipated, and they eventually settled on a strategy of "fire and blood," promising death and enslavement to all Chichimecas. After pressure from the Dominicans, the viceroy, Álvaro Manrique de Zúñiga, finally ended the "fire and blood" method and attempted to ease hostilities while keeping the mines open. Many soldiers were recalled from the area. The Chichimecas were slowly Christianized, and hostilities in the region ceased for a time.

Along with Peru, Mexico was the Spanish Empire's greatest source of wealth. But, to keep the mines open and the minerals and metals traveling along roads to the ships that carried them along the trade routes, Spain was forced to spend a good deal of money in protecting its interests. Other European countries, especially the English, were constantly trying to undermine Spain's power. English pirates attacked ships and ports on Mexico's coastlines.

Indigenous people continually rose against cruel treatment from Spanish colonists. Conditions in the mines of Mexico were some of the worst working conditions in recorded history. People were quite literally worked to death. The conditions were similar to the Aztec requirements for labor, but only in principle. The Spanish required natives to work underground for days, with crude light and little access to fresh water.

All the while, the Catholic missionaries worked tirelessly to turn natives away from their own religions and toward the Roman Catholic Church.

Because of the vast amount of trade, many Mexican cities were ethnically diverse. Filipino sailors, Spanish conquistadors, Maya, Catholic monks, Zapotec, Africans, and many others traded, gossiped, drank, prayed, loved, and died in these cities—and none more so than in Mexico City.

The massive Metropolitan Cathedral of Mexico City was built on the site of the Templo Mayor of Tenochtitlan. The building was proposed in 1552, but the first stones weren't laid until 1571, and it wasn't consecrated until 1667. Three kings of Spain died during this time: Philip II, III, and IV. The cathedral was not considered complete until the end of the eighteenth century, but of course, work must be continually done to maintain and improve it. The last Spanish king to provide significant funds towards the cathedral was Charles II, also known as "the Bewitched." Charles would be the last Spanish king of the Hapsburg family, and the crown would pass to his nephew, Philip V of the House of Bourbon after the War of Spanish Succession.

Born in 1662, Fernando de Alencastre Noroña y Silva, 1st Duke of Linares, was an example of a relatively good viceroy. Representing Philip V, Alencastre was appointed viceroy and captain general of New Spain in 1711. Mexico was hit by a massive earthquake in the first year of his time there, and two years later, Mexico City experienced an unprecedented snowfall. The snow resulted in crop failure, leading to famine and the outbreak of a plague. Alencastre suffered it all stoically and gave personally to colonists to help relieve suffering where he could and rebuild destroyed buildings. He increased the number of ships in the coast guard and bought 600 muskets for the colonial militia. After trade from Spain was halted during the War of Spanish Succession on two separate occasions, Alencastre suggested to the governing body which oversaw Spain's possessions in the New World, the Council of the Indies, that Mexico and Peru should trade between themselves. The council rejected the idea, believing Alencastre would profit personally from such an arrangement. The viceroy authorized expeditions to reoccupy Spanish Texas and missions to Nuevo Mexico, or New Mexico. He also founded the first public library and the first natural history museum in Mexico. In 1716, he retired from his position and died the following year in Mexico City.

For an example of an unpopular viceroy of New Spain, we need look no further than Carlos Francisco de Croix, 1st Marquess of Croix. He took office in 1766 and had the immediately difficult job of expelling the Jesuits from Mexico. The Jesuits, members of the Society of Jesus, had become unpopular among European royalty for their influence over the pope. Troops were called to force the priests from their positions. They were put onto ships, unable to take their possessions with them, and deported to Italy. The Jesuits were quite popular in many areas where they gave aid to the poor and provided schooling. The viceroy's actions led to rebellion in the cities of Guanajuato, Pátzcuaro, Valladolid, and Uruapan. De Croix dealt with the rebels severely, hanging the leaders. Angry citizens defaced images of King Charles III. Non-Jesuit clergy began to speak out against de Croix, and he threatened to punish them. He began to censor books of literary and scientific articles for fear that they might speak against the Crown. However, when mine workers demanded higher wages, de Croix convinced the mine owners to increase wages. He retired in 1771 and returned to Spain. He died in Valencia in 1786.

During the colonial period, Mexico, being the heart of New Spain, was subservient to the Crown in almost every way. It was kept from trading among the other colonies of the Americas or trading directly with other nations. At a time when it could take months to cross the Atlantic, orders from Spain could arrive long after their usefulness expired. This was the reason for the viceroy, but even he was not free to act however he saw fit.

This lack of independence undermined the effectiveness of the Spanish Empire to deal with things in a timely manner. It lacked some of the subtleties of the Aztec Empire, which was driven by tribute and did not require the emperor to keep track of everything in his domain. Yet, for three centuries, New Spain was the greatest colony in the New World. During the same period, Spain remained the greatest nation in Europe—and perhaps the world. There was, however, constant warfare, especially between the Spanish and English, often with Spain siding with France against the British. After the Seven Years' War (1756-1763), Spain lost control of Florida but gained the massive Louisiana Territory, which included the port of New Orleans.

While New Orleans was never as large as Mexico City, the two cities had diverse populations. In New Spain, criollos were full-blooded Spanish people born in the colonies. The *peninsulares* were Spaniards born in the Iberian Peninsula but living in the New World. To some, Race was a matter of purity of blood and could be traced back to the history of Moorish and Jewish people in Spain who converted to Catholicism. These conversos and their descendants were not considered to have blood as pure as Spaniards who had "always" been Christian. Thus, a hierarchy was established that was sometimes, but not always, applied to laws and restrictions.

Famously, in eighteenth-century Mexico, there was a tradition of *casta* paintings, which depict many of the racial configurations that could be seen in the colonies. Some casta paintings show mixed-race couples in beautiful settings, and it has been suggested that these were a contribution to those identifying themselves as Mexican and not with far-off Spain. Also, there was the idea that mixed couples who produced offspring would result in a re-purification of the blood. As one person explained in 1774, "It is held as systematic that a Spaniard and an Indian produce a mestizo; a mestizo and a Spaniard, a *castizo*; and a castizo and a Spaniard, a Spaniard." So, after three generations, the blood was considered purely Spanish. A Spaniard and a black person, according to this system, created a mulatto/a. A black person and a native would produce a *china cambuja*. A mestizo and an Amerindian would produce a *coyote*, and so on.

A census conducted in the 1790s of Mexico City showed a population of well over 100,000 people. Of these, those born in Spain only made up about 2 percent of the population, while colonists recognized as Spanish made up 48 percent. Mestizos and castizos made up about 18 percent combined. The mulatto population was 6.8 percent, and the Amerindians in Mexico City accounted for over 24 percent. In the rural areas beyond the capital, the population was made up of 71 percent native people, and Spaniards only accounted for 12 percent.

Mexico City was a lynchpin of power and business in New Spain. It was not just the capital of the viceroyalty but also the seat of the archbishopric and the center of official and religious organizations of all kinds. All the goods from the east passed through Mexico City on their way to the port of Veracruz and then to Europe. In 1594, a merchant's guild was founded in Mexico City. For many years, it was controlled by peninsular wholesale merchants, many of whom were members of the cabildo, a governing colonial council. The Crown Mint was also in the city. During the eighteenth century, Mexico City's economy boomed, and many merchants, religious leaders, and government officials became very rich.

Unlike settlers in the British colonies farther north, many Mexican colonists were or became part of the nobility. Titles were gained after several generations had amassed huge fortunes through trade, real estate, or mining. For example, Pedro Romero de Terreros, born to a common family in Spain, made his fortune investing in silver mines and married the noblewoman María Antonia de Trebuesto y Dávalos. In 1768, he was raised into the nobility and became the first Count of Regla.

The Spanish nobility in Mexico was required to maintain a certain level of luxury, especially regarding their houses. Thus, Mexico City became "the city of palaces" due to the lavish residences of wealthier citizens. Some had estates the size of small kingdoms. The Marquis of San Miguel de Aguayo amassed a domain that was two-thirds the size of Portugal. The marquis left his estates to be managed by administrators while his family owned four palatial residences in Mexico City. Many palaces lined San Francisco Street. Near the Alameda, one could find the houses of the Marquis of Guardiola of the Borda family, the Marquis of Prado Alegre, and the Counts of the Valley of Orizaba. Perhaps most famous was an old convent converted into a replica of the palace of Palermo, which was a wedding present from the Marquis of Jara to his daughter and her Sicilian husband. It was later owned by Agustín de Iturbide and is now known as the Palace of Iturbide.

Mexico City has also consistently struggled with a large population of urban poor. The low-born Pedro Romero de Terreros, Count of Regla, ordered the creation of the Nacional Monte de Piedad, a non-profit organization that offered no-interest loans to the poor. Much of the relief for the urban poor was provided by individual donors and by the church. Very early on, Hernán Cortés paid for the building of the Hospital de Jesús. The Mexico City Poor House was also established in 1774 by funds from Cortés. The Casa de Cuna ("House of the Cradle") was created in 1767 for the city's abandoned infants. The Spanish Crown maintained a monopoly on tobacco, so the creation of the Royal Cigar Factory was seen not just as a source of revenue for the king but as a means to provide work to the poor, especially women. Still, little could be done about bad harvests and poor crisis management, which led to two significant bread riots in Mexico City in 1624 and 1692.

While the Manila galleon continued to sail regularly from Acapulco to the Philippines laden with Mexican silver, the decrease in the native population meant changes in how haciendas and mines maintained labor forces. Instead of laborers being drafted from the indigenous villages, workers became free and salaried. Still, a small group of businessmen dominated the main economic activities. Pedro Romero de Terreros' silver mine in Real del Monte tried to cut labor costs, which resulted in a major strike. While the viceroy convinced Terreros to concede, it was only momentary. Labor relations remained volatile, and the output of the mines waxed and waned with the amount of silver found and the number of miners willing to endure the conditions of the mines. While the mines remained volatile investments, Mexico continued to produce large quantities of silver. By the end of the seventeenth century, Mexico overtook Peru as the world's largest producer of silver. However, the wealth that this produced was not evenly distributed.

By the end of the eighteenth century, New Spain was headed for crisis. The living standard decreased for the poor as wages remained static. All the while, the population increased. Private charities and the church could not meet the needs of the lower classes. Food crises were common, and shortages led to increased prices and lower production. All the while, Mexico's needs always came after the needs of the Crown and Spain, especially in times of war. As in other colonies, the pressure of taxation was also keenly felt. Things were reaching a boiling point.

Chapter 6: War of Independence and the First Empire

As the sun rose on December 9, 1531, a Chichimec peasant named Juan Diego was walking across the hill of Tepeyac in the countryside north of Mexico City when he was visited by a vision of the Virgin Mary. She told him to have a chapel built in that place so that she could help those who called on her in need. Juan was instructed to go to the Bishop of Mexico, Juan de Zumárraga, to request that a chapel be built. Juan did this but was turned away by the bishop. He came upon the Virgin again, and she told him to return to the bishop. He did, and the bishop asked for a sign. Juan again saw the Virgin, and she agreed to provide a sign the next day. Juan's uncle, Juan Diego Bernardino, became sick, and fearing that he would die, Juan left to find a priest. This time, he tried to avoid the Virgin, but she came to him anyway and scolded him for not coming to her. She asked him, "Am I not here, I who am your mother?" She told him that his uncle had recovered and gave him a sign, a depiction of the Virgin made from miraculous flowers on his cloak. He took this to the bishop, and the cloak has been revered ever since. The Virgin had also appeared to Juan's uncle and said she wished to be known as Guadalupe. She had spoken to both men in the Aztec language of Nahuatl. From then on, she would be known as Our Lady of Guadalupe or the Virgin of Guadalupe, and around her grew a devoted following.

A painting of Juan Diego's vision of the Virgin Mary.
Enrique López-Tamayo Biosca, CC BY 2.0 <https://creativecommons.org/licenses/by/2.0>, via Wikimedia Commons;
https://commons.wikimedia.org/wiki/File:Our_Lady_of_Guadalupe_Shrine,_Irapuato,_Guanajuato_State,_Mexico_08.jpg

In 1709, a great church was completed at the foot of the hill of Tepeyac, which would become the Basilica of Our Lady of Guadalupe. In 1754, Pope Benedict XIV declared in a papal bull that Our Lady of Guadalupe was the patroness of New Spain. Juan Diego was eventually made a saint, and the image on his cloak brought pilgrims from all over the world. One of the key elements of this apparition of the Virgin Mary was that she spoke in a native language and looked like a native, with dark hair and brown skin. To indigenous people suffering from the Spanish conquest, she represented a source of help and protection. The Virgin of Guadalupe watched over them, and her image became prominent throughout New Spain. For Mexicans of mixed ancestry who felt distant from Spain and the concerns of Europe, she was a symbol of independence and strength. She became a champion of the underdog, the native Mexicans, of those who lacked power. Her choice of messenger, the Chichimec Juan Diego, indicated that she was a saint for the common people, women, and those of mixed racial backgrounds. Reverence of Our Lady of Guadalupe came to represent a key component of a new cultural identity, that of the Mexican people. In 1810, Father Miguel Hidalgo even began the Mexican War of Independence with the words, "Long live the Virgin of Guadalupe!"

In 1808, King Charles IV of Spain abdicated the throne, and it was presumed his son Ferdinand would take over. But a presence in Europe had changed the status quo—Napoleon Bonaparte. Napoleon, having brought a large number of French soldiers into Spain, arranged matters so that Ferdinand would not become king. Instead, the crown of Spain would pass to Napoleon's brother, Joseph. This caused rebellions to spark in several parts of Spain and growing concern in New Spain. The Mexican people had grown unhappy under Spanish rule, but now they would be subject to completely foreign rule and under the thumb of the dreaded Bonaparte family.

The Congress of Chilpancingo convened in 1813, and a declaration of independence was ratified along with a constitution. The concept of "Creole Nationalism" was more clearly defined in the *Sentimientos de la Nación* (Sentiments of the Nation) document presented by Morelos. "Creole," in this sense, more accurately presented as criollo, refers to those of Spanish descent born in New Spain. In the document, they refer to themselves as Americans. The *Sentimientos de la Nación* established Catholicism as the only tolerated religion and reserved jobs only for Americans. It also established a national holiday on December 12 to celebrate the Virgin of Guadalupe.

Despite his early victories against royalist forces, Morelos was defeated several times after the Congress of Chilpancingo. By this time, Ferdinand VII was being reinstated to the throne of Spain, but many of the people of Mexico saw independence from Spain as crucial for the nation's future. In

1813, a brilliant royalist general named Félix María Calleja del Rey became the viceroy of New Spain. He acted quickly, seizing the property of the disbanded Inquisition and farming out tax collecting. He restructured the treasury and, by so doing, generated enough wealth to build a large and powerful army.

As Ferdinand returned to the throne, he sent the Jesuits back to Mexico and re-instituted the Inquisition. Calleja had finished his goal, however. He surrounded and captured Morelos in November of 1815. Found guilty by the Inquisition, Morelos was executed by firing squad on December 22.

With Morelos' death, it seemed for a while that the revolution was over. However, guerilla fighters continued to harass royalists for the next several years. Out of these groups came two leaders: Guadalupe Victoria in Pueblo and Vincente Guerrero in Oaxaca. Calleja responded by becoming more dictatorial in his leadership of the colony. This led to complaints from royalists that his brutal tactics were only making matters worse. He was relieved of his position in 1816.

Calleja's successor was Juan José Ruiz de Apodaca y Eliza. Apodaca began by offering amnesty to all rebels who turned themselves in and agreed to peace. Thousands of rebels accepted the offer, but Victoria and Guerrero remained in open rebellion.

In 1817, Francisco Javier Mina arrived in Mexico. Mina was a Spanish military officer who opposed King Ferdinand's absolute monarchy. He had been part of a failed coup to oust Ferdinand. He fled to France and then to England, where he boarded a ship for Baltimore. Mina and Mexican agents in the United States gathered together men and two ships for an expedition to New Spain in hopes of ending the monarchy's rule there. An American merchant named William Davis Robinson, who traded extensively in Mexico, wrote a memoir that highlighted Mina's campaign. According to Robinson, Viceroy Apodaca received orders from the Spanish government to stop Mina at all costs. Being from Spain, Mina represented a new type of revolutionary leader, arousing the republican ideals of the Mexican intellectuals. For a time, Mexico City coffee houses were full of people who openly supported Mina's cause.

In May of 1817, Mina, with a force of 300 men, made their way to Fuerte del Sombrero, a fortification held by Pedro Moreno, a revolutionary who had organized the farmers in his area to fight against the Spanish. Apodaca sent a force to defeat him, led by Inspector General

Don Pasqual Liñán. Mina and Moreno held off the royalist forces until August, when they were forced to flee from Pascual Liñán's forces. The revolutionaries fought a few battles before returning to Fuerte del Sombrero, where they were trapped without provisions. Their second escape ended with the death of Moreno and the capture of Mina. Mina was eventually brought before Field Marshal Liñán and executed by firing squad. It seemed, yet again, that the war for independence was at an end.

Yet, international politics helped keep the idea of Mexican independence alive. The United States, Great Britain, and France were all interested in the benefits that could be had if Spain was no longer in control of Mexico. But even more important than this was the growing desire of the Mexican people to be independent from Spanish control. This took various forms within the viceroyalty. Some wanted a complete break with Spain and the establishment of a republic. Others were willing to let Ferdinand continue as king of both Spain and Mexico. In this way, Mexico would have equal standing and not be forced to provide for Spain with nothing in return. Others wanted something in between. Some desired equality for all people in Mexico, while others believed in adherence to the *casta* system. However, events in Spain once again shaped the future of the struggle for independence in Mexico.

It was not just New Spain that balked against the yoke of the Spanish monarchy. Much had occurred in the Viceroyalty of New Granada, which was composed of the nations of Colombia, Ecuador, Panama, and Venezuela. There, revolutionary figures like Simon Bolívar and Francisco de Paula Santander had been fighting royalist forces and fostering alliances with Spanish enemies like England. In 1819, however, royalist forces controlled both New Granada and Chile. Spain sent large numbers of troops across the Atlantic to fight, but many died upon arrival from tropical diseases. The vast majority of royalist forces were, in fact, Spanish Americans.

Peru's war for independence had begun in 1810. The viceroy in Peru was busy dealing with Lord Cochrane, a somewhat disgraced Scottish naval officer who had come to South America after being discharged from the British Royal Navy on accusations of fraud in the stock exchange. By 1819, Cochrane had taken the strategically important city of Valdivia in Chile.

In January 1820, King Ferdinand of Spain organized a massive military operation to end the wars of independence in the Spanish colonies.

Ferdinand commanded the formation of ten battalions. He put a Liberal soldier named Rafael del Riego y Flórez in charge of the Asturian Battalion. This proved to be a mistake, as Riego soon organized a mutiny. Many joined his cause, which was the restoration of the Constitution of 1812, which Ferdinand had abolished. After the royal palace was surrounded by soldiers, Ferdinand agreed to restore the constitution.

Viceroy Apodaca of New Spain had received the order to reinstate the Constitution of 1812, but he had delayed its publication. He was working on a secret agreement in which New Spain would be declared independent and Ferdinand would be offered the position of absolute monarch with no mention of the constitution. To facilitate this scheme, Apodaca had chosen General Agustín de Iturbide to represent the viceroy's wishes in the clandestine meetings that would become known as the La Profesa Conspiracy, named after the church where Conservative leaders met to avoid the restoration of the constitution. However, Iturbide proved to be a more dynamic player in the political intrigue of Mexican independence than perhaps the viceroy had suspected.

Agustín had been born into a Basque noble family that owned extensive lands in Valladolid. Iturbide studied at the Colegio de San Nicolás, where both Hidalgo and Morelos studied. However, he joined the military and soon began fighting for the royalists against the insurgents. Hidalgo had even offered Iturbide a high rank in the peasant army, but he had turned it down. Iturbide distinguished himself by fighting against Morelos' forces. However, Iturbide's rise in the ranks was sullied due to accusations of cruelty and corruption, and he was relieved of his command. In 1820, his fortunes were reversed when he was reinstated by Viceroy Apodaca.

Iturbide's task, besides involvement in the Profesa Conspiracy, was to stamp out the guerilla fighter Vincent Guerrero. Thanks to letters discovered in 2006, we know that Iturbide and Guerrero struck up a correspondence during their campaigns against each other. In these letters, both leaders express their regret at the clashes. Then, Iturbide explains that he is interested in the same goal as Guerrero, specifically the liberation of Mexico.

To understand this seemingly one-hundred-and-eighty-degree turn from General Iturbide, we must better understand the complicated dynamics at work within New Spain. The early rebellions centered on the lower classes, among common people (peasants) and indigenous people.

Iturbide was not of these classes and was not interested in their desires. He was a criollo, a Mexican-born Spanish who was motivated by what was best for himself and his class. Iturbide supported the Bourbon dynasty's right to rule the Spanish Empire. After the reinstatement of the constitution, Ferdinand VII was no longer the absolute ruler of Spain. This worried the elites in Mexico, who were not interested in a constitutional monarchy. The elites did not trust the new government of Spain and so lost confidence in the viceroyalty. Iturbide's social class began to think that if Ferdinand were deposed, which seemed likely, he could rule as an absolute monarch of the newly free and independent Mexico. Therefore, the interests of the peasants and the elites were aligned in wanting to remove the viceroyalty from New Spain.

Iturbide did not want to see republicanism take over Mexico, and he felt the only way to ensure this was for Mexico to become free of Spanish rule and institute its own monarchy. Iturbide knew that, to do this, he would need an alliance between the commoners, the landed aristocracy, and the Catholic Church. He wrote out his plan to do just this, called the Plan of Iguala. The plan held three guarantees: freedom from Spain, Catholicism as the only accepted religion, and the equality of all inhabitants of Mexico. This is often summarized as independence, religion, and union. The plan envisioned that a monarchy would be established in Mexico. Iturbide believed this would meet all the demands of the various groups needed to ensure independence: the insurgents, royalists, criollos, and the Catholic Church. After careful negotiations, the plan was published on February 24, 1821, by Iturbide, Guerrero, and Guadalupe Victoria. Iturbide was then placed as the head of the Army of the Three Guarantees. They had asked Viceroy Apodaca to become the leader of the movement, but he had refused and named Iturbide a traitor. Apodaca sent troops under the command of Antonio López de Santa Anna, but they, too, joined the rebels. Apodaca was eventually deposed by a group of royalists who declared him inept. He was replaced by Juan de O'Donojú y O'Ryan.

O'Donojú signed the Treaty of Cordoba when the Army of the Three Guarantees marched into Mexico City in August 1821. This treaty essentially ratified Mexican independence. The fledgling Mexican government quickly sent an offer to Ferdinand to become the king of Mexico, with the idea that, if he refused, another member of the Bourbon family would be selected to rule. Ferdinand rejected the offer and refused to accept the conditions of the Treaty of Cordoba.

In May of 1822, a movement to place Iturbide on the throne of the newly created Mexican Empire began, mainly focused in the Mexican military. Eventually, the movement spread to the general public, who crowded the streets demanding to put Iturbide on the throne. The new Mexican Congress deliberated the idea. They eventually held a vote and decided the best course of action would be to make Iturbide emperor, as this would please both the Liberal and Conservative factions of the government. Iturbide was crowned Emperor Agustín I on July 21, 1822, in the Metropolitan Cathedral in Mexico City.

Chapter 7: Santa Anna and the Mexican-American War

The Emperor of Mexico was not destined for a long reign, nor was the First Mexican Empire. The administration of the empire seemed to be plagued with difficulties from the start. When it was first conceived, the empire was quite large, expanding well beyond the modern borders of Mexico into Texas, New Mexico, Arizona, California and the Central American nations of Honduras, Guatemala, Costa Rica, El Salvador, and Nicaragua. Emperor Iturbide grasped for more control, but Liberal elements in the Congress wanted him to abide by the restrictions of the Spanish Constitution of 1812. Iturbide balked at this, declaring that Congress had accomplished nothing in its six months of existence, and dissolved it altogether. Due to the clashes between the emperor and Congress, Congress had been unable to establish a constitution of its own. Their respective powers remained unclear, which led to more clashes.

To replace Congress, Iturbide created a National Institutional Junta. However, a revolt was developing within the military against Iturbide. It began with Antonia Lopez de Santa Anna in Veracruz, who was declared a traitor. But he was soon joined by the guerilla fighter Guadalupe Victoria. After clashing with imperial troops, the so-called "Liberating Army" was joined by Vincent Guerrero and Nicolás Bravo, a military leader and politician. A general was sent by Iturbide but defected to the revolutionary cause, much like Iturbide had done only a few years before. Iturbide was forced to reconvene Congress. Then, seeing no other choice, he abdicated. The former emperor was allowed to leave the capital with his family before the rebels took control.

A provisional government was formed upon the empire's fall in April 1823. Sovereignty passed to Congress, which appointed a triumvirate to hold executive powers. This consisted of Guadalupe Victoria, Nicolás Bravo, and Pedro Celestino Joseph Negrete, a former royalist and supporter of Iturbide. Negrete, who had been Iturbide's friend, had pressured the emperor to abdicate. In October of 1824, the Constitution of the United Mexican States was adopted, establishing a system of republicanism consisting of representative, popular, and federal government. The first president elected in the United Mexican States was General Guadalupe Victoria. The general had served under Morelos and had fought alongside Iturbide but had clashed with the emperor when Congress was dissolved. Victoria's first term began in April of 1825.

Upon the fall of the First Mexican Empire, several territories broke off to form their own nations, such as the United Provinces of Central America, British Honduras, and the Mosquito Coast. President Victoria recognized the sovereignty of these nations and focused on the troublesome task before him. His goal to maintain the Mexican Republic was hindered at almost every turn. He had to deal with three separate revolts, one started by his own vice-president, Nicolás Bravo. Under Victoria's leadership, the last holdout of Spanish control, the fort of San Juan de Ulúa in Veracruz, finally surrendered. To do this, Victoria created Mexico's navy. The new president faced economic problems and was forced to borrow from firms in the United Kingdom, but he kept the economy afloat. In 1824, the Mexican government enacted the Great Colonization Law, which incentivized foreign immigration. This led to a flood of American immigrants to Coahuila y Tejas, north of the Rio Grande. This was followed by a brief rebellion led by Texan settler Haden Edwards, who declared his small part of the state free from Mexico and formed the Republic of Fredonia. Edwards was forced to flee after Victoria sent the Mexican army to quell the rebellion. Victoria also joined Simón Bolívar's Pan-American Union.

In the election of 1828, Victoria did not run but put his support behind Manuel Gómez Pedraza. This angered a large faction that wanted to see Vincent Guerrero as the next president. Pedraza won the election, but this sparked an outcry among Guerrero supporters. Pedraza was forced to flee, and a general revolt arose in which General Antonio Lopez de Santa Anna began taking cities in the name of Guerrero. Rebel forces entered

Mexico City and took control of the Acordada, a building that contained a large amount of ammunition. The revolution would be known as the Mutiny of the Acordada. After a few days of fighting in the capital, Congress disregarded the constitution and declared Vincent Guerrero the next president of the United Mexican States. President Victoria respected Congress's decision and handed the presidency over to Guerrero in April of 1829. The new president was liberally inclined and was a Yorkino. (After independence, a freemason lodge called the York Rite Masons had been established in Mexico by US diplomat Joel Robert Poinsett. The members of this lodge were called Yorkinos. They were Liberals opposed to a lodge known as the Scottish Rite Masons, which had been established before independence and was staunchly Conservative.) However, some Yorkinos opposed Guerrero because they felt he was too radical.

Guerrero's vice-president was the Conservative Anastasio Bustamante. Because Guerrero was mixed-race and from a lower class, many hailed him as a folk hero who was taking the country back from European descendants. Others, especially the criollos, were concerned about what the president would do. Because of the questions of his legitimacy, Guerrero faced problems from the beginning of his term. His greatest achievement was the complete abolition of slavery in Mexico. Within the first year of his term, a rebellion was formed by his vice-president. Guerrero had left Mexico City to fight the rebellious Nicolas Bravo in the south. While he was gone, the city's garrison deposed him. In the south, Guerrero was betrayed, captured, and tried in a court martial. He was eventually executed by firing squad in 1831. Anastasio Bustamante was eventually named president. He expelled Joel Roberts Poinsett and banned the immigration of Americans into Texas.

However, a revolutionary faction was developing that opposed Bustamante's conservatism and what it felt were autocratic policies. This faction put forward Antonio Lopez de Santa Anna, the revolutionary many times over, as their leader.

Santa Anna was born in Veracruz in 1794. His military and political career was noted for many reversals and side-switching. He had been a royalist and then joined the insurgents along with Agustín Iturbide during the War of Independence. During the First Empire, Santa Anna had command of the vital port of Veracruz. When Iturbide removed him from this post, he rebelled against the emperor. Originally, Santa Anna had supported the Conservative Scottish Rite Masons but then threw in with the Liberal Yorkinos and supported Guerrero as president. In 1829,

Spain made one last attempt to retake Mexico. Santa Anna marched against them with a much smaller force and defeated the Spanish "Barradas Expedition." This made Santa Anna a national hero.

After declaring his rebellion against Bustamante in 1832, Santa Anna was eventually successful and forced Bustamante's resignation. While Santa Anna was elected president, he was not much interested in governing. From the start of his term in 1833, his vice-president, Valentín Gómez Farías, handled the job of running the country. Santa Anna spent most of his time in his *hacienda*, Manga de Clavo, in Veracruz. Farías was essentially a moderate, but the country was in incredible debt after the spending of the Bustamante administration. So, Farías and the Liberal Congress enacted reforms to reduce the size of the army, which was the nation's chief expenditure, and restrict the Catholic Church's demands for tithing. This had the obvious effect of drawing Conservatives out in protest. However, the Conservatives' solution was to put Santa Anna back in power as a central authority, overriding Farías' reforms.

Santa Anna agreed to restore the army and repeal the restrictions on the Church, but only if the Church agreed to pay the government a monthly sum of 30,000 to 40,000 pesos. This essentially had the same effect as the Liberal reforms but pleased the Conservatives. In 1834, Santa Anna dissolved Congress and announced his adoption of the Plan of Cuernavaca, which made Mexico a Catholic, centralist, and Conservative government. In October 1835, the former constitution was abandoned, and the Centralist Republic of Mexico was created. A new constitution called *Las Siete Leyes* (The Seven Laws) was adopted. The Seven Laws can be abbreviated as follows:

1. Citizenship was granted to anyone who could read Spanish and had an annual income of at least 100 pesos.
2. The president could close Congress and suppress the Supreme Court.
3. The establishment of a Congress of two assemblies of deputies and senators.
4. The Supreme Court, the Senate of Mexico, and the ministries would each nominate three candidates, and the lower house of Congress would select the president and vice-president from these nominees.
5. The eleven-member Supreme Court was elected in the same manner.

6. The states were replaced with "departments" whose governors and legislatures were appointed by the president.
7. The last law prohibited returning to the previous constitution for six years.

Santa Anna again stepped down, and in 1836, José Justo Corro became president. Just before Corro's term began, however, the Texas Revolution broke out.

Anglo-Americans who had settled in Texas were angered by the move to a centralist government, especially concerning their desire to continue their practice of chattel slavery. Santa Anna personally led his troops against the Texian Army. (Early Anglo-American settlers in Tejas were called Texians, while Mexican settlers were Tejanos.) Santa Anna had Congress pass a resolution that soldiers fighting against the Mexican army and not under the flag of a recognized country would be considered pirates and executed immediately. Only 100 men were stationed at the Alamo Mission in Bexar, which was strategically important. Only 100 reinforcements had reached the fort when 1,300 Mexican troops arrived and besieged it for thirteen days. Finally, Santa Anna ordered a general assault, and after fierce fighting, no quarter was given. Almost all those inside the Alamo were killed. A few survivors, maybe seven or eight men, surrendered, but Santa Anna had them executed according to the laws of piracy.

Santa Anna moved on and faced the volunteer army of Sam Houston. The Mexicans lost the Battle of San Jacinto in April of 1836. This time, it was the Texians who showed no mercy while chanting, "Remember the Alamo! Remember Goliad!" Goliad had been another defeat. Mexican soldiers cried out, "Me no Alamo," but were shot down by Texian sharpshooters. Santa Anna had been wounded and was captured and brought before Houston. The two began negotiations that resulted in the removal of all Mexican troops from Texas and led to the creation of the Republic of Texas. However, Mexico refused to recognize the new republic, citing that Santa Anna had made these agreements as a prisoner of war and not in good faith. A truce would not be declared by the two nations for several years. Santa Anna remained in exile, meeting US President Andrew Jackson in 1837, but was then allowed to return to Mexico.

In 1838, French forces were sent to the port of Veracruz as part of what would be called the Pastry War. At the time, the presidency was back in the hands of Anastasio Bustamante, the Conservative who had been ousted by Santa Anna. The French had demanded that the Mexican government pay them 600,000 pesos for damages incurred by French citizens in Mexico. The chief complaint came from a pastry chef who had petitioned French King Louis Philippe, stating that in 1832, some Mexican officers had looted his shop in a town on the outskirts of Mexico City. He believed the property in question to be worth about 60,000 pesos. This was at a time when the typical daily wage in Mexico was one peso, and the pastry chef's shop was believed to be worth only 1,000 pesos. Nonetheless, the French prime minister demanded the extraordinary sum from the Mexican government, who refused to pay. The French king then ordered part of the French Navy to form a blockade on Mexico's eastern ports and seize the city of Veracruz. Santa Anna quickly offered his military services to rid the country of their French incursion. At the Battle of Veracruz (1838), Santa Anna was wounded, and his leg had to be amputated. It was buried with full military honors. The French soon signed a peace treaty in which the Mexican government agreed to pay the 600,000 pesos in damages. Santa Anna used the battle and his wound to promote himself back into power.

In 1839, Santa Anna returned as the president. This time, perhaps feeling that his countrymen did not deserve liberty, Santa Anna ruled in a more dictatorial fashion. Dissidents were jailed, and newspapers were censored. In October of that year, the remains of Emperor Agustín Iturbide were placed in an urn in the Chapel of San Felipe de Jesús in the Metropolitan Cathedral. Iturbide, who had been in exile, had returned to Mexico in 1824 and been executed by firing squad. Santa Anna had his body exhumed and ordered that it be brought to the capital with honors. This was carried out by Bustamante. Iturbide, who had been seen as the enemy of the Mexican Republic, had his memory cleansed. In the chapel is a plaque that reads, "Agustín de Iturbide. Author of the independence of Mexico. Compatriot, cry for him; passerby, admire him. This monument guards the ashes of a hero. His soul rests in the bosom of God."

From 1839 to 1844, the office of the president of Mexico was passed around to a handful of individuals, chiefly Bustamante, Nicolás Bravo, Santa Anna, and Valentín Canalizo—a puppet president controlled by Santa Anna. In 1843, Santa Anna introduced the Bases Orgánicas (Organic Bases), which he saw as a new constitution for the Centralist Mexican government. Bustamante had been overthrown by a rebellion begun by Mariano Paredes y Arrillaga, who was joined by Santa Anna. Bravo was placed in the presidency by Santa Anna, who was looking to dissolve the Federalist Congress. Though Bravo was a centrist like Santa Anna, he did not support the general's schemes. Congress was dissolved anyway, and the Organic Bases were put into place. The new constitution set out the following:

1. For a male citizen to vote, he must have a yearly salary of 200 pesos. Women could not vote.
2. As in the Seven Laws, the country would be divided into departments whose governors were appointed by the president.
3. The president was elected by the department assemblies for a term of five years.
4. The legislature and Supreme Court would be much the same as they were set up under the Seven Laws.

However, by 1844, resentment against Santa Anna's centralist government had grown. Yucatan and Lerado declared themselves independent republics. Santa Anna had little choice but to step away from power and leave Mexico City. His honored leg was dug up and dragged around the streets until it broke into pieces. He was captured, momentarily imprisoned, and then exiled to Cuba.

That same year, James K. Polk was elected to the presidency of the United States. Polk had campaigned on the promise of territorial expansion. He wanted to annex Texas and had designs on California, New Mexico, Arizona, Nevada, Utah, and parts of Colorado. In early 1845, before Polk was instated, President John Tyler put forward a motion to Congress to annex Texas, which it did. Mexico responded by breaking off all diplomatic ties. When Polk became president, he ordered the American ambassador in Mexico to make offers to purchase Mexico's northern regions. Mexico refused, and the ambassador was forced to flee. Polk then sent General Zachary Taylor to the Rio Grande, feeling that Mexico had acted in a threatening manner. For Mexico, this was seen as an act of war. They believed the Mexico-Texas border was some 100 miles to the north at the Nueces River. Thus, Taylor's army was illegally in Mexican territory. It was clear to those involved that Polk was antagonizing the Mexicans. Skirmishes followed, and eleven Americans were killed in a firefight. According to the Americans, this meant "American blood shed on American soil." Polk asked for and received a declaration of war, and on May 13, 1846, the Mexican-American War began.

This was not a good time for Mexico to enter a war with a power like the United States. In 1946 alone, the Mexican presidency had changed hands four times. This political instability was worsened by economic issues. Public opinion supported the war, and those who questioned it were considered traitors. But there were no great movements by common people to expel the invading army. The Americans, on the other hand, were driven by the concept of "Manifest Destiny," which led them to believe that God desired for the United States to stretch from the Atlantic to the Pacific. To fulfill this destiny, many reasoned, the US needed to capture the Mexican territories to the west. For some, this was seen as a way to expand chattel slavery and thus give an upper hand to the South in the political conflict of free versus slave states. It was no coincidence that Polk was a North Carolinian who had been the governor of Tennessee and a supporter of Andrew Jackson. Northerners were mostly opposed to the war, including a young Abraham Lincoln. Americans called it the Mexican War; the Mexicans call it the North American Intervention.

General Taylor crossed the Rio Grande and slowly made his way south, capturing towns as he went. At the same time, a general uprising had begun by mostly Americans in the Mexican region of Alto, California. Marion Paredes was ratified as the Mexican president in June of 1846, and Nicolás Bravo was selected as his vice president and the leader of Mexican forces against the American invasion. However, the early defeats at the hands of Taylor and the worsening situation in California led to Paredes' resignation in July. Vice-president Bravo replaced him but was ousted by José Mariano de Salas, who declared the beginning of a Second Federal Republic. Salas then handed the presidency to Valentín Gómez Farías, who, along with many others, had become convinced that only Santa Anna could save Mexico. He began talks with the exiled dictator.

Santa Anna then began to communicate with Polk, telling him that, if allowed safe passage through the American blockades into Mexico, he would take power and quickly surrender to the United States, giving Polk the territory he wanted. Polk allowed Santa Anna to pass through the blockades and, once again, Antonio Lopez de Santa Anna was the head of the Mexican government. Once inside Mexican territory, Santa Anna made it known that he would not surrender to the Americans and that they should expect to face the might of the Mexican army.

Santa Anna gathered an army of between 18,000 and 20,000 troops in the city of San Luis Potosí, leaving his vice-president, Gómez Farías, to raise the funds needed and manage the unruly populace—the same arrangement from the previous decade. Gómez Farías again tried to acquire funds through the Church, but the clergy refused to give him the silver he needed.

Meanwhile, Polk had decided on a new strategy: invade Mexico through the port of Veracruz. He put General Winfield Scott in charge of this campaign. Gen. Taylor was to give half his army to Scott. Santa Anna saw this as an opportunity and marched against Taylor, catching the Americans by surprise with superior numbers. However, the Battle of Buena Vista would not give him the decisive victory he hoped for. Mainly, this was because of the superior cannons the Americans employed. Santa Anna was forced to retreat back to Potosí, though he claimed victory because he had inflicted many casualties on Taylor's army. Taylor claimed the victory for himself, pointing out that his army had held their ground.

Santa Anna returned to Mexico City and, due to overwhelming criticisms, removed Gómez Farías from power and replaced him with Pedro Maria Anaya. Santa Anna then demanded two million pesos from the Church and received that sum. He planned to head off Winfield Scott's army, which had already landed at Veracruz.

Scott's predicament did not look good. His soldiers began to die in large numbers thanks to the diseases of the tropics. He was outnumbered and in rugged, foreign territory. Santa Anna awaited Scott at Cerro Gordo, a spot he felt was impenetrable. However, he did not account for America's West Point-trained engineers, who dug ditches and built bridges in ways the Mexicans had never seen. This led to Scott being able to position his powerful guns on either side of Santa Anna's position. The Mexicans were shattered and fell back to the capital.

Things began to fall apart even more among the leaders of Mexico. No one trusted Santa Anna, but no one else could be trusted. His promises to Polk became well known, and his "victory" at Buena Vista was doubted. However, there was no one else.

Santa Anna raised another army. However, the officers below the general were uncooperative and mutinous. They disobeyed orders, and Scott took them out one by one. He made his way towards the capital, taking strategic locations and fortresses. Nicolás Bravo tried to defend Chapultepec Castle (then a military academy), but he had only cadets. Six cadets bravely lost their lives in a hopeless defense against the American army on September 13, 1847. Santa Anna's army fell apart, and the council of Mexico City ordered the white flag of surrender to be flown.

Santa Anna tried to hold out, but another loss at Puebla cost him all his credit. The moderates now in control of the government wanted only peace. José Manuel de la Peña y Peña, the head of the Supreme Court, took the reins as president. He surrendered to Scott, who quickly worked out a treaty. In the Treaty of Guadalupe Hidalgo, signed in February of 1848, Mexico agreed to give 55 percent of its territory to the United States, land that would become the states of California, Arizona, New Mexico, Nevada, Utah, much of Colorado, and a portion of Wyoming. The Rio Grande would be the recognized border between Texas and Mexico. The US, in turn, paid Mexico $15 million and paid off any debts owed by American citizens to the government of Mexico. Mexico also agreed to acknowledge the Republic of Texas's right to be annexed by the United States. At that time, Texas also included what would become Oklahoma and Kansas.

While the treaty's terms were by no means harsh, the treaty concluded a progression that had been started many years before. After Guadalupe Hidalgo, Mexico was forced to a second-place status on the continent. For centuries, the Spanish and then Mexicans had created empires and enjoyed influence far beyond their borders. Mexico would continue to be a large and important nation, but from then on, the United States would be the primary power of North America.

Chapter 8: Liberal and Conservative Reforms (1850–1880 CE)

President José Joaquín Antonio de Herrera.
https://commons.wikimedia.org/wiki/File:Jos%C3%A9_Joaqu%C3%ADn_de_Herrera.jpg

After the defeat against the Americans, Mexico looked to José Joaquín de Herrera as their next president. Herrera had been president twice before and would be the first president to serve his full term since 1824. He passed the presidency on to José Mariano Arista, a soldier who had commanded the Mexican forces in the disastrous early battles of the Mexican-American War but had regained popularity as Herrera's Minister of War.

Arista became president in 1851. Soon after, the American money ran out and Mexico faced an income of eight million pesos with expenditures of about twenty-six million. Arista made extreme cuts, but it was not enough. Government employees became dissatisfied, the military was unpaid, and local commandants issued ominous pronouncements that seemed a precursor of more rebellion. Even though Arista had been elected, he had been forced to put down revolts in San Luis Potosí, Veracruz, and Tlaxcala. By 1853, things were out of Arista's control. He resigned after a new revolt called the Plan of Jalisco was taken over by supporters of Santa Anna, called Santanistas, intending to put the dictator in power once again. They were eventually successful, and Santa Anna was once again president in April of 1853.

Santa Anna was brought back into power mainly with the help of the Catholic Church. Some clergymen felt that Mexico needed to be ruled by a strong Catholic dictator since the Church was felt to be the only thing that still united the country. Santa Anna returned from exile and repealed previous Liberal laws that had restricted the Church. He also allowed the Jesuits to return to Mexico after their banishment in 1767. This time, Santa Anna declared himself dictator for life and gave himself the title "Most Serene Highness."

In 1853, The United States approached Santa Anna's government with an offer to buy contested land in northwest Mexican Mesilla Valley. This was called the Gadsden Purchase, which is today the southern portion of Arizona and the southwest corner of New Mexico.

Santa Anna didn't want to wait for the money to come, so he arranged a deal with US bankers in which Mexico netted only $250,000 while the banks took $650,000. For a new generation of Liberals that had risen to power, this was going too far. Santa Anna had control over all the states of Mexico except Guerrero, which was governed by General Juan Álvarez. It was in Guerrero that the Plan of Ayutla was drafted, which aimed to overthrow the dictator and write a new constitution for the country.

Álvarez, Tomás Moreno, and Nicolás Bravo were declared the leaders of this new movement. Supporters of the plan included Liberals exiled to New Orleans by Santa Anna, including the *indio* Liberal lawyer Benito Pablo Juárez. The plan became the Revolution of Ayutla, which focused on Liberal reform and not solely on the ousting of Santa Anna. In 1855, Juárez returned to Acapulco to ally himself with Álvarez.

Benito Juárez played an important role in the Liberal reforms of the mid-nineteenth century.
https://en.wikipedia.org/wiki/File:Photograph_of_Benito_Juarez.jpg

Born in 1806 in the Oaxaca region to Zapotec parents, Benito Juárez was the first Amerindian to gain national prominence in Mexico. In 1818, he walked to Oaxaca City looking for an education. He was illiterate and couldn't speak Spanish, only his native tongue. In the city, he worked with his sister and found a benefactor in a lay Franciscan who sent him to seminary, but Juárez chose law over the priesthood. He graduated from the seminary in 1827 and went on to get his law degree. He was known to have Liberal views, so he was exiled by Santa Anna.

Upon Juárez's return and the rising of the Revolution of Ayutla, Santa Anna had already led an army to crush the rebellion. Though he was victorious in several battles, he took heavy losses. His treatment of prisoners (typically ending in execution) and use of scorched earth tactics led to more uprisings and the spread of Álvarez and Juárez's desire for reform. After months of indecisive battles, Santa Anna returned to Mexico City, where he was denounced by government officials.

On August 12, 1855, Santa Anna abdicated the presidency. It would be the last time he held an official role in Mexico. Juan Álvarez took over as president. Santa Anna was exiled to Cuba and then spent some time in the United States, where he introduced Americans to chicle, a natural gum that he believed could replace rubber. While his dreams of developing a market never materialized, chicle would be used to produce chewing gum. However, Santa Anna never profited from this industry. He returned to Mexico in 1874. Blind and crippled, he died in 1876.

Nicolás Bravo, who had once been considered a leader in the revolution, had died in 1854 when Santa Anna had been nearby. Bravo coincidentally died on the same day as his wife, which led to rumors that they had been murdered by order of the dictator. Juan Álvarez was an old soldier, having fought alongside Morelos, Guerrero, and Bravo. He had always stayed true to his Liberal ideals and had opposed the Conservatives—and Santa Anna, in particular—whenever he could.

Álvarez's Minister of Justice was the radical Benito Juárez, and his Minister of War was the moderate Ignacio Comonfort. With direction from his cabinet, he tried to face his two main obstacles: writing a new constitution and tackling Mexico's chronic financial troubles. The president's new cabinet was made mostly of a new generation of Mexican leaders who had grown up under the turbulent revolutions, empires, invasions, and crises of the nineteenth century. They wanted to bring peace and prosperity to Mexico through what would be called La Reforma.

In November 1855, Álvarez enacted the Ley Juárez, or Juárez Law, which ended the special jurisdiction of clerical and military courts over civic cases. The cabinet was often conflicted, and the government faced widespread criticism from Conservatives. Álvarez resigned as president at the end of 1855 and handed the presidency over to his Minister of War, Ignacio Comonfort.

Comonfort held Liberal sympathies, but he was first and foremost a military man. When Juárez and another cabinet member, Melchor Ocampo, supported the idea of dissolving the military and starting over,

Comonfort had opposed them. When Comonfort became president, he replaced Juárez, and Ocampo resigned and returned to his home territory in Michoacán. Comonfort faced two revolts while in office but defeated both. The Constitutional Congress met and produced the Federal Constitution of the United Mexican States of 1857. This constitution included personal rights, universal male suffrage, and the abolition of slavery, debtor's prison, and the death penalty. It created a federal government with a strong Congress and a relatively small executive branch to avoid dictatorships. It also abolished communal property, which affected the Catholic Church and indigenous people. This had been established a few years earlier by Ley Laredo, but it was codified in the Constitution of 1857.

The clergy openly rejected the constitution and Ley Laredo to the point that several Franciscans were arrested and their property confiscated. Not only that, but one of the northern governors was in open revolt. Another revolt led by a priest erupted in Puebla City.

Comonfort replaced his entire ministry with more moderate politicians. Conservatives who had opposed the Liberal reformation now hatched the Plan of Tacubaya, intending to abandon the new constitution. One of these was General Félix María Zuloaga. He was indicted for plotting to overthrow the government but then led a brigade into Mexico City, where he arrested the president of Congress and the president of the Supreme Court, Benito Juárez. Comonfort, who had supported the Plan of Tacubaya, now changed his mind. He released Juárez and resigned as president in December of 1857. The presidency now fell to the next in line according to the constitution, the president of the Supreme Court. Comonfort went into exile in Europe and then to Texas, where he was able to come back to Mexico.

Some states would recognize Benito Juárez as president, while others recognized the Conservative Félix Zuloaga. This would lead to a civil war in Mexico known as the Reform War. Juárez and his cabinet were forced to flee Mexico City to the state of Querétaro; he ultimately made his capital in Veracruz. He named Santos Degollado as the head of the Liberal Army. The Conservative Army was better equipped and better trained, so Degollado faced defeat after defeat in the field. Still, the Liberal government remained, and the army fought on. However, Zuloaga's government could not create a constitution, and this led to his ousting. The Conservative presidency was finally taken by Miguel Miramón, a Conservative general who was just twenty-seven years old.

Each side attempted to attack the other's capital but was defeated or gave up.

In 1859, Miramón again had plans to lay siege to Veracruz. He wanted to meet up with a naval squadron, but the United States Navy was blocking Conservative vessels attempting to disembark in Mexico. The Liberals had gained war funds by confiscating church possessions, while the Conservatives were running out of resources. Degollado began to gain victories across the country. The new Liberal general, Jesus Gonzalez Ortega, now approached Mexico City. The decisive battles took place at San Miguel Calpulalpan on December 22, 1860. Miramón, outnumbered two-to-one, was defeated, and the Conservatives agreed to surrender. After the Liberal victory, Miramón went into exile in Havana.

In March of 1861, Juárez was elected president of the republic by a large majority. However, protection and recognition of the Liberal government by the United States soon evaporated with the outbreak of the American Civil War. Mexico, with a debt of fifty-one million pesos, put a moratorium on debt payments for two years. England, Spain, and France agreed to occupy Mexican customs houses to force debt repayment. The English and Spanish withdrew when it became apparent that the French, led by Napoleon III, had decided to bring troops for a full-scale invasion.

This second French intervention was due to a perceived opportunity to gain a new foothold in North America. Napoleon III wanted to remove Juárez's government and replace it with a monarchy ruled by a European prince. He chose the Austrian-Hapsburg Archduke Ferdinand Maximilian. What followed was the Second Franco-Mexican War from 1862 to 1867. The French finally placed Maximilian on the throne in 1864 as the head of the Second Mexican Empire. However, the French could never completely stamp out the republican government embodied in Juárez, who always evaded their grasp.

France had several problems with the intervention. One was that they hoped for a strong alliance with the Conservatives of Mexico. However, Maximilian proved somewhat Liberal-leaning and did not appoint Conservatives to important roles in his court. By 1866, growing costs, political issues in Europe, domestic opposition, and opposition from the newly unified United States led to a withdrawal of French troops. Maximilian chose to remain in Mexico and called on the help of General Miramón to stage a last stand against the encroaching Liberal armies. The Liberal commanders, Mariano Escobedo and Porfirio Díaz, achieved the final victories over the Conservatives, with Díaz capturing Mexico City in 1867. Maximilian, Miramón, and General Tomás Mejía were brought before a court-martial under treason laws established in 1862. All three were found guilty and executed by firing squad. It did not go unnoticed that Maximilian, a Hapsburg descendent of the Spanish Emperor Charles V, was put to death on a hill outside Mexico City and killed by the mestizo soldiers of a republican army. It was intended as a warning to any European monarchs with intentions to meddle in the affairs of American republics. Benito Juárez, who had maintained the Mexican Republic through the Reform Wars and French intervention, once again became president—this time over a seemingly unified Mexico.

Section Three: Revolution and Evolution (1870–Present)

Chapter 9: Porfirio's Mexico

Porfirio Díaz was born in Oaxaca in 1830, the son of a criollo father and a mestizo mother. His father was a modest innkeeper who died of cholera when Porfirio was only three. Despite the family's financial difficulties, Porfirio was sent to school when he was six. It was eventually determined that he should pursue an ecclesiastical career. However, Díaz, like many other students during the Mexican-American War, joined the military instead. In 1846, Díaz met the governor of Oaxaca, Benito Juárez. He became a Liberal and remained loyal to Juárez even after Santa Anna returned to power, joining guerilla groups fighting Santa Anna's government. Díaz was rewarded when the Liberals regained power, and he quickly rose to the rank of general. When the French invaded, he proved himself to be a more than able tactician. He had victories at the Battle of Puebla, Nochixtlán, and La Carbonera. He was captured by the French but escaped and was asked to join the Conservatives; however, he pledged loyalty to the Liberals. In 1867, Emperor Maximilian offered Díaz command of the Imperial Army, but Díaz turned him down. By the end of the war with France, Díaz was a national hero. Juárez returned to the presidency, and Porfirio Díaz resigned from the army and returned home to Oaxaca.

However, Díaz soon expressed his opposition to Juárez's presidency. The general championed term limits and ran against Juárez in 1870. When Juárez won, Díaz made accusations of fraud. In open defiance of Juárez, he created the Plan de la Noria and was joined by other disgruntled leaders. He was defeated in the battle of La Bufa in March of 1872.

Then, in July of that same year, Benito Juárez, who had served as the twenty-sixth President of Mexico for over fourteen years, died of a heart attack in the capital. Sebastián Lerdo de Tejada, head of the Supreme Court, became interim president. After elections were held, Lerdo became the twenty-seventh president. Despite Porfirio's rebellious outbursts, Lerdo offered him amnesty. The general took it and retired to a hacienda in Veracruz.

The new president was honest but cold. He refused to allow railroads to be built connecting the United States and Mexico, which angered railroad interests in the US. This also added to tensions concerning Mexican and Amerindian bandits who crossed the border to raid US property and then disappeared back into the Mexican desert. Lerdo grew unpopular in Mexico, as well. When he announced he would run for the presidency again, Díaz and his supporters announced the Plan of Tuxtepec, which called for "effective suffrage" and "no reelection." This resonated with educated Mexicans.

Díaz gathered troops, support, and money in Texas, but his planned invasion was defeated. Díaz then took a ship to Veracruz, disguised as a worker. He entered Oaxaca, gathered a small army, and marched towards the capital. He might have been defeated again if not for the new head of the Supreme Court, José María Iglesias. Iglesias voided Lerdo's reelection on the grounds that votes from states in open revolt should not be counted and made himself interim president. Amid the confusion, General Porfirio Díaz, at the head of his small army, captured the capital and was praised as the savior of the country. He rode in triumph through the streets while Lerdo and Iglesias quickly boarded a ship into self-imposed exile.

Díaz was made provincial president and took office as the constitutional president in 1877. He quickly stamped out any plans to reinstate Lerdo or Iglesias. However, he avoided mistakes made by previous presidents. He did not take a hard line against the Catholic Church or military but won over political enemies with favors. When his term expired in 1880, he stayed true to his dictum of no reelection but ensured that the presidency went to his friend, Manuel González Flores.

Though Díaz stepped down, he remained close to the center of power, first as governor of Oaxaca and then as Chief Justice of the Supreme Court, second in line to the president. Possibly with Díaz's approval and perhaps his prompting, González began to make bold moves. He sold off large tracts of "uninhabited" land to foreign companies and large Mexican landowners even though the land was the home of a large number of Amerindians. Railroad and mining operations, largely in northern states, were sold to American interests. This might have been a delivery of promises Díaz had made while gaining support in Texas.

What caused the greatest uproar in Mexico was not necessarily the selling of Mexican land and resources but the fact that the González's administration made such a mess of these sales that the treasury remained bare. Díaz received no criticism, but González was hung out to dry. Also, during this period, American soldiers made several incursions into Mexico to hunt bandits without permission from the Mexican government. These border crossings remained etched in the Mexican memory. Every school child could name them, while most in the United States didn't even know they happened.

When 1884 came, many were pressuring Díaz to return to the presidency, and he did. The old slogan of "no reelection" was seemingly forgotten in favor of stability. This began a period known as Porfiriato, in which Díaz would lead the country as a dictator for the next twenty-six and a half years. Díaz did not lead with a particular governing philosophy. He was a pragmatic ruler who valued order and obedience above all else.

However, some intellectuals sought to define the period in political terms. These *Científicos,* or "men of science," promoted positivist scientific politics that sought to modernize Mexico. This group included the writer and historian Justo Sierra Méndez and Secretary of Finance José Yves Limantour. The focus for these men and for the president was a steady and reliable government above all else. Those in power knew that Mexico needed a stable government to progress into the twentieth century, and they sacrificed their republican and democratic ideals to this end. Elections had often been messy affairs in Mexican history, and Díaz sought to end that. Elections were not rigged during the Porfiriato as much as the winning candidate was selected beforehand and was typically handpicked by Díaz. This is how Díaz won every election from 1884 to 1910.

To revitalize the Mexican economy, Díaz continued the tradition of Ley Lerdo and continued to sell national land to developers. The government adopted a plan in which railroad surveyors, almost all US-based, would gain a third of the land they mapped. Wealthy Mexicans also benefited from these laws and made huge land grabs. By 1910, 2 percent of the country's population owned 98 percent of the land. Three major railways were able to reach from the United States into Mexico.

The main goal of foreign and domestic investors was to gain rights to the rich minerals in the Valley of Mexico. As far back as 1550, all subsurface minerals belonged to the Spanish Crown. After the War of Independence, this distinction was not so clear. In 1884, the Díaz administration introduced a new mineral mining code that clearly stated mining rights belonged to the investors who owned the land. In 1876, there were only forty mining concessions. By 1910, this number had reached 13,000. While the Spanish had only been interested in silver, these new operations searched for lead, zinc, and the crucial mineral of the electric age—copper. They found all these in abundance, and soon, the largest corporations in Mexico were mining companies, usually with US owners.

But mining created mining towns that were unsanitary, with people living in squalid conditions. Mines were run with severity, and the once-precious skills of the miners became unneeded in the age of open-pit and strip mining.

Still, in the north, the railroads and mines created boom states like Chihuahua. There, the Terraza family ruled a petty fiefdom, owning seven million acres of land and half a million cattle. The patriarch, Don Luis, would joke, "I'm not from Chihuahua, I own Chihuahua."

A unique culture developed in the north, where native people like the Yaqui, Mayo, and Tarahumara still held onto their traditions and way of life. Under Díaz's rule, the native people of Mexico suffered greatly and lost their lands to developers. Linguistic barriers kept these people isolated from society and from one another. Only two groups remained somewhat autonomous: the Yaqui of Sonora and the various Maya of the Yucatan.

The people of the north were not overtly religious but respected self-reliance, horsemanship, and the ability to handle a gun. At the same time, Chinese and Japanese immigrants began to enter the region, pushed out of their land by dense populations and economic issues or, in the case of many, moving away from the United States and its new anti-immigration laws.

Dams were built, and rivers that had previously run dry could be used to irrigate vast cotton fields in places like Coahuila. Commercial estates, growing sugar or henequen fiber used for twine, grew to consume whole villages. A few became immensely wealthy, while the majority struggled with high prices, soaring property values (which meant the loss of land), and the decline of personal freedoms. Then, oil was found near Tampico, an oil field second only to those in the United States.

Into the twentieth century, Díaz's political machine continued. Real power eventually fell into the hands of governors' handpicked administrators—*jefes políticos*. By 1910, jefes wielded considerable power over their appointed districts. They reported back to the governors, who then reported to Mexico City. But their reports were always fictitious accounts of what they thought Díaz wanted to hear. Dissenters were often deported or simply shot without a trial.

The Catholic Church presented a larger problem. Díaz kept the anti-clerical, Liberal laws on the books but chose not to enforce them in most cases. Religious schools were allowed, as were processions, but if a priest became a troublemaker, he was dealt with quickly.

For the elite, this new Mexico was amazing. Young men, who would have previously chosen between seminary or the military, went to universities in large numbers. Young women could legally marry who they liked and did not need their parents' permission. Mexico City buzzed with telegraph lines, telephone poles, movie theaters, and gramophones. Mexican thinkers now had access to a wider range of writers. They liked none more than Auguste Comte, whose positivism justified their country's transition from a place ruled by religion and superstition to a scientific age founded on reason and observation.

However, these changes came at a cost. The Porfiriato benefited a few at the cost of increased suffering for many. Foreign investors owned huge swaths of Mexican land, and the rest was held by a single-digit minority. Landless workers were the largest growing sector of the population. The outright violence of early generations had been replaced by systematic repression. Díaz's government was clearly aware of the danger of encroaching foreign investors. Still, by 1910, Díaz appeared to be at the height of his power, and many felt Mexico was far from any signs of revolution. Andrew Carnegie gushed that Díaz was "one of the greatest rulers in the world" after a trip to Mexico. Carnegie added, "The idea of revolution in Mexico is now impossible."

In 1909, President William Howard Taft became the first US president to visit Mexico while in office. This was a great chance for Díaz to show off his Mexico and get his picture taken side-by-side with the leader of the most powerful American nation. Taft was there to check on the stability of a nation that was, in so many ways, owned by a large number of US investors. However, even as Taft and Díaz stood together before the cameras, cracks were appearing in the Porfiriato. Though many did not realize it, and many more would spend years trying to understand it, the Mexican Revolution was about to dawn.

Chapter 10: Revolution!

The twentieth century saw many revolutions. They all shared a similar plot: radical elements overthrowing an aging power. These changes occurred in Russia, China, Cuba, Nicaragua, and many others, but the first was in Mexico. The debate continues about what ultimately led to the revolution. Certainly, there was growing discontent over the reapportionment of land and an overwhelming need for land reform. This was particularly conspicuous in states like Morelos and Chihuahua, where wealthy families took land for self-enrichment. In Morelos, sugar profits caused planters to aggressively take village properties. This would incite an insurgency led by a man named Emiliano Zapata.

Yet it was not just the confiscation of land that led to the revolution. In 1910, President Díaz was once again facing a reelection at eighty years old. Many felt that Díaz should have picked a successor long ago. Díaz had, in fact, indicated he would retire but changed his mind and decided to run again in 1910. Díaz allowed the moderate but left-leaning Francisco Madero to run against him. Madero was intended to be a consolation candidate, but he was never supposed to win.

The election took place in June and July. Madero had gathered significant public support, but when the results were announced, Díaz had won for the seventh time. If Díaz thought Madero would accept these results placidly, he must not have been paying close attention. Madero, the son of a wealthy family in Coahuila, had been the leading opponent to Díaz's reelection. Madero had even written a book, *The Presidential Succession of 1910*, which quickly became a bestseller. Madero was hailed as "the Apostle of Democracy" because he argued that, though Díaz had brought peace and stability to Mexico, it was at the price of freedom. To circumvent Madero's resistance, Díaz had his opponent arrested and imprisoned. However, Madero's family convinced his jailers to allow him to ride around San Luis Potosí on horseback. He was then able to easily escape. Madero was smuggled out of Mexico and set up shop in San Antonio, Texas. From there, he issued the Plan of San Luis Potosí, which called for an armed rebellion against President Díaz.

Emiliano Zapata Salazar, born in Anenecuilco in the state of Morelos in 1879, was thirty-one years old and already the president of his village council when Madero issued his plan. Zapata joined Madero's cause along with Pascual Orozco and Francisco "Pancho" Villa. Zapata was wary of Madero but allied with him because of Madero's promises of land reform. Zapata then led an army against the federals in the Battle of Cuautla. After six days, he emerged victorious. Orozco led an army in Chihuahua, where he enjoyed several victories against loyalist forces and helped oust the powerful Creel-Terrazas family. Pancho Villa, a bandit living in Durango, joined Madero to expand his activity.

Against Madero's wishes, Orozco and Villa took Ciudad Juárez in May of 1911. Not long after this, Díaz sued for peace. The result was the Treaty of Ciudad Juárez, which required Díaz to finally resign from the presidency. The interim president would be Francisco León de la Barra, former ambassador to the United States. By May 31, Díaz was leaving the country, never to return. As he left, the man who had once been the most powerful person in Mexico told reporters, "Madero has unleashed a tiger; let us see if he can control it."

In fact, Madero had called for the revolutionaries to lay down their arms, but Zapata refused to comply. In November, Madero was officially elected to the presidency. He retained the federal army, keeping many of the generals that had served Porfirio Díaz before him. Madero's efforts on land reform appeared too little, too late for many of the revolutionaries that had supported him. Zapata declared that Madero's democracy was not different from Díaz's tyranny.

General Victoriano Huerta had fought for Díaz and then pledged allegiance to Madero. He was now ordered by the new president to put down these continued revolts. Meanwhile, Zapata drafted the Plan of Ayala, which denounced Madero and would become the key document to those who supported Zapata, known as the Zapatistas. The plan called

Madero a traitor and named Pascual Orozco as the leader of the revolution.

Orozco had grown to oppose Madero after the new president had looked him over for key government positions and also because of Madero's lackluster attempts at land reform. Still, Orozco waited until the spring of 1912 to announce his intention of revolting against Madero. He would finance his war from his own pocket and from confiscated livestock sold in Texas for guns and ammunition. He soon defeated a federal army sent against him. Seeing the danger of this new resistance, Madero sent General Huerta to stop Orozco. The aging general defeated the rebels in three consecutive battles and captured Ciudad Juarez. Orozco was eventually injured and fled to the United States.

Meanwhile, Zapata was fighting in the south with federal forces and trying to take control of the rebellion in Morelos politically. He eventually succeeded, and locals pulled resources to give Zapata 10,000 pesos to continue his fighting.

Pancho Villa, unlike his fellow revolutionaries, had remained allied to Madero and fought on the federalist side against the rebels. Eventually, he met up with General Huerta, who made Villa a brigadier general. Villa was not so easily bought, so Huerta tried to discredit him by claiming he had stolen a prize horse. Villa struck the general, who demanded Villa be shot for insubordination. Villa was about to be executed when an order from Madero saved him. Villa was then taken to Belem Prison in Mexico City. In prison, Villa was educated in reading and writing and was informed of Zapata's Plan of Ayala. He escaped on Christmas Day 1912 and snuck into the United States.

Huerta was now conspiring to overthrow Madero along with Porfirio Díaz's nephew Félix Díaz, General Bernardo Reyes, General Madragón, and the United States ambassador, Henry Lane Wilson.

In February of 1913, a coup d'etat known to Mexicans as the "Ten Tragic Days" took place from the ninth to the nineteenth. Fighting began in Mexico City, where a group of military cadets and a few soldiers were led by General Madragón to force the release of Félix Díaz and Bernardo Reyes from prison. An assault on the presidential palace forced Madero to Cuernavaca in the state of Morelos. Madero made Huerta the head of the Capital Army, not knowing Huerta had allied with Díaz and Reyes. However, Huerta did not yet show his hand, and several days of bombardments rocked Mexico City, killing soldiers and civilians.

Then, in a flurry of exchanges between the conspirators, Ambassador Wilson, and reports back to US President Taft, it was arranged for Madero to resign and Huerta to become the interim president. After Madero signed the papers, he prepared to go into exile but was detained by Huerta's forces. Huerta became president on February 20, 1913. Madero and Vice-president José María Pino Suárez were taken by car to Lecumberri prison, where they were unceremoniously shot. The fighting had ceased, but Mexico City was littered with bodies that were burned because there was not enough time to bury them all.

While Díaz and his supporters hoped Huerta would be only a temporary president, they soon learned that the general had plans of his own. Huerta reached out to Pascual Orozco to gain his support. Orozco, who had not so long before been fighting Huerta on the battlefield, laid out his demands, which Huerta quickly agreed to. Orozco threw his support behind Huerta on February 27. Huerta also tried to gain Zapata's support, but the head of the forces in Morelos refused to defect to a federalist general. Zapata soon revised the Plan of Ayala and named himself the head of the revolution.

Pancho Villa had returned to Mexico and, finding the man who had tried to kill him in power, quickly joined forces with other revolutionaries in opposition to Huerta. This included Venustiano Carranza, the governor of Coahuila who had penned the Plan of Guadalupe, which denounced Huerta and called for the reinstatement of the constitutional government by a Constitutional Army.

Huerta wanted to restore Mexico to the "order" of the Porfiriato but lacked the nuanced political savvy that had kept Díaz in power. More likely to execute critics than turn them to his side, Huerta's regime was one of increased militarization. He called for more and more troops to join the Federal Army, relying on forced conscription (*leva*). Indigenous people, criminals, the homeless, and men simply leaving work at the end of the day were rounded up and added to the roster of an army that was, on paper, a quarter of a million men. However, Huerta's tactics in recruiting did not instill loyalty, and soldiers continually defected to the Constitutional Army rather than fight for Huerta.

US President Woodrow Wilson felt Huerta had gone too far and refused to recognize the newest Mexican government. Huerta used this as fuel to increase the size of his army, claiming an imminent US invasion. When middle-class Mexicans joined up, they were disappointed to learn they would be fighting other Mexicans and not Americans.

However, seeing the situation in dire straits, Wilson ordered the port of Veracruz to be occupied in what was known as the Tampico Affair in April of 1914. Ambassador Henry Lane Wilson was recalled, and President Wilson sent his representative, John Lind, to inform him of the developments in Mexico.

Álvaro Obregón, a politician born in Sonora, now joined the revolution against Huerta. He would prove to be a natural soldier and an excellent organizer. With elections approaching, Huerta ordered the army to surround the legislature building and had any congressman who might oppose him arrested. Congress was thus shut down, and the elections that followed were a sham.

In 1914, Zapata took the cities of Chilpancingo, Acapulco, Iguala, and Buenavista de Cuéllar. He then moved towards the capital. At the same time, Pancho Villa had several victories against the Federal Army, with Mexico City before him undefended. Obregón moved from Sonora and defeated Federal forces, including attacking gunboats with an airplane. Huerta, seeing his position deteriorate, resigned in July of 1914. He fled Mexico City to the United States, where he was arrested and died in captivity.

General Victoriano Huerta.
https://en.wikipedia.org/wiki/File:Victoriano_Huerta,_Retrato.png

After Huerta's resignation, the Federal Army simply ceased to function. The various revolutionary factions realized the need to meet and determine the future of Mexico. Villa and others devised the Pact of Torreón, a modification of Carranza's Plan of Guadalupe. The pact affirmed Carranza as chief of the Constitutional Army and called for the surrender of the Federal Army. However, the pact was radical in its language, and Carranza strove to lessen the power of the more radical elements in the Constitutional Army. The revolutionary generals met in October of 1914 in Aguascalientes, and Carranza faced harsh opposition. Carranza agreed to resign if his two opponents, Pancho Villa and Emiliano Zapata, also resigned and went into exile. None of this took place, and the convention settled on General Eulalio Gutiérrez to serve as president for twenty days.

Villa and Zapata allied against Carranza and Obregón, taking Mexico City when Carranza's forces evacuated it. After this, however, Zapata returned to Morelos while Villa set out to defeat the Constitutional Army. The United States favored Carranza, feeling that Villa and Zapata were too radical. They exited Veracruz so that the Constitutionalists could take the port and receive supplies and ammunition. When Villa met Obregón's forces in the Battle of Celaya, the Constitutionalists were victorious, and Villa was forced to flee north.

From 1915 to 1920, Carranza became the head of the constitutional government. To counteract his radical opponents, he issued additions to his Plan of Guadalupe that called for judicial, labor, and land reform. He became the constitutional president from 1917 to 1920. All the while, Zapata was a problem in the south until his assassination by order of Carranza in 1919. Villa was a problem in the north. There, Villa provoked the US by raiding an American settlement in New Mexico. On top of this, Félix Díaz had returned and was causing trouble in Veracruz with an army he had gathered there.

On the global stage, World War I had broken out, and Carranza decided to remain neutral— though he did toy with the idea of aligning with Germany, which resulted in the famous "Zimmerman Telegram" used to bring the United States into the war.

Carranza prudently decided not to run for reelection in 1920, but he did not support General Obregón as expected because he believed Mexico should have a civilian president. Obregón then opposed Carranza and forced the president out of Mexico City. Carranza left for Veracruz but was betrayed and assassinated on May 21, 1920.

This began a period of consolidation in the country that lasted for approximately the next twenty years. Álvaro Obregón served for four years as president; then he, too, was assassinated. He was succeeded by Plutarco Elías Calles, who also served for four years. After this came a period known as Maximato, in which Calles continued to wield power without holding the presidency. This lasted until 1934 with the election of Lázaro Cárdenas. At this time, the presidential term was extended to six years, but it became illegal to run for the office more than once. Cárdenas served until 1940, when World War II had broken out and Mexico's condition was about to improve.

Chapter 11: The Mexican Miracle and Post-War Evolution

President Manuel Ávila Camacho.
https://commons.wikimedia.org/wiki/File:Manuel_%C3%81vila_Camacho_in_the_1930s.jpg

President Plutarco Elías Calles founded the National Revolutionary Party (PNR) in 1929. Since Calles was not allowed to run again due to the 1917 Constitution, he put forward a relatively unknown candidate, Pascual Ortiz

Rubio. The PNR conducted various forms of voter fraud to give Rubio the victory by a landslide. Abelardo Rodríguez, the next candidate put forward by Calles' PNR, also won in a rigged election and acted as a subordinate to Calles.

Next came President Cárdenas, who took his own path even though Calles had handpicked him. Part of this was to change the name of the PNR to the Party of the Mexican Revolution (PRM). Cárdenas envisioned a party system that united working-class people in a form of socialism, but this was never realized. However, the separation of the party into sectors remained. There were four sectors: labor, peasants, "popular" (teachers and civil servants), and the military. This did not include the private business sector or those connected to the Catholic Church. These two interest groups would unite in the National Action Party (PAN), a major opposition party. This method of corporatism is often associated with the Nazi Party in Germany, which rose around the same time. However, Cárdenas was strongly opposed to fascism. He picked his successor, Ávila Camacho, who again won thanks to a fraudulent and violent election.

Camacho had joined the revolutionary army in 1914 and was a colonel by 1920. He had fought under Cárdenas in the Escobar Rebellion of 1929. In the 1930s, he entered political life and became Secretary of National Defense in 1937. Unlike some of his predecessors, Camacho was openly Catholic, and the struggles between the Church and the government largely ended during his term. In 1943, Camacho created the Mexican Social Security Institute to benefit the working class. He promoted literacy programs and land reform and instituted a rent freeze to help low-income Mexicans. Despite being elected fraudulently, Camacho promoted election reform to discourage the creation of far-right and far-left parties. In 1946, he again changed the name of the PRM to the Institutional Revolution Party (PRI).

Camacho increased the industrialization of Mexico and sided with the Allies in World War II. Mexican raw materials then went to the US to help the war effort. Industry grew by 10 percent annually from 1940 to 1945. His administration invited the Rockefeller Foundation to bring new technology that greatly increased the country's crop yields. By declaring war against the Axis powers, Camacho eased years of strain between the United States and Mexico.

The only Mexican troops involved in World War II were the 201st Fighter Squadron, whose pilots were nicknamed the "Aztec Eagles." The squadron flew in ninety-six combat missions and aided in the bombing of Luzon and Formosa against the Japanese. Out of its 300 men, the squadron only lost six pilots, who either crashed or were shot down.

Mexico also provided 300,000 workers to replace enlisted men in the United States under what was known as the Bracero Program. This agreement was extended with the Migrant Labor Agreement of 1951, keeping the program in place until 1964. Temporary agricultural workers were allowed via H-2 and then H-2A visas, according to the Immigration Reform and Control Act of 1986. In all, the Bracero Program provided five million workers to the US. Still, Mexico banned workers from going to certain states, such as Texas, because of the mistreatment and lynching suffered by Mexican workers there.

Under Camacho, Mexico also began diplomatic relations with the United Kingdom and the Soviet Union. After his term was finished, Camacho retired to his farm. Though they were far from perfect, Camacho and Cárdenas would be among the most beloved twentieth-century Mexican presidents.

The PRI became the major party of Mexico, and the only path to the presidency was through the party structure. Miguel Alemán Valdés was president from 1946 to 1952. He had served as Secretary to the Interior under Camacho and had been a rising star in the PRI for many years. He was handpicked by Camacho to be his successor. However, Alemán did not have a military background, something that had been true for every president in the modern era. This turned out not to be a drawback. The election of 1946 was free of violence, and there was a peaceful transition of power. The beginning of his term in office until 1970 has been called the "Mexican Miracle" due to the growth and rapid industrialization the country experienced. He supported spending on infrastructure and a decrease in spending on the military. Dams, river diversions, highways, and railways were all constructed and improved. A new campus was built for the National University. Still, corruption and cronyism were rampant during his time in office.

The PRI dominated Mexican politics to the point that the government was often considered a one-party organization. From 1929 to 1982, the PRI consistently won the presidential elections by over 70 percent, almost always due to election fraud. With help from party advisors, the incumbent president would pick his successor in a procedure known as *el dedazo* ("the tap of the finger"). Yet the PRI's dominance was not just at the presidential level but all levels throughout the government. During its period of dominance, it held every seat in the Senate and an overwhelming majority in the Chamber of Deputies.

Voter turnout was low, and the only real opposition the PRI faced was from the Conservative National Action Party, which would sometimes garner a majority of votes. However, the PRI would use its control of local government to rig the votes in its favor. The PRI controlled the labor unions and farmers and had the backing of intellectuals due to its support of universities and the arts.

Due to the policies introduced in the 1930s, Mexico was essentially closed off from foreign investment, so most Mexican companies relied on large government contracts. This resulted in urbanization and massive welfare programs to benefit the poor. Inflation remained low during this period, and the economy was stable. Due to this stability, most Mexicans did not oppose the lack of democracy, so the country remained free of internal instability. The population grew, especially in the north, where Monterrey became the country's second-largest city.

President Alemán expressed a desire to run for a second term, but the party leaders dissuaded him from this course. Instead, he chose Adolfo Ruiz Cortines, previous Secretary of the Interior and Governor of Veracruz, as his successor. Ruiz had fought in the Constitutional Army and had opposed Huerta and supported Carranza in the revolution. One of Ruiz's first actions when he took office in 1952 was to put forward an amendment to the constitution that would give women the right to vote. This was eventually passed. Under his administration, infrastructure increased, spending was reduced, and malaria was eradicated from the country. His freeze on government contracts caused a severe blow to employers, who were forced to lay off many of their workers. However, he shifted his focus and began to spend once again on government projects. While Ruiz was president, the Mexican Miracle continued, and he experienced little opposition. As his successor, he chose the relatively obscure Adolfo López Mateos.

Mateos, like the two presidents before him, favored industrialization and looked to capitalism over the needs of the labor sector. However, he needed labor organizations to cooperate to continue the policies of the Mexican Miracle. Labor unions were becoming uneasy about their position within the government hierarchy. Labor was mainly organized within the PRI in the Confederation of Mexican Workers (CTM), run by

Fidel Velázquez Sánchez. Velázquez had helped found CTM in 1936 and forced its leader, Vicente Lombardo Toledano ("the dean of Mexican Marxism"), out of power and out of the organization. Velázquez was a heavy-handed leader, and the organization grew more corrupt and Conservative as time went on. Some who had served in the PRI the longest were derisively called "dinosaurs," and Velázquez would outlast them all. Still, he could do nothing about the growing restlessness within labor. Workers called for higher wages and better working conditions.

In 1958, militant railroad workers' unions began to go on strike. Mateos' Secretary of the Interior, Gustavo Díaz Ordaz, responded by arresting the union leaders. Yet Mateos also updated the constitution to provide certain guarantees to workers as long as they joined the federal workers' union. The minimum wage was at an all-time high during his presidency. He opened several museums and encouraged healthcare and land reforms. Mateos also implemented a free textbook program and adult classes to reduce illiteracy. He picked Gustavo Díaz Ordaz as his successor.

Gustavo Díaz Ordaz served from 1964 until 1970. He was authoritarian in his manner of governance. Under his presidency, there was continual unrest, with many protests and strikes. A union of medics went on strike early in his term, and his response was to use force to end the protests.

Ordaz's authoritarian style is perhaps best seen in an incident that occurred on October 2, 1968. A group of students had organized themselves to publicly oppose the PRI at the Autonomous National University of Mexico and the National Polytechnic Institute in Mexico City. The protests became larger and larger over the summer of 1968. The students were particularly opposed to the 1968 World Olympics, which were to take place in Mexico City. On October 2, about 10,000 university and high school students gathered in the Plaza de las Tres Culturas (Plaza of the Three Cultures) to hear speeches. They chanted, "We don't want Olympics, we want revolution!" Local residents, including children, began to gather to watch. Around 5,000 soldiers, two helicopters, and several tankettes arrived at the scene. Flares were shot into the ground, believed to have been a signal to the soldiers—particularly the Olympia Battalion, made of soldiers, police officers, and federal agents—to begin firing into the crowd. Snipers were positioned on the roofs, and machine gun nests had been set up in buildings surrounding the plaza. The soldiers fired indiscriminately, killing protestors and onlookers alike, including children.

This would be known as the Tlatelolco Massacre, and the details of the incident would not be fully understood until 2001. The death toll, originally reported to be around twenty-eight people, was actually closer to 400. The Olympia Battalion appears to have been most instrumental in the killings and subsequent arrests of protesters, onlookers, and passers-by, who were held in makeshift prisons around the square.

Díaz Ordaz chose Luis Echeverría to be his successor. Echeverría served from 1970 to 1976. As the former Secretary of the Interior, he was among those responsible for the Tlatelolco Massacre. However, as president, he ignored any accusations associated with the incident. He released those still in prison from the 1968 protests, which was seen as an effort to distance himself from the event. Echeverría instituted political and economic reform, nationalized mining operations, and redistributed land in the Sinaloa and Sonora regions. He increased spending on food subsidies, education, healthcare, and housing. Under Echeverría, the number of people covered under social security almost doubled.

At the end of Echeverría's term, the Mexican Miracle began to fall apart. The federal debt to other countries had risen from $6 billion to $20 billion. Still, the Mexican economy grew during Echeverría's time in office. He chose José López Portillo, a close friend of the president and his finance minister, to follow him.

Despite some changes in election law, López Portillo ran unopposed due to internal struggles within the National Action Party. He would serve from 1976 to 1982. His solution to Mexico's deep economic crisis was to derive revenue from new oil reserves discovered in Veracruz and Tabasco through the publicly owned oil company Pemex. Mexico also joined with Venezuela in the Pact of San José, an agreement to sell oil at preferential rates to countries in Latin America and the Caribbean. Thanks to López Portillo's efforts, Mexico received a short reprieve from economic hardships, but this did not last past López Portillo's term. López Portillo also nationalized the country's banking system.

There were reports of corruption within the government, and it also became apparent that López Portillo did not shy away from nepotism. He hired his sister to run the General Directorate of Radio, Television, and Cinematography. His cousin was hired to be the first and only head of the newly created National Institute of Sport, and his son became the Subsecretary of Programming and Budget.

López Portillo remains one of Mexico's most unpopular presidents. He chose Miguel de la Madrid as his successor.

Chapter 12: From Crisis to Contemporary: Modern Mexico

The 1980s have been called "La Década Perdida" (The Lost Decade) in many Latin American countries. This was due to a number of economic factors but primarily the drop in the value of raw materials, particularly oil, at the end of the 1970s. The downturn was not just experienced in Mexico but in almost every country in Central and South America. The decade was noted for high inflation, huge external and unpayable debts, and unemployment.

Miguel de la Madrid, who came from Colima, Mexico, might have seemed like a good candidate to deal with this crisis. He had a background working for the Bank of Mexico. He had also worked for Pemex and served as the Secretary of Budget and Planning before becoming president. The election of 1982 had a massive turnout, unlike previous elections, and De la Madrid, who did not face a strong opponent, won by a large margin. Still, he could do little in the face of such an economic crisis. His attempts to remedy the situation included cutting spending, reorganizing the bureaucracy, fiscal reforms, and job protection. But these actions did little to deal with the problems Mexico faced. The country saw negative economic growth during his entire six-year term.

President de la Madrid was a market-focused leader and introduced neoliberal ideas into the government, including privatizing state-run companies and encouraging foreign investment. Though he stated that the country needed more democracy, he was hostile towards the growing influence of political parties besides the PRI.

It was during his presidency that the National Action Party (PAN) began to gain significant popularity, especially in Northern Mexico. PAN had been founded partly out of a desire to oppose state-imposed education. This concept of educational freedom had enticed the Jesuit organization Unión Nacional de Estudiantes Católicos (UNEC), founded in 1931, to team up with the politician Manuel Gómez Morín to promote a more Conservative ideology than that espoused by the PRI. Morín founded PAN in 1939. The party had existed in the PRI shadow for several decades, but during La Década Perdida, it came to be seen as a reasonable alternative to the corruption and missteps of the PRI. In particular, the PAN was pro-democracy and pro-rule of law, which stood in contrast to the previous decades under the PRI.

In 1983, the PAN won several elections in the state of Chihuahua. PRI officials claimed voters had been influenced by the Catholic Church and foreign interests. In 1989, the PAN candidate, Ernesto Ruffo Appel, won the governorship of Baja California. He was the first state governor not affiliated with the PRI since 1929. By that time, the presidency had passed on to Carlos Salinas de Gortari.

Carlos Salinas de Gortari's father had served in the cabinet of President Mateos but was passed over for president in favor of Gustavo Díaz Ordaz. Salinas had been an undergraduate at the National Autonomous University of Mexico when the 1968 Tlatelolco Massacre occurred. The future president joined and was active in the PRI at a young age. He went on to attend Harvard University and eventually graduated from the Harvard Kennedy School. In 1982, he became the Minister of Planning and Budget under President de la Madrid when he was just thirty-four. His chief rival in the cabinet was the Minister of Finance, Jesús Silva-Herzog, whom Salinas sought every opportunity to disgrace. He formed an alliance with the Minister of the Interior, which eventually led to Silva-Herzog's resignation.

In the 1988 election, the PRI faced serious opposition for the first time. On the left was the National Democratic Front, which ran Cuauhtémoc Cárdenas (son of previous President Lázaro Cárdenas), and on the right was the PAN, which ran Manuel Clouthier, a well-to-do businessman, as its candidate.

Carlos Salinas de Gortari won the election, but not without doubts about the legitimacy of his victory. The Minister of the Interior, who oversaw the election process, had installed new voting computers that had mysteriously crashed during the election. When they were restored, the vote came out in favor of Salinas. Mexicans continue to use the phrase *se cayó el Sistema*, or "the system crashed," to denote election fraud.

When Salinas took office, he appointed many of the PRI "dinosaurs" to his cabinet and continued the neoliberal reforms of his predecessor. He privatized the Mexican Telephone Company (Telmex) and the banks previously under the government's control. However, he also bailed out toll roads and banks during his term. The president was able to decrease inflation and stabilize the *peso*. He also instituted a direct welfare program to aid the country's poor, which did not align with neoliberalism. However, this program lacked oversight and did not target the poorest states. Instead, it focused on states that had been the most contested during the election. This convinced critics that Salinas' motives were purely political.

In 1994, the Zapatista Army of National Liberation (EZLN), named after revolutionary hero Emiliano Zapata, conducted an uprising in the state of Chiapas. It had been created largely in opposition to Salinas' amendment to the constitution, which took away protections for national land. These Zapatistas were indigenous people who had organized themselves. On the first day of the year, they simultaneously attacked city halls and other civic buildings. They wore ski masks and, once inside the buildings, barricaded themselves in using office furniture. In the city of San Cristóbal de las Casas, the Zapatistas freed 240 indigenous prisoners from jail and destroyed land records. They fought police and government forces in many of the cities they attacked. The rebels were eventually driven out of the towns by the Mexican Army and into the Lacandon Jungle. Zapatista supporters used the internet to spread the word about the events as the Mexican government sought to suppress news of the rebellion on radio and TV. A ceasefire was agreed to, but after a meeting in February, the EZLN rejected the government's proposals. Peace was not fully realized until 1996. The agreement was not particularly beneficial to the EZLN, but the uprising has been cited as an influence on the further democratization of Mexico.

Salinas chose Luis Donaldo Colosio Murrieta as his successor in the PRI. During the campaign of 1994, Colosio gave a controversial speech that echoed many of the talking points of the EZLN. It is believed that this speech caused a break between Salinas and Colosio. On March 23, 1994, Colosio was shot in the head at a campaign rally. He died a few hours later. The shooter was identified as Mario Aburto Martínez, who confessed and said that he had acted alone. Aburto was found guilty and sentenced to forty-two years in prison. Still, many critics pointed out that the investigation seemed rushed, and much was made confidential. Many claim that Salinas and cabinet member Manuel Camacho Solís were behind the assassination. In Colosio's place, the PRI put forth Ernesto Zedillo as the presidential candidate. He had been the Secretary of Education and was running Colosio's campaign at the time of his death. Though Zedillo won the election, he received only 48.69 percent of the vote.

Zedillo inherited one of the worst economic climates in Mexican history. Still, he continued to approach the crisis with the neoliberal attitude of his predecessors. Many thought he would be simply a puppet president controlled by Salinas. To show his independence, he had Salinas' older brother, Raúl Salinas de Gortari, arrested for involvement in the murder of PRI General Secretary José Francisco Ruiz Massieu. To validate the investigations into the various assassinations that had occurred, Zedillo appointed Antonio Lozano Gracia, of the opposing National Action Party, to the post of attorney general.

Though Salinas had helped finalize the program, the North American Free Trade Agreement (NAFTA) was first tested under Zedillo. During a steep devaluation of the peso in 1994, the United States provided a multi-billion-dollar loan to help stabilize Mexico's economy. Zedillo continued to privatize state-owned companies like the railway system. Zedillo's approval rating was particularly low during the first years of his term but steadily improved with an easing of economic woes. He was also viewed favorably for the peaceful transition of power to the next president in 2000.

That president was Vincente Fox. For the first time in seventy-one years, the newest leader of Mexico was not from the PRI but was the candidate from an alliance between PAN and the Ecologist Green Party of Mexico (PVEM) called the "Alliance for Change." Fox had won 42.5 percent of the popular vote, and the alliance also won 46 out of 128 seats in the Senate the same year.

Vincente Fox, previously an executive at Coca-Cola and later Governor of Guanajuato, pursued the same neoliberal goals as his predecessors despite the party differences. During his term, Fox sometimes appeared subservient to the United States, particularly to President George W.

Bush. Fox's several missteps and scandals led to a view of him as a "lame duck," but there were periods when he enjoyed high approval ratings.

Fox was succeeded by Felipe de Jesús Calderón, also of PAN and previously the Secretary of Energy. Calderón won by a hairline margin over the Party of Democratic Revolution (PRD) candidate Andrés Manuel López Obrador. The PRD disputed the results and called for a complete recount, but Calderón's victory was affirmed by the Federal Electoral Tribunal.

One of Calderón's first actions was to declare war on the Mexican drug cartels in what would be known as the "Mexican Drug War." Two years later, 45,000 troops were involved. The success of this war is hotly debated. By the end of Calderón's term, his administration claimed there had been only 50,000 drug-related homicides in the country, whereas other groups placed the number closer to 120,000.

The president who served after Calderón, Enrique Peña Nieto (EPN), tried to de-escalate the war and focus on stopping drug violence without arresting or killing leaders of the cartels. Peña Nieto was from the PRI and won a narrow victory against López Obrador and the PRD, who contested the vote but could not secure change. EPN's time in office has largely been viewed as harmful to the PRI and Mexico. A mass kidnapping in 2014 and the escape of drug lord "El Chapo" tarnished the president's reputation. Economic woes from falling oil prices and alleged connection to illegal campaign funds have led to him being viewed as one of Mexico's least popular presidents.

After Peña Nieto, the presidency finally went to López Obrador, who had so narrowly lost the previous two elections. Obrador came into office in 2018 after winning a landslide victory. He is a center-left, progressive populist who has been working towards improving the conditions of the working class and rolling back the neoliberal actions of his predecessors. However, critics have claimed he failed to respond appropriately to the COVID-19 pandemic and has not been successful at dealing with Mexico's drug cartels. He is the head of a new political party—Movement for National Regeneration, or MORENA. Obrador has pledged to conduct a crusade of anti-corruption but has fallen short of international expectations. He has been accused of theatrics with little substance. However, he has gained attention for his work on the Maya Train, an intercity railway line connecting sites in the Yucatan region.

Section Four:
A Thematic Overview

Chapter 13: Legendary Battles and Events

The Battle of Calderón Bridge (1811)

It was January of 1811, and revolutionary forces had failed to take Mexico City and had retreated towards Guadalajara. The total number of soldiers under the command of Miguel Hidalgo, Ignacio Allende, Juan Aldama, and Mariano Abasolo numbered about 100,000, but they were ill-equipped and largely untrained. At the bridge of Calderón, which crossed the Calderón River, they took up a defensive position and awaited the arrival of the Spanish forces. This royalist army was under the command of Félix María Calleja del Rey, who would become the viceroy of New Spain in 1813. Calleja's forces, which numbered no more than 8,000 with ten cannons, arrived at the bridge on January 16. As the battle got underway, the royalist artillery struck an ammunition wagon among the revolutionaries. The resulting explosion caused the rebels to disperse and gave the victory to the much smaller but better-trained royalist army. This defeat directly led to the capture and eventual death of Hidalgo, showing the insurgents that they required better training and arms if they were going to defeat the skilled armies of New Spain.

The Assassination of Emiliano Zapata (1919)

The rebel Emiliano Zapata once said, "Men of the South, it is better to die on your feet than live on your knees." After the revolution seemed finished and Carranza had taken power, Zapata continued his fight in Morelos. He knew Carranza was a moderate and would not redistribute land or remove the foreign investors that Zapata felt were ruining the country. Carranza would not stop the sugar plantations from spreading through Morelos and causing more and more farmers to lose their land and livelihoods. Zapata saw this and knew he had to continue to fight.

General Pablo González had been sent by Carranza to capture Zapata, but though the general laid waste to the state of Morelos, he could not capture the rebel. So, González instead relied on treachery. Zapata received a message from a man named Jesus Guajardo, a colonel in the González army, saying that he wanted to defect and join Zapata's rebellion. Zapata was suspicious, but when Guajuardo captured some of González's troops and had them shot, Zapata took the claim more seriously. A meeting was arranged at a hacienda in San Juan Chinameca. When Zapata arrived, he was greeted by a flourish of trumpets followed shortly by a hail of gunfire. Zapata was killed instantly. His body was picked up and taken to Cuautla, where it was dumped in the street.

The Battle of Puebla (1862)

During the Second French intervention in May of 1862, French forces under the command of Charles de Lorencez attempted to storm the forts of Loreto and Guadalupe, which were situated on top of hills overlooking the city of Puebla. The Mexican commanders included Ignacio Zaragoza and Porfirio Díaz. The French troops used advanced weaponry that outclassed the Mexican's antiquated muskets and cannon. However, the French had underestimated the fortifications they faced and the skill of the Mexican commanders. After a full day of trying to take the forts with heavy casualties, the French were forced to retire. On the second day, the French attempted to surround the forts but were defeated in each engagement and were forced to retreat by evening. The day of victory was May 5, remembered in Puebla as "The Day of the Battle of Puebla." It would come to the United States as Cinco de Mayo, a celebration of Mexican heritage. Though the battle was not a turning point in the war, it was an inspirational victory for the Mexican people.

The Siege of Guanajuato (1810)

When Father Miguel Hidalgo issued his "Cry of Dolores," he found himself the leader of an ever-increasing mob of disaffected Mexicans sick of Spanish rule. As the mob traveled through towns, its numbers increased. Eventually, they came to the city of Guanajuato in the region also known as Guanajuato. Royalist forces there were prepared to stand against the disaffected Mexicans and fortified themselves in a large granary in town. Inside were wealthy Creoles and Spanish, loyal soldiers, and the intendant of the town, Juan Antonio Riaño y Bárcena. The peasants of the town joined Hidalgo's mob. For five hours, the mob sieged the granary fortress. Four hundred defenders were killed, including Riaño, who was shot. The granary was overcome by overwhelming forces. Some of those inside the granary wished to surrender, while some of the soldiers continued to fight. Once the revolutionary forces broke through, they killed those still inside. The siege has also been called the Capture of Alhóndiga de Granaditas. It was the first victory of the fledgling revolution and boosted the Mexican people's confidence.

Pancho Villa's Attack on the United States (1916)

In 1915, the United States recognized Venustiano Carranza as the legitimate head of the Mexican government. This was a slap in the face to Carranza's rival, Francisco "Pancho" Villa. The US further supplied rail transport for Carranza's soldiers to attack Villa at the Battle of Agua Prieta, where Villa's forces were defeated. Villa responded by attacking US citizens in Mexico and taking their property.

In March of 1916, Villa and a small army crossed the border and attacked Columbus, New Mexico, including the army outpost, Camp Furlong. Villa's forces killed eight soldiers and ten civilians in the raid and made off with ammunition, machine guns, and other supplies. They burned the town and stole all the horses and mules. However, Villa's men suffered significant casualties, including sixty-seven deaths.

This prompted an immediate response from the US. Major General John Pershing was put in charge of an expeditionary force ordered to cross into Mexico in pursuit of Villa. All told, Pershing had a force of about 10,000 men, mostly composed of cavalry and horse artillery. Pershing also used the 1st Aero Squadron for aerial reconnaissance missions. However, Villa had a six-day head start, and his band broke up and hid in the mountains of Northern Mexico. A few engagements resulted in over a hundred Villa supporters being killed. Pershing's forces suffered a total of sixty-five deaths during the whole expedition. The Americans were not able to capture or kill Villa. Eventually, they had to abandon the operation when Carranza threatened to begin attacking the expedition's supply lines and force them out of Mexico.

Chapter 14: Key Figures

Former President Cárdenas.
Eneas De Troya from Mexico City, México, CC BY 2.0
<*https://creativecommons.org/licenses/by/2.0*>, *via Wikimedia Commons;*
https://commons.wikimedia.org/wiki/File:Conf%C3%ADo_en_la_palabra_del_PRI_respecto_a_Pemex_Cuauht%C3%A9moc_C%C3%A1rdenas_(8434851979).jpg)

Cuauhtémoc Cárdenas

Born in 1934 in Mexico City, Cuauhtémoc Cárdenas was the son of former president Lázaro Cárdenas and was named after the last Aztec emperor. After his father left office, he worked with the elder Cárdenas to pull the PRI more to the left politically. He was eventually driven out of the PRI for his anti-privatization rhetoric. In 1988, he ran against the PRI's centrist candidate, Carlos Salinas, supported by a coalition of small left-wing parties calling themselves the National Democratic Front. This was the election in which the "system crashed" and Salinas was crowned the victor. The next year, undaunted, Cárdenas formed the Party of Democratic Revolution (PRD) and was named the party's first president. In 1994, he ran again for the presidency and placed third behind the PRI and PAN candidates. In 1997, he was elected the Head of Government of the Federal District, a spot between the mayor of Mexico City and the state governor. He ran for president again in 2000, once again coming in third. He no longer ran for the presidency, but in 2018, his ally and PRD candidate, Andrés Manuel López Obrador, did win the election. In 2014, he stunned many by leaving the PRD, which spurred speculation of inter-party difficulties.

Father Miguel Hidalgo.
https://commons.wikimedia.org/wiki/File:Miguel_Hidalgo_y_Costilla.png

Don Miguel Hidalgo y Costilla

Born May 8, 1753, Hidalgo was a Catholic priest and revolutionary who has been called the "George Washington of Mexico" and "Father of the Nation." The son of a criollo father who owned a hacienda, Hidalgo moved to the city of Valladolid when he was fifteen, where he spent the majority of his life. (Today, it is more commonly called Morelia.) He studied with the Jesuits, but when they were expelled, he went to the Universidad Michoacana de San Nicolás. Today, the school adds "y Hidalgo" to its name. He excelled in school and gained the nickname "El Zorro" or "The Fox" for his cleverness. He read Enlightenment works that were banned by the Catholic Church.

In 1778, at twenty-five, Hidalgo was ordained a priest, one of the few professions available to middle-class men. He became a teacher of grammar, arts, and theology at the school he graduated from. He was eventually removed from the college for his revised teaching methods and was sent to be a priest in Colima and San Felipe Torres Mochas. In 1803, he was then sent to Dolores in Guanajuato. The parish was made mainly of indigenous people struggling to survive. He taught them useful trades and tried to better their lives.

There, he owned three haciendas and had relationships with women. He clearly challenged the traditional views of what a priest should be and had grown to oppose Spanish control of Mexico. He was brought before the Court of the Inquisition, but they did not find him guilty.

Around this time, a conspiracy was developing in the city of Querétaro, which involved Ignacio José de Allende, a captain of the Spanish army who favored independence. At one of these meetings, Hidalgo met Allende and another captain, Juan Aldama. All three would become important figures in the War of Independence. However, it was Hidalgo who cast the dice when he gave the Cry of Dolores on September 16, 1810, and began the Mexican War of Independence. When it was finished, Mexico would finally be free from the Spanish yoke, but Hidalgo would not live long enough to see his dream come true. On July 30, 1811, he was captured and sentenced to death by firing squad. His head was put on display to warn other revolutionaries. He was fifty-eight years old.

Santa Anna

Antonio López de Santa Anna.
Gnew20, CC BY-SA 4.0 <https://creativecommons.org/licenses/by-sa/4.0>, via Wikimedia Commons; https://commons.wikimedia.org/wiki/File:Antonio_Lopez_de_Santa_Anna,_president_of_Mexico.jpg

Santa Anna's full name was Antonio de Padua María Severino López de Santa Anna y Pérez de Lebrón. As detailed in previous chapters, perhaps no other figure in Mexican history has been pushed out only to come back more times than Santa Anna. He served as president eleven different times throughout the nineteenth century, a time that is often referred to as the "Age of Santa Anna." He fought in the War of Independence, participated in the fall of the First Empire, helped establish the Constitution of 1835, created the Centralist Republic, fought against the Texans in the Texas Revolution, led troops in the Pastry War, helped create the Constitution of 1843, and fought against the Americans in the Mexican-American War.

For three decades, Santa Anna dominated the political and military world of Mexico. He switched parties multiple times, put people into power only to overthrow them, and was exiled from his country on several occasions. He was a tireless self-promoter, calling himself the "Napoleon of the West." He was a figure larger than life. He had glorious victories, such as when the Spanish attempted to retake Mexico and Santa Anna defeated them with an inferior force. He also had terrible defeats, such as the many defeats he suffered at the hands of United States forces in the Mexican-American War.

Americans perhaps know him best as the butcher of the Alamo, but his story is infinitely more complex and is sewn into the very fabric of the path of Mexico from independence from Spain to the revolution of the early twentieth century.

Victoriano Huerta

Victoriano Huerta.
https://commons.wikimedia.org/wiki/File:Victoriano_Huerta.(cropped).jpg

As we've discovered, Victoriano Huerta is an intriguing figure. His parents were both Huichol, or Wixárika, an indigenous people living in both Mexico and the United States. He decided on a military career at a young age and became the personal secretary to General Donato Guerra in 1869, not long after the end of the Second French intervention. With the help of Guerra, he attended the Mexican National Military Academy, graduating in 1877. He worked as an engineer but eventually came under the patronage of General González, a close friend of Porfirio Díaz and eventually the 35th President of Mexico.

Huerta was eventually put in command of fighting units and distinguished himself. He was known for ensuring his men were paid, sometimes by extra-legal means. (He was accused of stealing from a church to get silver to pay his men and of emptying a bank at gunpoint for the same reason.) Huerta's hero, like Santa Anna, was Napoleon. He gained a reputation for ruthlessness, often refusing to take prisoners and killing captives.

In 1901, Huerta was made a general and soon advanced to a brigadier general. Despite appearances, Huerta had developed a heavy drinking problem, and his health was in decline. In 1907, he retired from the army. Huerta was teaching mathematics when the revolution broke out in 1910. He came out of retirement to attempt to crush Zapata in Morelos on behalf of the new Madero government. He became Madero's most trusted general and tried unsuccessfully to have his rival, Pancho Villa, executed. Huerta's forces defeated the forces of Pascal Orozco in 1912, and he became a national military hero.

Seeing the opportunity for greater power, Huerta joined forces with people in the government who wanted to overthrow Madero. Huerta became president but eventually resigned after being defeated by Villa and others in 1914. He went into exile in the United States and planned to return to Mexico to once again overthrow the government. However, he was found out by US agents and put in prison, where he died. The cause of death was given as natural, but many suspect he was poisoned.

Nuño Beltrán de Guzmán

Nuño de Guzmán was born in 1485 in Spain to a noble family. He served for a time as a royal bodyguard of Charles V of Spain. In 1525, he was made governor of a region on the Gulf Coast in northeast Mexico, a territory called Pánuco. He traveled to Mexico and assumed his position in 1527. His appointment was a direct challenge to Hernán Cortés, who had already extended his reach into Pánuco.

Cortés and his supporters opposed Guzmán, but he had the backing of the Council of the Indies, the Spanish Crown, and many Spanish settlers who felt blocked by Cortés and his associates, who seemed to be taking all the land for themselves. Governor Guzmán dealt harshly with pro-Cortés factions and natives in his territory. In 1529, Nuño Beltrán de Guzmán was named president of the First Audiencia, a governing body meant to check the expansion of individual power in Mexico. With Cortés in Spain, defending his actions, Guzmán became the head of New Spain.

The next year, Cortés returned to Mexico, and Guzmán stepped down to become governor of Nueva Galicia. The name of this territory was changed to the "Kingdom of New Galicia," and Guzmán continued his cruel treatment of indigenous peoples and anyone who opposed him, gaining a reputation as a depraved ruler. He was eventually arrested in 1536 and returned to Spain, where he was released and again became a royal bodyguard. He died there in 1561.

Chapter 15: The America Question

The United States and Mexico share a complicated past. Originally home to cultures of indigenous people, they both became home to European colonies. First, Spain established New Spain in what would become Mexico. The United States was home to English, French, Dutch, and Spanish colonies fighting with each other for supremacy. The native population faced disease, slavery, and oppression in both areas. New Spain was certainly the wealthier and more powerful colony, and Mexico City was the greatest of North American cities, overshadowing Boston, New York, and New Orleans.

When the colonists expelled the British and formed the United States at the end of the eighteenth century, they looked to New Spain for some of their inspiration. For instance, they called their currency "dollars" in the Spanish fashion. In turn, the people of Mexico were most likely inspired to get rid of the Spanish after the successful American Revolution.

In the early decades of the nineteenth century, the United States grew exponentially by taking land from native peoples and purchasing the Louisiana Territory in 1803. Mexico, after the War of Independence, struggled through bouts of civil war and instability. Whereas Mexico had once been the dominant power in North America, the United States rose in global prominence. The scales were finally tipped in the Mexican-American War. After the breaking off of Texas from Mexico and the desire of Americans to gain control of western territory, Americans invaded their southern neighbor to secure California, Texas, Arizona, New Mexico, and parts of Colorado, Utah, and Nevada. With their victory, the Americans secured their place as the new great power in the Americas.

The United States came out of its own Civil War more industrialized and a greater power than before, while Mexico fell behind in the Industrial Revolution. Americans took advantage of the situation and began to buy up Mexican land and bring American companies into Mexico to corner markets. Mexicans began to see Americans as greedy foreign investors taking away their sovereignty and wealth. By the end of the nineteenth century, the Mexican people had developed a sincere distrust and dislike of the United States.

The Americans, for their part, used their position to dictate the political landscape of Mexico to their advantage. The recognition of Mexican governments became a powerful tool that allowed the US to shape who gained power in Mexico. For instance, even though western European powers had recognized President Huerta as the legitimate president, US President Woodrow Wilson's refusal to acknowledge Huerta helped the Constitutional Army force him out of power. The US's assistance to President Carranza fueled Pancho Villa's attacks on American soil, leading to the US's unapproved expedition into Mexico. This disregard for Mexico's sovereignty continued to add to the dislike of Americans.

Things remained this way until the 1940s and World War II when Mexico and the US became allies with a common goal. Past differences were quickly forgotten, and Mexican pilots were training in Texas while Mexican workers came to take the place of Americans fighting overseas. The good economy Mexico enjoyed in the post-war years, the "Mexican Miracle," helped ensure that the governments of Mexico and the United States remained on good terms.

Racism still played a large part in the treatment of Mexican immigrants crossing the border into the US, but it was not regarded as a particular problem at the time. However, once the Mexican Miracle was over, things quickly turned sour, especially at the border shared by the two countries. The major issues from the American point of view became the illicit drug trade and the number of illegal immigrants crossing the border. From the Mexican perspective, the issue was American involvement in the Mexican Drug War, which was an American operation conducted with the approval of the Mexican government for a time. Also, the neoliberal presidents of the PRI were selling large tracts of land to buyers, including many American investors. This outside money concerned some Mexican citizens because it represented the overreaching of American power. Once again, the U.S. seemed to dismiss Mexican sovereignty and treat Mexico as if it were unimportant.

The US has created the Border Patrol to deal with potential illegal immigration, especially focused on those smuggling drugs into the country. The number of encounters Border Patrol has in a given year fluctuates. The highest numbers were reported in 1986, 2000, and 2021, while the lowest number of encounters were seen in the years before 1980 and between 2005 and 2010. These numbers can be misleading because many encounters are with repeat offenders. For example, in 2021, Border Patrol reported 1,659,206 encounters, but the number of individuals encountered was much lower. This is partly due to Border Patrol policy, which sometimes requires that every individual is detained and put through the criminal justice system but at other sends people back into Mexico. US President Donald Trump famously proposed building a wall along the border to stop illegal immigration, but he was unable to complete it in his term.

Interestingly, Mexican nationals only make up about 37 percent of people encountered by Border Patrol. The rest come from many other countries, including Honduras, El Salvador, Cuba, and Brazil.

In 2019, Mexican President López Obrador declared the Mexican Drug War was over, and his administration focused on government spending and directing military services to combat gasoline theft rings in the country. However, the drug cartels have continued their violence throughout the country.

Obrador's decision remains very controversial. The US State Department says that 90 percent of the cocaine (mostly made in Columbia) in the United States arrives across the Mexican border. Mexican cartels are known to smuggle Asian methamphetamines across the border, as well. A large portion of the heroine in the US comes via the same border. Mexican cartels grow billions of dollars' worth of marijuana in US federal and state parks and forests.

A decrease in the drug supply into Mexico results in a proportional rise in drug violence within the country. Yet, drug use in Mexico is lower per capita than in the United States. While many in the US believe the solution to the drug problem is to stop smuggling across the border, many others have pointed out that the smuggling is driven by the fact that the

United States is the largest consumer of illicit drugs in the world. If that demand were decreased, the drug trade across the southern border would most likely follow suit.

Chapter 16: Pop Culture and Stereotypes

The United States has long been the supplier of mass media and pop culture to much of the rest of the world, and Mexicans have often suffered as a result. Some Americans fail to consider that before Americans were living in states like Texas and California, these places were home to Mexicans, indigenous people, and people who were a combination of both. When those areas were annexed into the United States, these people and their descendants remained. This means that some of the first Mexican-Americans were not truly immigrants but lived on land that was once Mexico. Yet, Mexican-Americans, or Mexican Nationals, are often portrayed as immigrants, legal and illegal, who lack education and work menial jobs or are criminals or sex objects. Mexicans are grouped with all Latinos, and the details of their history and culture are often lost to the minds of American writers of film and TV. Mexicans are often shown as non-English speaking, even though many Mexicans can speak English well. They have generally been portrayed as lazy and dirty.

However, mass media has sometimes created favorable characters, if perhaps unknowingly. Warner Bros.' Looney Tunes, for instance, once featured the character Speedy Gonzales, who wore an oversized sombrero and talked with an exaggerated Mexican accent. He was often found outsmarting Sylvester the Cat and yelling "Arriba! Andale!" (roughly "Hurry up" in Spanish). Speedy was the "Fastest Mouse in Mexico" and was known for being quick-witted, while his cousin Slowpoke was the

"Slowest Mouse in Mexico." In 1999, Cartoon Network, which had purchased the rights to the cartoons, opted not to air Speedy cartoons anymore because of their use of "ethnic stereotypes." However, Speedy was again on the air in 2002 after he was declared an icon by the League of Latin American Citizens. Many people in Latin America remember the character fondly for his speed and quick wit.

However, negative stereotypes are perpetuated regularly. Former US President Donald Trump has made statements that imply Mexicans are drug dealers, criminals, and rapists. The Mexican-American maid who can barely speak English and works for a white family (and is almost certainly undocumented) is a common recurring character in many forms of mass media. When Hollywood decided to make a biopic of Emiliano Zapata in 1952, Marlon Brando was cast as Zapata and wore brown makeup to look the part. Danny Trejo, a Mexican-American actor, is almost always cast not as a leading man but as a fierce criminal. In almost every movie or TV show, Mexico is shown as a lifeless desert, while the actual country ranges from beautiful coastlines and snow-covered dormant volcanoes to windswept plains and jungles bursting with life. Why does American pop culture seem to miss so much of Mexico and only focus on a few parts and a few people?

This is not to gloss over the fact that Mexico has its own pop culture. In fact, from 1936 until well into the 1950s, Mexico experienced a cinematic "Golden Era." While other countries were more focused on World War II and most movies made in Hollywood were war films, Mexican film studios produced classic films like *Allá en el Rancho Grande*, a romantic drama directed by Fernando de Fuentes, the 1943 film *Wild Flower*, starring one of the greatest stars of the era, Dolores del Río, and the film *María Candelaria*, which won the Golden Palm in Cannes in 1946. The Mexican film industry produced a wide range of films, including comedies, horror films, and noir films like *Gangster Versus Cowboys* (1948).

In visual arts, Mexican artists are perhaps best known as muralists. Diego Rivera (1886- 1957) was a very well-known painter of murals in Mexico City and Cuernavaca, as well as in San Francisco, Detroit, and New York City in the US. Rivera was married to one of the most well-known Mexican painters, Frida Kahlo, known for her many self-portraits. Kahlo was part of the post-revolutionary Mexicayotl movement, which sought to revive ancient religion and philosophy among the Mexican people. Mexicayotl was especially well-known in the 1950s and spawned the Native Mexican Church. Frida Kahlo has become a pop culture icon with biopic Hollywood movies and cameos in Disney animated films. Her signature self-portraits that take a traditional European portrait style and infuse it with Latin American colors, animals, and surrealist elements have become some of the most sought-after works of art in the world. Her art has become so precious to the Mexican people that it is now illegal to export her work out of the country.

In writing, Mexico has become one of the preeminent Spanish-speaking countries both in volume and recognition. In the modern era, Mexican poet Octavio Paz was awarded the Nobel Prize in Literature in 1990, while the novelist Alfonso Reyes was nominated five times for the Nobel Prize. He is often regarded as one of the greatest authors of the Spanish language. One of the most praised Mexican novels is *Recollections of Things to Come* by Elena Garro. The book was published in 1963 but is set just after the Mexican Revolution. In it, the fictitious southern Mexican town of Ixtepec suffers during the tumultuous period of Madero, Huerta, and Carranza's presidencies. The story is told by the town itself and includes small hints of what would become known as magical realism—a term that Garro did not care for but is often associated with Latin, especially Mexican, writers.

Mexico, including in its pre-Columbian past, was the site of many architectural wonders and is home to more UNESCO World Heritage sites than other country in the Americas. Mexican cuisine is among the most celebrated in the world, blending Mesoamerican ingredients with European and Asian influences. Maize, beans, potatoes, tomatoes, and a wide range of peppers constitute the main part of most dishes, as well as white and red meat and seafood. Mexico is the home to some of the world's favorite flavors, including chocolate and vanilla. While Mexican music is sometimes identified as only Mariachi bands, the country actually has a large variety of music, including traditional music, rock, pop, and folk music. Often, the music is accompanied by dancing. One of the best-known folk dances of Mexico is the "Mexican Hat Dance" or *Jarabe Tapatío,* which is the national dance of Mexico.

Conclusion

Mexico's history is truly epic—a grand, sweeping narrative of powerful individuals, ideas, and movements. From the first humans to call Mexico home to the political ambitions of the next generation, Mexico will certainly continue to command an important place among Spanish-speaking countries and the world. Those who remain ignorant of Mexico's history will fail to understand the country's current, evolving situation and will be unable to appreciate the role Mexico has played in world events. They will also be missing out on a gripping tale. The Mesoamerican cultures were among the most productive and interesting ancient cultures. The Spanish conquest and subsequent colonization is a tale both brutal and moving in the complexities of the clash and combination of two great civilizations. The struggle for independence from a European empire is understood on almost every continent. The plight of the indigenous people of Mexico is echoed in the stories of native peoples in almost every corner of the world. Mexico's history is the history of humanity.

Part 2: History of Ancient Mexico

An Enthralling Guide to Pre-Columbian Mexico and Its Civilizations, Such as the Olmecs, Maya, Zapotecs, Mixtecs, Toltecs, and Aztecs

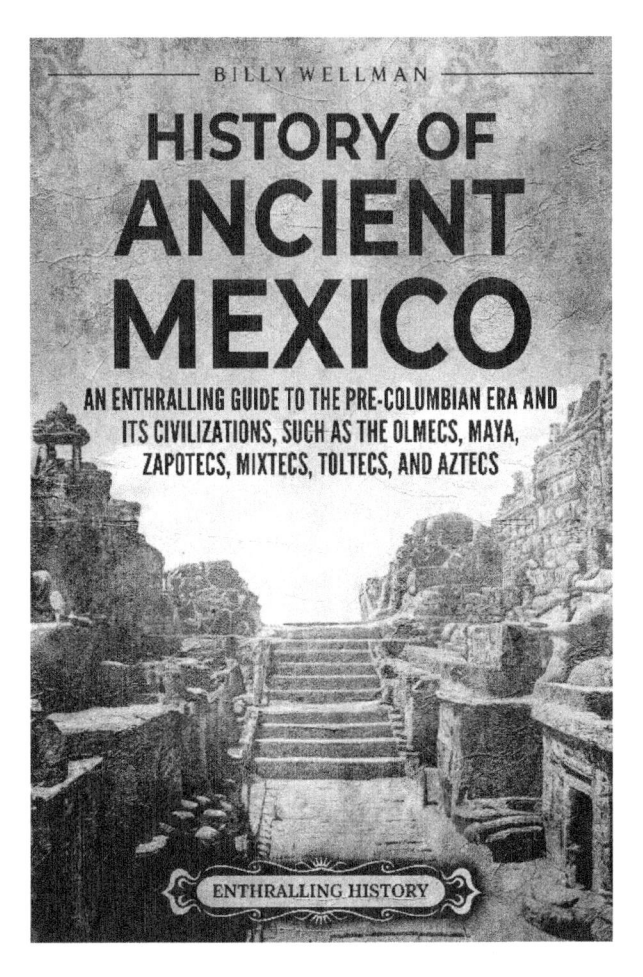

Introduction

On the Lake of the Moon sat the idyllic island city of Aztlán, where elegant white herons stood regally among the reeds. The lake teemed with large fish, ducks paddled in the shallows, and brilliant yellow and red songbirds flitted among the trees. In the middle of this picturesque island rose a high hill, and under its craggy slopes were seven caves. Seven tribes emerged from these seven caves, according to the Mexica genesis myths. Collectively called the Aztecs for their island of origin, the seven tribes left the island one by one. The last to go was the Mexica, around nine centuries ago.

Why did they leave their island of abundance? This part of the story is unclear; perhaps some traumatic event happened, such as an invasion or an earthquake. But their comfortable life abruptly ended when they started to wander through Mexico's northwestern desert in "a land turned against them." Jagged rocks, cacti, and thistles tore at their feet as they dodged slithering rattlesnakes and venomous Gila monsters. The Mexica finally emerged in the Valley of Mexico, the highlands plateau in central Mexico encompassing today's Mexico City, where their six kinsmen tribes had already settled.[1]

For thousands of years before the seven Aztec tribes arrived in central Mexico, other fascinating civilizations ruled central and southern Mexico. The Olmecs erected pyramids and palaces on the Gulf Coast beginning

---

[1] Wayne Elzey, "A Hill on a Land Surrounded by Water: An Aztec Story of Origin and Destiny," *History of Religions,* 31, no. 2 (1991):105-49. http://www.jstor.org/stable/1063021.

around 1600 BCE. Later, the Teotihuacanos built the largest city in the Americas in the Valley of Mexico's northeastern corner. Although they are crumbling today, the majestic ruins stand as an astonishing testament to the two advanced civilizations that existed when the Mexica arrived.

The Maya, contemporaries of the Olmec, built their spectacular cities in the jungles and highlands of the Yucatán Peninsula, southern Mexico, and Central America. The artistic Zapotecs and Mixtecs arose in the later days of the Olmec, thriving in the Puebla and Oaxaca regions of southern Mexico, stretching to the Pacific coast. The mighty Toltecs arrived in central Mexico about the time of Teotihuacan's fall, but their grand civilization imploded before the Aztecs arrived.

This book explores the interrelated stories of the remarkable civilizations that left an indelible mark on Mexico's history. We will unwrap the tales of their legendary figures, examine the art and architecture of these magnificent cultures, and learn about their epic wars, mythology, and religious practices. Finally, we will discuss what happened when Spanish ships arrived on Mexico's shores in the early sixteenth century.

Learning history has multiple benefits. It helps us understand why things are the way they are today. We capture valuable knowledge we can apply to modern-day scenarios from the phenomenal victories and dismal failures of the past. While some of Mexico's ancient cultures stand in stark contrast to today's Mexico, some things haven't changed much at all. Let's explore the magical mysteries of ancient Mexico and uncover a legacy that continues to impact our world today.

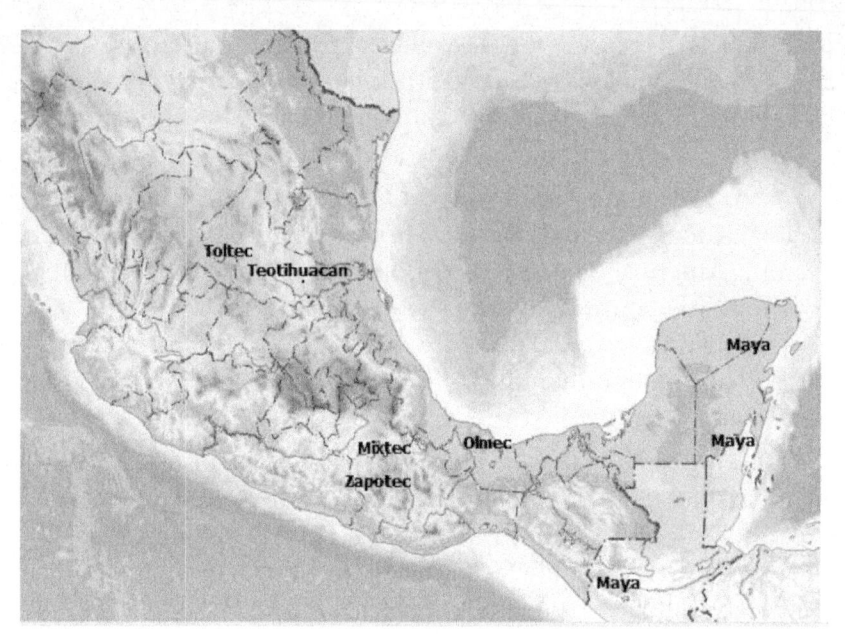

Pre-Aztec civilizations in Mexico.
Photo modified: zoomed in, labels added. Credit: Addicted04, CC BY-SA 3.0 <https://creativecommons.org/licenses/by-sa/3.0>, via Wikimedia Commons; https://commons.wikimedia.org/wiki/File:Mexico_topographic_map-blank_2.svg

Section One:
Key Civilizations

Chapter 1: The Olmecs

Chocolate, colossal heads, and rubber balls: the Olmecs invented them all! They also built the first known pyramid in North America. As the "mother culture" of Mesoamerica (the region from central Mexico to Costa Rica), the Olmec culture evolved into a higher civilization without any known outside influence. Their cultural prototypes, which later Mesoamerican civilizations copied, included pyramids, glyph-writing, and aligning their cities according to their 260-day religious calendar.[2]

The Olmec civilization emerged in the marshy, warm region near the Gulf of Mexico, today's Veracruz and Tabasco. Around 8000 BCE, the beginning of the Mesoamerican Archaic period, hunters and gatherers began segueing into a more sedentary agricultural lifestyle. Corn became the staple crop in the farm villages of the pre-Olmec around 2500 BCE. The Olmecs morphed from primitive farmers into Mesoamerica's first complex civilization around 1800 BCE, near the beginning of Mesoamerica's Preclassic period. The Olmecs introduced North America to its first cities, pyramids, calendar, writing system, and aqueducts.

We have no idea what the Olmecs called themselves, but in the Nahuatl language of the Aztecs, "Olmec" meant "rubber people." The Olmecs discovered that if they mixed sap from rubber trees with sap from morning glory vines, the resulting goo was pliable enough to wrap around

---

[2] Ronald A. Grennes-Ravitz and G. H. Coleman, "The Quintessential Role of Olmec in the Central Highlands of Mexico: A Refutation," *American Antiquity* 41, no. 2 (1976): 196. https://doi.org/10.2307/279172.

rocks. Rubber has many practical uses, but for the Olmecs, the main point of inventing rubber was for bouncy balls.[3]

The Olmecs played a ball game with these rubber balls. The game consisted of two teams in a sunken courtyard with a goal on each end. In this soccer-like game, which the Aztecs later called ulama, the players hit the ball with their hips, forearms, and heads to move it to their goal. The game became an intrinsic part of Mesoamerican culture and was connected to religious festivities. Almost two thousand ancient ballcourts have been unearthed In Mexico and Central America. Villagers in Sinaloa, Mexico, still play a version of ulama today.

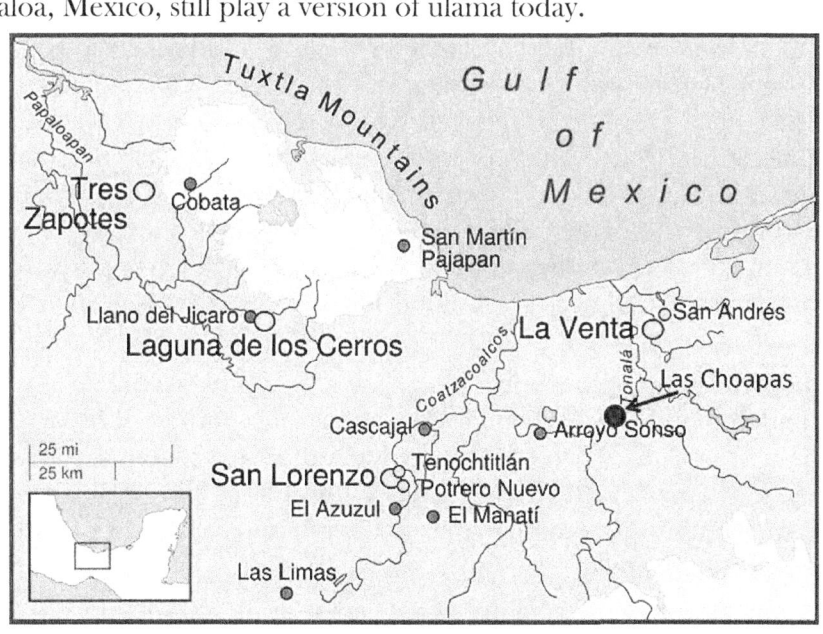

Olmec heartland.
Original Version author Madman2001, edited version author:RG, CC BY 3.0 <https://creativecommons.org/licenses/by/3.0>, via Wikimedia Commons; https://commons.wikimedia.org/wiki/File:800px-Olmec_Heartland_Overview_5.jpg

The Olmec's earliest known ceremonial center was El Manatí, built around 1700 BCE at the foot of Cerro Manatí (Manatee Hill) in the swampy floodplains of the Coatzacoalcos River. And, yes, they already had rubber balls. Archaeologists found twelve balls, thirty-seven carved

---

[3] Dorothy Hosler, et al., "Prehistoric Polymers: Rubber Processing in Ancient Mesoamerica," *Science*, June 18, 1999, 1988-91. doi:10.1126/science.284.5422.1988. OCLC 207960606. PMID 10373117.

wooden human busts, jade axe heads, and the skeletons of newborn babies, possibly human sacrifices.

The early Olmecs were drinking chocolate about 3,700 years ago. Researchers tested residue at the bottom of a ceramic vessel in El Manatí and found theobromine, an alkaloid chemical in the cacao plant. Later, archaeologists uncovered over twenty cups with chocolate residue at the Olmec site of San Lorenzo. The ingenious Olmecs had figured out how to ferment and roast cacao beans to make a chocolate drink.[4]

When the Olmecs weren't playing ball or drinking chocolate, they were hard at work building cities. After settling along the Coatzacoalcos River around 1450 BCE, the Olmecs hauled tons of dirt in baskets to construct a 140-acre plateau with terraces descending to the wetlands. They built their first small city, known today as San Lorenzo, around 1200 BCE on this plateau on the banks of the Coatzacoalcos River in southeast Veracruz. San Lorenzo was a religious and trade center with a population of about five thousand, although it served around thirteen thousand people in the surrounding farming communities covering thirty square miles. Two other Olmec towns stood next to the river to the north and south of San Lorenzo.

Another Olmec pioneering marvel was a complex aqueduct system with underground pipes moving fresh spring water into San Lorenzo. The Western Hemisphere's first known conduit drainage system featured 300 tons of U-shaped basalt troughs with removable covers traveling over a 550-foot mainline. It emptied into a duck-shaped cistern that had the carving of a duck on it.[5]

A hallmark of Olmec culture was its colossal heads, which were about ten feet high and weighed around eight tons. The Olmecs carved them from basalt, a rock formed by rapidly cooling lava, from the Cerro Cintepec and San Martín volcanoes of the Tuxtlas Mountains. Cerro Cintepec was sixty miles north of San Lorenzo, and the San Martín volcano was almost one hundred miles away. How the Olmecs transported these eight-ton sculptures over that distance without the wheel or beasts of burden is mind-boggling. Were they dragged over land or moved by raft on the river system? Either transport method was a jaw-

---

[4] T. G. Powis, et al., "Cacao Use and the San Lorenzo Olmec," *Proceedings of the National Academy of Sciences*, 108(21) (2011): 8595-600.

[5] Alison Bailey Kennedy, "Ecce Bufo: The Toad in Nature and in Olmec Iconography," *Current Anthropology* 23, no. 3 (1982): 286-7. http://www.jstor.org/stable/2742313.

dropping engineering feat requiring tremendous manpower.

An Olmec colossal head with a helmet.

TomClark18, CC BY-SA 4.0 <https://creativecommons.org/licenses/by-sa/4.0>, via Wikimedia Commons; https://commons.wikimedia.org/wiki/File:Olmec_colossal_head_5_.gif

The faces of the colossal heads are distinctive. The colossal heads probably represent a real person, such as a king. They wear helmets, suggesting they might have been warriors or ball players. Their almond-shaped eyes, broad noses, and full lips seem Polynesian or even African. However, the mitochondrial DNA of two Olmec skeletons dating from 1200 and 1000 BCE found they belong to haplogroup A, the indigenous American population. The Olmecs painted these carvings with bright colors, although that has worn off over the past three millennia. Ten of these enormous carvings were in San Lorenzo, although there were several in other Olmec cities.

The Olmecs' primary food was maize (corn), but they also consumed avocado, beans, chocolate, squash, and sweet potato. They raised dogs for food, hunted white-tailed deer and peccaries, and harvested fish from the river. Their extensive trade network used the river system and penetrated four hundred miles northwest into the Basin of Mexico and five hundred miles southeast into Guatemala. They traded rubber, figurines, and ceramics for jade, colorful feathers, and the razor-sharp volcanic obsidian they used for knives and spearheads.

San Lorenzo had elite residences at the highest point of its artificial plateau. Its palatial structures included the "red palace," which featured basalt columns supporting the roof and a basalt drain. Red ochre (iron oxide mixed with clay) covered the plastered walls and floors. Next to the red palace were a basalt workshop and another workshop that recycled older sculptures by carving fresh faces on them. Non-elite residents lived in wattle and daub homes on the city's lower terraces. These houses had a wooden lattice framework covered with a mixture of clay and straw.

San Lorenzo declined, with its population dispersing, around 850 BCE, probably due to the river changing course. Meanwhile, a new Olmec city sprang up on an island on a Tonalá River tributary ten miles from the Gulf of Mexico. La Venta, the new Olmec capital, was considerably larger, with an estimated population of twenty thousand. The Stirling Acropolis was a temple complex adjacent to a ballcourt and the Great Pyramid.

La Venta's pyramid and other significant structures are aligned eight degrees west of north. Some other major Mesoamerican cities, like Teotihuacan, had an astronomical northern alignment. This alignment is probably related to where the sun rose at the beginning and end of their 260-day ritual year, which fit into their 365-day solar year (they had both). Scholars believe the 260-day calendar used throughout Mesoamerica began with the Olmecs at La Venta around 800 BCE but was possibly used earlier in San Lorenzo. Using lidar imaging technology, researchers recently found hundreds of ancient Mesoamerican cities aligned with the 260-day calendar. This new study supports the hypothesis that the Olmecs initially developed the Mesoamerican calendar system and the astronomically-oriented alignment of cities.[6]

What appears to be a hill rising over a plateau is actually the remains of La Venta's Great Pyramid, the first in Mesoamerica. Erected in the core of the city's ceremonial center, it stands over one hundred feet high. The tallest manmade structure in Mesoamerica at that time, it was built of packed clay, and stepped sides covered with stone slabs rose from its rectangular base. Eight stelae (stone pillars or slabs) stood in a row on the southern side of the pyramid, facing away from it.

---

[6] Ivan Sprajc, et al., "Origins of Mesoamerican Astronomy and Calendar: Evidence from the Olmec and Maya Regions," *Science Advances* 9, no. 1 (2023). doi:10.1126/sciadv.abq7675.

Great Pyramid of La Venta.
Photo modified: zoomed in.
https://commons.wikimedia.org/wiki/File:La_Venta_Pir%C3%A1mide_cara_norte.jpg

Tres Zapotes was another significant Olmec city about sixty miles west of La Venta. Built around 1000 BCE, it encompassed about two hundred acres but did not display the ostentatious wealth of La Venta. In 1862, a farmer's hoe clanked on something, which turned out to be a colossal head, and that's how Tres Zapotes was discovered. Unlike San Lorenzo and La Venta, which each had an extravagant central administrative and religious complex, Tres Zapotes had four plazas about one-half mile apart. Each plaza was built around 400 BCE with a pyramid on its west side and a similar platform arrangement.

The Olmecs developed the first writing system in North America: a primitive form of hieroglyphics. The Cascajal Block is a foot-long serpentine stone with sixty-two symbols running horizontally. Some glyphs appear to depict corn, fish, insects, and pineapple; others are more abstract. Road builders discovered the stone in the late 1990s in a pile of debris close to ancient San Lorenzo, and scholars dated it to the late 900s BCE. In 1997 and 1998, another stone and a cylinder seal were discovered only three miles from La Venta, with glyphs dating to around 650 BCE.

Like San Lorenzo, La Venta experienced an abrupt depopulation around 400 BCE. This time, the city and the entire eastern Olmec heartland lost their population, leaving the region almost empty for two millennia. Only Tres Zapotes, one hundred miles west of La Venta, survived. Tens of thousands of Olmecs suddenly died or vacated the eastern area. What happened? Apparently, a horrific environmental catastrophe thrust the culture into extinction.

What sort of apocalyptic disaster could do this? Three enormous tectonic plates lie under Mexico, and earthquakes and volcanoes result when they shift and upheave. Mexico ranks number nine worldwide for volcanoes in the Holocene epoch (going back almost twelve thousand years). The El Chichón volcano is about sixty miles from La Venta and is still active, erupting last in 1981. It is part of the Chiapanecan Volcanic Arc, where three great tectonic plates collide: the North American Plate, the Caribbean Plate, and the Cocos Plate.

Mexico experiences thousands of earthquakes annually and averages about one earthquake a year that is greater than a 6.1 magnitude. The Olmec territory was slightly out of the most active earthquake range, yet with its soft, marshy soil, even mild tremors could have damaged buildings. Tectonic shifting could also have generated volcanic activity and changes in the river system on which the Olmecs depended.

An insidious aspect of active volcanoes is carbon dioxide in the plumes and fumaroles. Carbon dioxide is heavier than air and can collect in low-lying areas, such as the Olmec marshy heartland. Air with over 3 percent carbon dioxide causes dizziness, headaches, and trouble breathing. If it reaches 15 percent, this lethal gas will kill all human, animal, and plant life. Carbon dioxide could have suddenly and silently wiped out life in the low-lying areas of the Olmec territory.

Although what happened to La Venta and the eastern Olmec heartland is unclear, an exodus of survivors moved to Tres Zapotes in the west. This was when the Tres Zapotes residents built the four similar ceremonial plazas at equal distances from each other, hinting at a co-ruling situation or a more egalitarian society. Some eastern Olmecs also flooded into the Olmec town of Cerro de las Mesas, northwest of Tres Zapotes.

A new culture called the Epi-Olmec, apparently an extension of the Olmec civilization, flourished in Tres Zapotes and Cerro de las Mesas until around 250 CE. Tres Zapotes persisted for two thousand years through the Olmec, Epi-Olmec, and Classic Veracruz civilizations. The Epi-Olmecs did not display the flamboyant wealth of La Venta and San Lorenzo, and they didn't import luxury goods from afar. The Olmec trade empire collapsed, and most of what the Epi-Olmecs had was locally produced.

Although the Epi-Olmec didn't have the lavish Olmec lifestyle, they still made cultural strides. They used the Long Count calendar, which kept track of the years going back to their perceived date of the creation of humans: 3114 BCE. Interestingly, that date was close to when the pre-Olmecs began settling the Veracruz and Tabasco areas and engaging in more formal agriculture. Although the Olmecs had simple hieroglyphics, the Epi-Olmec developed the more sophisticated Isthmian hieroglyphic script. A farmer in the Tuxtlas mountain region unearthed the Tuxtla Statuette: a half-man and half-duck creature. Seventy-five glyphs were carved into the figurine with a date from the Long Count calendar (162 CE in our calendar).

In 1939, part of a rectangular stone block called Stela C was unearthed in Tres Zapotes, and thirty years later, the rest of it was discovered. Stela C had Isthmian script on one side and a Long Count calendar date corresponding to 32 BCE. In 1986, anthropologists were thrilled when the four-ton La Mojarra Stela was found in the Acula River, close to Tres Zapotes. It had a portrait of an elaborately costumed man etched in part of the stone, and 535 glyphs and 2 dates, corresponding to 143 and 156 CE, covered the rest.

The Olmecs left an incredible legacy of innovations, spreading their cultural contributions through trade and establishing colonies. The Maya civilization, which emerged partway through the Olmecs' history, adopted many of their cultural elements. We owe our enjoyment of chocolate and rubber balls to these creative pioneers who introduced many historical firsts to Mesoamerica and the world.

Key Takeaways:
- Three main phases of the Olmecs
    - San Lorenzo
    - La Venta
    - Epi-Olmec and Tres Zapotes
- Firsts in Mesoamerica and the world
    - First Mesoamerican pyramid
    - First chocolate in the world
    - First rubber balls in the world
    - First to align a city according to the 260-day religious calendar
    - First glyph-writing in the Americas
    - First Mesoamerican city
    - First Mesoamerican aqueduct
- Unique cultural contribution: colossal heads

Chapter 2: The Maya

Who were the Maya, and why were they such brilliant influencers of Mesoamerican culture? And is it Maya, Mayas, or Mayan? To answer the second question, most of today's scholars use Maya (never Mayas, even when plural). Mayan refers to the language family of the Maya, which includes twenty-eight languages that are used today, such as K'iche,' Mam, and Tostsil (Tzotzil).

The Maya independent city-states spread through the Yucatán Peninsula, southern Mexico, Guatemala, Belize, Honduras, and El Salvador. Although the Maya never unified into a political empire, they shared the Mayan language family and a common culture. The Maya are among the world's oldest continuous civilizations, from their inception as a complex society around 950 BCE to the present, albeit with periods of decline and near collapse.

The early Maya settled in agricultural villages, growing corn in Mesoamerica's Formative or Preclassic period (1900 BCE–250 CE). Around 1500 BCE, the southern Guatemala Maya developed the "nixtamalization" process: soaking corn in water with a chunk of heated limestone. Nixtamalization enabled the ground corn meal to form a dough for making tortillas. More importantly, it increased the availability of niacin, an essential B vitamin. Corn nixtamalization spread throughout Mesoamerica, where it is still used today.

Around 950 BCE, the Maya built their first known ceremonial center, Ceibal, in Guatemala's Petén region at the Yucatán Peninsula's base. The Maya built Ceibal about 750 years after the Olmec built El Manatí and slightly earlier than La Venta. Ceibal was continuously inhabited for two thousand years, with a maximum population of ten thousand. In its earliest phase, the Maya built an artificial plateau at least twenty feet high and about one-half mile long.[7]

In June 2020, archaeologist Takeshi Inomata, who investigated Ceibal, announced the discovery by lidar aerial survey of another Maya ceremonial center, Aguada Fénix. This center had an even more extensive artificial plateau than Ceibal, as it was nearly a mile long and at least thirty-three feet high. With an estimated establishment date between 1000 and 800 BCE, Aguada Fénix might have predated Ceibal. Aguada Fénix is in Mexico's state of Tabasco, across the border from Guatemala.

In 1930, aerial photographs revealed an ancient city hidden in the Mirador Basin jungles fifty miles north of Ceibal. Recent archaeological studies show that agricultural villages existed there as early as 1400 BCE. Around 600 BCE, the Maya began building pyramids and temples, forming the ceremonial center now known as Nakbé, which was home to the earliest ballcourt in Maya history.

The first Maya city-state was probably Kaminaljuyú, now mostly covered by the western suburbs of Guatemala City. A city-state was a large, primary city and the small towns and agricultural villages surrounding it. Sometimes, a powerful city-state would gain control over other cities, forcing them to pay tribute and provide men for the military. Each city-state had an independent government, although they might ally with other city-states in war.

---

[7] T. Inomata, et al., "Artificial Plateau Construction during the Preclassic Period at the Maya Site of Ceibal, Guatemala." *PLoS One*, 2019 Aug 30;14(8):e0221943. doi: 10.1371/journal.pone.0221943. PMID: 31469887; PMCID: PMC6716660

Kaminaljuyú figurine of a monkey holding her baby.
Simon Burchell, CC BY-SA 4.0 <https://creativecommons.org/licenses/by-sa/4.0>, via Wikimedia Commons; https://commons.wikimedia.org/wiki/File:Museo_Miraflores_093.jpg

Kaminaljuyú grew into a large city around 800 BCE. When archaeologists Edwin Shook and Alfred Kidder investigated Kaminaljuyú in the 1930s, they found over three hundred ancient buildings and thirty-five Maya towns nearby. They also discovered that the Maya had ceramic-making factories in the city, uncovering a half million broken pottery items in one location.[8]

Kaminaljuyú had the largest population in the Maya southern highlands of the Sierra Madre mountain range. Located sixty miles from the Pacific Ocean, the city served as a trade conduit for seashells and salt from the ocean. Cacao beans (used to make cocoa) and brilliantly colored feathers came from the rainforests. The Mesoamericans prized large conch shells, which they used as trumpets, and colorful smaller shells to decorate festive clothing.

---

[8] Edwin M. Shook and Alfred V. Kidder, "Mound E-III-3, K'aminaljuyu, Guatemala," *Contributions to American Anthropology and History*, Vol. 9 (53) (1952): 33-127.

Twenty-five miles east of the city was the El Chayal quarry for volcanic obsidian glass. Mesoamerica did not develop metalworking until the 7th century CE, so obsidian was a coveted product for knives and spearheads. Obsidian artifacts from El Chayal have been found in the Yucatán Peninsula and El Salvador. Kaminaljuyú also grew cotton, a sought-after product for clothing throughout Mesoamerica.

Kaminaljuyú declined around 400 BCE, the same time as the Olmec city of La Venta. For unclear reasons, other Maya urban centers in southern Mexico and the Guatemalan Highlands also collapsed in this period. Perhaps earthquakes or volcanic activity destroyed some cities, breaking down the bustling trade routes. Cities that continued, like Tres Zapotes, were no longer engaging in long-distance trade but surviving on what they could locally produce.

Although Kaminaljuyú declined significantly, it didn't end. It stumbled along for a few centuries and then bounced back, bigger and brighter than before, surviving until 1200 CE. The city displayed its recovered wealth by building clay pipes that carried drinking water through the city. A spectacular network of canals, aqueducts, and pools transformed the metropolis into a watery paradise decorated with stone carvings of fish and turtles.

The Maya Golden Age flourished in Mesoamerica's Classic period, beginning about 250 CE. About forty major Maya cities with breathtaking temples and pyramids thrived in the jungles and highlands of southern Mexico and Central America. Maya agricultural technology included irrigation and terraced farming along hillsides. The Maya adopted the Olmec rubber balls and played games in ballcourts, as did most other Mesoamerican cultures.

Several notable Maya cities in Mexico include Cobá, which flourished in the Classic period (250–900 CE) in the Yucatán Peninsula. Located between two lakes, an impressive network of elevated limestone causeways meandered along the lakes and through the wetlands to other Maya cities, one of which was over sixty miles away. One nearby city, Ek' Balam ("Black Jaguar"), features winged men on a mesmerizing stucco façade at the entrance of the tomb of King Ukit Kan Le'k Tok', who died in 801 CE.

Ornate tomb of King Ukit Kan Le' at Ek' Balam.
*Elijahmeeks at the English-language Wikipedia, CC BY-SA 3.0
<http://creativecommons.org/licenses/by-sa/3.0/>, via Wikimedia Commons;
https://commons.wikimedia.org/wiki/File:Ekbalam-Jaguar-Altar-Right.png*

In Maya society, kings held godlike status in the city-states they ruled. Maya rulers descended from royal dynasties, which occasionally meant a queen ruled the city-state if the royal family had no suitable male available. Royal lineage was bilateral; it could go from the bloodline of the father or the mother or both. The Maya knew their kings could get sick, injured, and die like everyone else. For them, "godlike" meant they were hybrid divine-human creatures.

The Maya did not hold the Western concept of an infinite, all-powerful, unchanging, and infallible deity. In Maya metaphysics, gods and supernatural beings were born, could die, and were vulnerable, unpredictable, and inconsistent. Their theology allowed for an imperfect, mortal king to call himself "Ajaw" (divine lord). Kings often used names associated with Maya deities, such as K'inich (sun) or Balam (jaguar).[9]

Since there was a strict divide between nobility and commoners, only the elite could wear elaborate clothing decorated with feathers and shells. In the Maya feudal system, the nobility controlled most of the farmland, and the serfs farmed it in return for part of the harvest. Kings, administrative officials, military commanders, scribes, and high priests

---

[9] Stephen Houston and David Stuart, "Of Gods, Glyphs and Kings: Divinity and Rulership among the Classic Maya," *Antiquity* 70, no. 268 (1996): 289-95. doi:10.1017/S0003598X00083289.

were all part of the nobility and were literate.

In addition to clothing, Maya people demonstrated their status through cranial modifications. Newborn babies and toddlers would lie in a special cradle or have padded wooden frames tied to their heads to change the shape of their skulls. The shape of the adjusted skull depended on kinship and status. Another status symbol was drilling holes in teeth for jewelry and filing teeth into different shapes.

Examples of how the Maya shaped the skulls of their small children.
https://commons.wikimedia.org/wiki/File:Maya_cranial_deformation.gif

Commoners worked as craftsmen and merchants and served in the military. Warriors captured in battle faced one of two fates: enslavement or human sacrifice. Other people were enslaved because of crimes or debts, and orphan children were in peril of being sacrificed or enslaved. When a king or queen died, their slaves would often be sacrificed and buried in their tombs to serve them in the afterlife.

Since the Maya civilization was never a united empire but a collection of self-ruling city-states, the kings vied for power, access to coveted resources, and control of trade routes. As with most Mesoamerican cultures, they practiced human sacrifice and needed victims, although not on the gruesome scale of the Aztecs. Maya kings fought other Maya and nearby cultures, and warfare was especially rampant from around 600 to 900 CE when several stressors hit the Maya.

Conflict arose when some cities outgrew their agricultural output. When they cleared the jungle for more farmland, that led to soil erosion in the rainy season. Other times, they didn't get enough rain; even a moderately poor harvest due to drought could have led to near starvation in the overcrowded cities. These problems would have eroded the people's trust in their rulers and increased warfare with nearby city-states in the grab for land and resources.

When the Maya went to war, they bombarded the enemy with spears, arrows, blowgun darts, and stones from slings. The Maya adopted the atlatl or spear-thrower from the Teotihuacanos of central Mexico, which used leverage for lethal power and speed. The atlatl was a shaft with a cup or notch at one end into which the spear butt fit. The warrior held the other end of the atlatl and the spear and threw it, holding the atlatl but releasing the spear. The extra leverage from the atlatl sent the spear farther and faster than if simply thrown by hand.

How the atlatl spear-thrower worked.
Sebastião da Silva Vieira, CC BY 3.0 <https://creativecommons.org/licenses/by/3.0>, via Wikimedia Commons; https://commons.wikimedia.org/wiki/File:Nativo_do_Novo_Mundo_lan%C3%A7ando_flecha_com_o_propulsor_ou_est%C3%B3lica.jpg

Hand-to-hand combat in Maya warfare was brutal. They had a three-and-a-half-foot wooden club lined with razor-sharp obsidian blades, which could knock a man out or slice his head off. The Mesoamericans started working with metals in the mid-Classic era, and the Maya added copper knives and ax heads to their deadly repertoire by 650 CE. Their objective in battle was often capturing the enemy rather than killing them so they would have victims for human sacrifice or slavery. Hence, they often used the blunt end of their battle axes to knock their opponent out instead of killing him.

Some Maya built defensive walls around their cities, although this was rare. The Maya occasionally hurled gourds filled with hornet nests at enemy lines, confusing and panicking the warriors as a cloud of angry, stinging hornets flew out. The Maya carried small, round shields made of animal skins, woven reeds, or wood. They wore quilted cotton armor with rock salt sewn into the batting to deflect or break the enemy's obsidian blades.

The Maya produced an outstanding cultural heritage of literacy. From the earliest centuries of their civilization, they erected stone stelae with simple pictograph glyph inscriptions, as the Olmecs had done. By 300 BCE, they had developed a much more sophisticated hieroglyphic written language, which they carved into altars, around doorways, and on stone pillars. They also wrote on paper made from bark and made pictorial books with accordion folds.

The Maya logo-syllabic script used pictographs (picture symbols) for nouns and action verbs and glyph symbols for prepositions and adjectives. They used phonetic symbols to represent sounds like we use consonants and vowels. A Maya scribe worked with three to five hundred characters. If writing on bark paper or animal skin, the writer wrote with feather quill pens or a brush made from animal hair. If using quills, he or she (yes, some upper-class women could write) had quills with large and small tips for the basic glyph outlines and finer details.

The Maya wrote numbers with dots and bars. Dots represented the numbers one through four: one dot was the number one, two dots were the number two, and so on. A bar represented the number five. Two bars would be ten, three bars would be fifteen, and so on. The number six would be one bar and one dot, and the number twelve would be two bars and two dots.

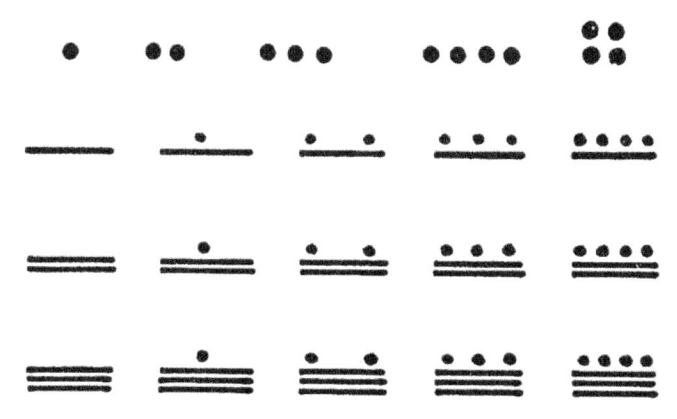

How the Maya wrote the numerals one to nineteen.
https://commons.wikimedia.org/wiki/File:Maya_Hieroglyphs_Fig_39.jpg

Like the Olmecs, the Maya used both a 260-day religious calendar (*Tzolk'in*) to keep track of special festival days and a 365-day calendar (*Haab*) for agricultural purposes. The 365-day calendar had eighteen 20-

day months plus a 5-day month. Around 36 BCE, perhaps two centuries earlier, the Maya started using the Long Count calendar, which kept track of all the days since creation in cycles of fifty-two years. The Epi-Olmecs also began using the Long Count calendar by at least 32 BCE.

The Maya used a "Calendar Round" with four circles to keep track of time. Around the outermost circle was a hieroglyphic sign for each of the 18 months of their 365-day solar year cycle. Immediately inside that outer circle was a second circle with the numbers for the twenty days of the month, with zero represented by a shell. The inner two circles of the Calendar Round were for the 260-day religious calendar. The third circle from the outside perimeter had glyphs for the twenty months of the Tzolk'in religious calendar, and the fourth circle had numbers for the thirteen days of each religious month.

Each day, the Maya would place four shells or pebbles on the calendar, marking the month and day of the solar calendar and the month and day of the religious calendar. It took fifty-two years for all four circles of months and days to line up the same way again. When this happened, a new cycle began. Most Mesoamerican cultures adopted this calendar system and were using it when the Spaniards arrived in the early 1500s CE.

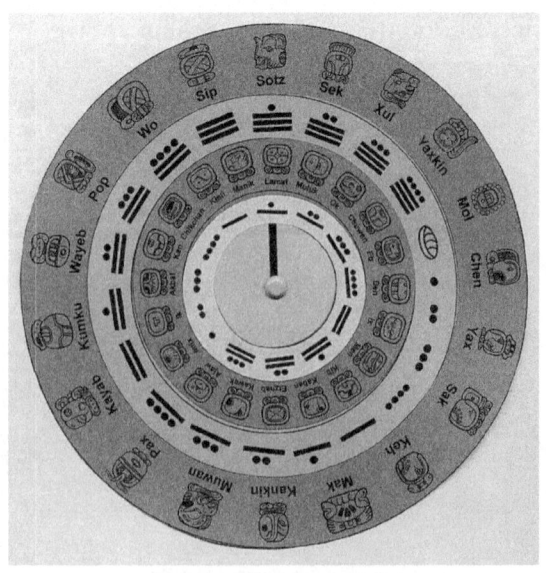

Maya Calendar Round.
Croppy Peace Sign, CC0, via Wikimedia Commons;
https://commons.wikimedia.org/wiki/File:Construction_paper_Mayan_calander.jpg

Key Takeaways:
- Who were the Maya?
    o Independent city-states sharing language family and culture
    o Settled in regions from southern Mexico to Central America
    o Early ceremonial centers and cities: Ceibal, Aguada Fénix, Nakbé
    o First city-state: Kaminaljuyú
- Maya Golden Age
    o Societal structure
        ▪ Kings and commoners
        ▪ Status symbols: clothing, cranial modification, tooth jewelry
- Warfare
    o City-states vying for power and access to land and goods
    o Weaponry, armor, and defense tactics
- Cultural heritage
    o Logo-syllabic script
    o Numbers
    o Calendar Round

Mexico's highest Maya pyramid (243 feet tall) at Toniná in Chiapas State.
Dge, CC BY-SA 4.0 <https://creativecommons.org/licenses/by-sa/4.0>, via Wikimedia Commons; https://commons.wikimedia.org/wiki/File:Tonin%C3%A1_(150).jpg

Chapter 3: The Zapotecs

They called themselves the Cloud People, the Ben 'Zaa, because they believed their ancestors descended from the clouds and that their spirits would ascend into the clouds when they died. The Cloud People dominated the Oaxaca Valley of southern Mexico for almost two millennia before the Aztecs arrived and called them "Zapotec." That name either meant "cloud merchants" or "people of the sapote tree," a type of persimmon common in the area. The Zapotec language family, still spoken with over fifty languages, is part of the Otomanguean language group, which includes the Mixtec languages.

The earliest significant Zapotec settlement was San José Mogote, about seven miles northwest of today's Oaxaca City.[10] The Zapotecs were the first to establish villages and make pottery in the Oaxaca Valley, and their Gray Ware ceramics later became a sought-after trade item. The Zapotecs developed into a complex civilization by 1300 BCE, erecting ceremonial buildings in San José Mogote surrounded by defensive stake fences. Their cultural advancements were several centuries ahead of the Maya and about five hundred years behind the Olmecs.

They began using irrigation ditches to enhance farming in the semi-arid region and constructing adobe buildings by 850 BCE. They developed trade networks, importing obsidian from the Guadalupe Victoria region in

---

[10] Susan T. Evans, *Ancient Mexico and Central America: Archaeology and Culture History* (London: Thames and Hudson, 2004), 122.

Puebla and El Chayal in Guatemala.[11] By 600 BCE, San José Mogote evolved into a socially stratified chiefdom of about one thousand people living on fifty acres, controlling forty nearby villages and towns. The stone-block ceremonial structures at San José Mogote were oriented eight degrees west of north. This alignment was the same as the Olmec city of La Venta 250 miles away, a trade destination for the iron oxide mirrors the Zapotecs produced.[12] By 500 BCE, San José Mogote had declined as Monte Albán sprang to power about twelve miles south.

Zapotec core area.
Photo modified: zoomed in. https://commons.wikimedia.org/wiki/File:Zapotecos.png

The Oaxaca Valley is a rough Y-shape, with three regional divisions of the Zapotec civilization, each with its own subset of the Zapotec language family. The Valley Zapotecs were located in the central Oaxaca Valley and held the most potent political power. The Sierra Zapotecs lived in the mountains north of the Oaxaca Valley, not far from Olmec territory. The Southern Zapotecs lived near the Pacific coast. For most of their history, the Southern (Pacific Coast) Zapotecs were independent of Monte Albán. Differences in pottery styles and decorative motifs showcase the cultural divide between the three sub-groups. Imports from other Mesoamerican regions differed, indicating the three areas had separate trade destinations.[13]

The Valley Zapotecs led the way in cultural innovations in the Oaxaca Valley. A carving with two glyphs found in San José Mogote dated to 650

---

[11] Arthur A. Joyce, "Interregional Interaction and Social Development on the Oaxaca Coast," *Ancient Mesoamerica* 4, no. 1 (1993): 69. http://www.jstor.org/stable/26307326.
[12] Evans, *Ancient Mexico and Central America*, 122-3.
[13] Joyce, "Interregional Interaction," 71.

BCE. Around 500 BCE, the Zapotecs of the Monte Albán area developed Mesoamerica's first complex hieroglyphics in the logo-syllabic system. This language development was close to when the Oaxaca Valley people segued from scattered chiefdoms into a more centralized and powerful government.

The Zapotec hieroglyphics were similar to the later Mayan hieroglyphics in that they both had pictorial symbols for nouns and action verbs and phonetic symbols for sounds. Yet, unlike the Mayan script, which read in blocks from right to left, the Zapotec script read from the top to the bottom of the page like ancient Chinese characters. The Zapotec stopped using their writing system by 900 CE, embracing the Mixtec and later the Aztec script. The old Zapotec script wasn't deciphered until 2022. In 2018, archaeologists discovered a fifty-foot frieze dating to between 650 to 850 CE in the Monte Albán archaeological site with the largest number of Zapotec glyphs ever found. Three years later, scholars completed a rough translation of the script, which included calendar notations.[14]

Like the Maya, the Zapotecs used bars and dots to represent numbers. They also used the 260-day sacred calendar, the 365-day solar calendar, and cycles of 52 years. They kept historical records of their calendars with notations for lunar and solar eclipses and might have calculated the timing of eclipses. The Saros eclipse cycle of 6,585 days, when the sun, moon, and earth return to almost a straight line, nearly coincided with 25 cycles of their 260-day sacred calendar.

Monte Albán served as the Zapotecs' first capital beginning around 500 BCE when the Zapotecs built it on top of a mountain about 1,300 feet above the Oaxaca Valley. Monte Albán means "white mountain" in Spanish; the Zapotecs called it Daní Baan, or "sacred mountain." Its elevated position provides a view of the surrounding valley, making it a superb defensive location. Although there is no evidence of a previous settlement on the summit, it might have served as an earlier ceremonial location.

The food supply for the mountaintop city came from the valley below. The valley was well suited for agriculture since there was no frost, a high

---

[14] Jane Recker, "Researchers Decipher the Glyphs on a 1,300-Year-Old Frieze in Mexico," *Smithsonian Magazine*, March 8, 2022. https://www.smithsonianmag.com/smart-news/researchers-decipher-the-glyphs-on-a-1300-year-old-frieze-in-mexico-180979691/

water table that made irrigation easy, and flat land with little erosion. The Zapotecs leveled off their mountaintop and built a paved ceremonial center. Temples and palaces sat on raised platforms next to a sunken ballcourt, and thirty-foot-high walls surrounded the city. The temples were two-roomed structures with porticos in the front.

Monte Albán's mountaintop ceremonial center.
https://commons.wikimedia.org/wiki/File:Ruins_field.jpg

More than three hundred stone slabs that date back to the city's beginnings depict rubbery, contorted men that early archaeologists naively called *danzantes* or "dancers." Closer inspection revealed closed eyes and gaping or grimacing mouths. Furthermore, Mesoamerican men usually covered their genitals, but these men were completely naked, and some were castrated. The men weren't playfully dancing—they were dead. Perhaps they were captured warriors who became sacrificial victims. A similar stone slab at San José Mogote shows a disemboweled man.

Intriguingly, some of the men have beards. Ancient Mesoamericans rarely wore beards, except the Olmecs. Did the carvings represent Olmec men? The Olmec civilization collapsed around 400 BCE, about a century after the Zapotecs built Monte Albán. The two cultures traded goods, and the Zapotecs adopted aspects of Olmec culture, such as ballcourts. But the violence portrayed in the carvings suggests a war between the Olmecs and Zapotecs.

The Zapotecs of Monte Albán enjoyed a friendship with the gigantic metropolis of Teotihuacan in the Basin of Mexico, about three hundred miles northeast of the Oaxaca Valley. Zapotecs began migrating to Teotihuacan by 200 BCE during the massive city's earliest days. Perhaps the Zapotecs were among the multiethnic city's founders. They had an Oaxacan barrio on the southwestern side of the city with fifteen Zapotec apartment compounds where they manned workshops producing Oaxacan Gray Ware pottery. The Zapotecs also lived alongside the Teotihuacanos in the Chingú, Acoculco, and El Tesoro colonies in Hidalgo, which were only 60 miles northwest of Teotihuacan but 330 miles from Monte Albán. The Zapotec population living with the Teotihuacanos in Hidalgo were probably from the Zapotec enclave in Teotihuacan.[15]

Archaeologists divide the city's history into four phases. Monte Albán I began in 500 BCE when the urban center was first built, perhaps by people who had moved out of San José Mogote. It controlled one thousand villages and small towns scattered throughout the Oaxaca Valley. Monte Albán II ran from 100 BCE to 200 CE when the Zapotecs began colonizing to the north and south of the Oaxaca Valley in what became the Sierra Zapotec and Southern Zapotec territories. Monte Albán III was the 200 to 500 CE era when the city's population grew to twenty-five thousand and was at its zenith of power. In Monte Albán IV (500–1000 CE), the city's influence declined as other cities in the Oaxaca Valley rose in power. By 1000 CE, Monte Albán was a ghost town.

Huitzo (San Pablo Huitzo) lay in the northernmost tip of the Oaxaca Valley at the border between the Mixtec and Zapotec territories divided by the Garcés River. Small farming villages dotted the area by 1000 BCE, and around 400 CE, the Zapotecs established a town with a fortress on top of a hill. Images of the Feathered Serpent deity, Quetzalcoatl in the Aztec Nahuatl language, decorated the citadel.

As with other agricultural centers in the Oaxaca Valley, the farmers of Huitzo used a pot-irrigation system. They buried unglazed, narrow-necked clay pots up to their rims in the fields next to where squash, tomatoes, chilis, or other plants grew. They kept the pots filled with water, and when the surrounding soil dried out, it created a suction force from soil

---

[15] Haley Holt Mehta, "Colonial Encounters, Creolization, and the Classic Period Zapotec Diaspora: Questions of Identity from El Tesoro, Hidalgo, Mexico" (PhD diss., Tulane University, 2019), 47-53.

moisture tension. The water in the pots seeped through the clay, disbursing water to the plant roots. For large grain fields, like maize, the Oaxaca Valley farmers used canal irrigation.

The Zapotecs practiced an "infield-outfield" agricultural system, relying on the annual flooding of rivers in the rainy season. The "infield" was the land closest to the river; the flooding brought fresh soil, renewing nutrients. In the "outfield" areas unreached by flooding, they used slash-and-burn cultivation, burning off the corn stubble or other remaining plants after the harvest. The fire left a nutrient-rich layer of ash that fertilized the soil. Since mountains on three sides surrounded the town of Huitzo, the farmers built terraces up the mountainsides to enlarge their farming areas.

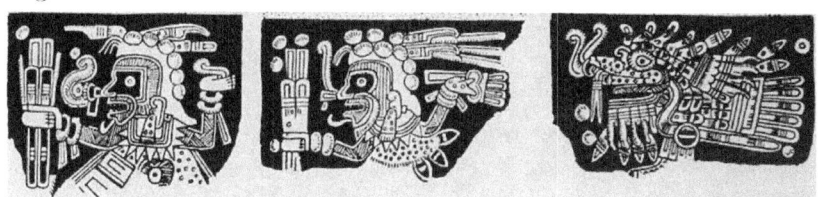

Zapotec deities on a Mitla tomb fresco, with the Feathered Serpent on the right.
Internet Archive Book Images, No restrictions, via Wikimedia Commons;
https://commons.wikimedia.org/wiki/File:Ancient_civilizations_of_Mexico_and_Central_America_(1917)_(18009178109).jpg

The mountain city of Mitla was a sacred Zapotec burial site with intricate stone mosaics not found elsewhere in Mexico. Early Zapotecs lived in the area from 900 BCE, and it grew into a city and powerful religious center by 450 CE, eventually replacing Monte Albán as the Zapotec capital. Instead of pyramids, Mitla features eight enormous, flat-roofed rectangular buildings called the Group of the Columns, which are renowned for their geometric relief carvings.

The Postclassic Zapotecs displayed engineering genius with complex designs on Mitla's Group of the Columns and massive blocks over the doorways. Trachyte volcanic-rock columns supported the roofs, and polished stone, cut and fitted together without mortar, formed "stepped-fret" geometric designs on the walls. The buildings, originally painted red, served as a palace and temple complex where regular human sacrifice occurred. The high priest's throne, covered with a jaguar skin, sat in one of the temples.

"Stepped-fret" geometric designs on a Mitla building.
Roman Israel, CC BY-SA 4.0 <https://creativecommons.org/licenses/by-sa/4.0>, via Wikimedia Commons; https://commons.wikimedia.org/wiki/File:Puerta_mitla_fachada.jpg

The Zapotecs lived immediately south of their neighbors and sister culture, the Mixtecs. The two groups frequently battled each other, especially as the Mixtecs grew stronger in the Postclassic age and began encroaching on Zapotec territory. But then, a new adversary arrived. The Mexica-Aztecs in the Basin of Mexico allied with two other Aztec tribes in 1428 CE. Within months, the new Aztec Empire invaded the Oaxaca Valley, conquering Mixtec strongholds and engaging the Zapotecs in several wars in which the Aztecs were victorious.

But then, the Aztecs faced their own ultimate nemesis when Spanish ships sailed toward the Mexican coast in the early 16th century. After the Spaniards brutally defeated the Aztecs, the Zapotecs decided upon a strategy of non-resistance. Nevertheless, the Zapotecs suffered huge losses from diseases the Spaniards introduced to the Americas, against which the indigenous people had no acquired immunity. The Spaniards forced them to convert to Catholicism, building churches on top of former Zapotec temples. But the Zapotec people survived, with about 400,000 still living in the Oaxaca Valley, many speaking their ancient languages.

Key Takeaways:
- Earliest settlement: San José Mogote
    o Complex civilization by 1300 BCE

- o Chiefdom of over forty towns
- o Oriented eight degrees west of north like La Venta
- Three divisions: Sierra Zapotecs, Valley Zapotecs, Southern Zapotecs
- Literacy and calendar
  - o Logo-syllabic script
  - o Recorded and possibly calculated eclipses with the sacred calendar
- Key Zapotec sites
  - o Monte Albán: capital
  - o Huitzo: an agricultural center
  - o Mitla: the second capital
- Conquest by Mixtecs, Aztecs, and Spaniards

Chapter 4: The Mixtecs

With stunning turquoise and gold jewelry, exquisitely painted ceramics, and deerskin fold-out books chronicling their history, the Mixtecs left an indelible imprint on ancient Mexico. Like their sister culture, the Zapotecs, the Mixtecs called themselves the "cloud people" or "Nusabi," which the Aztecs translated into "Mixtecatl." Their culture stretched back to 1500 BCE, yet they didn't rise to power until the Zapotecs peaked in the 8th century of the Common Era.

The Mixtecs had three geographic groups with distinct cultures speaking over thirty related languages. The first group to emerge was the Mixteca Alta, who established terraced farming around 1500 BCE. This densely populated culture lived at chilly elevations of up to 8,200 feet in the Sierra Madre del Sur range in today's states of Oaxaca and Guerrero. Some Mixtecs spread to the valley regions of northwest Oaxaca and the southwestern part of Puebla, known as the Mixteca Baja. Eventually, the Mixteca de la Costa settled along the Pacific coast of Guerrero and Oaxaca.

Before the early Mixtecs had cities, they were trading with the Olmecs, as archaeologists found Mixtec ceramics in the Olmec heartland and Olmec artifacts in Mixtec territory.[16] One of the Mixtec's earliest cities was Etlatongo in the northeastern Oaxaca state, which they built in approximately 500 BCE over an abandoned ceremonial center. The

---

[16] Kent V. Flannery and Joyce Marcus, "Las Sociedades Jerárquicas Oaxaqueñas y el Intercambio con los Olmecas," *Arqueología Mexicana*, 87, (2007): 73.

Olmecs might have constructed the earlier center almost a thousand years previously, as Olmec-type figurines were in the area.

Archaeologists recently uncovered an exciting find in Etlatongo: two ballcourts dating to approximately 1374 BCE. These ballcourts were there *before* the Olmecs constructed San Lorenzo but after they built El Manatí, both of which had rubber balls but no known ballcourt. Scholars are now wondering who made these ballcourts. Was it the Olmecs or another mysterious advanced civilization?[17]

Around 500 BCE, the Mixtecs built Monte Negro across the high mountains northeast of the Oaxaca Valley. With a population of 2,900, the city's temples and other buildings had limestone foundations and columns, adobe walls, and thatched roofs. Like the Maya, the Etlatongo and Monte Negro elite used cranial modification to mold their children's skulls into rounded coneheads. The Mixteca Alta built Tilantongo, or Temple of Heaven, in the northwestern Oaxaca Valley around 300 BCE, which eventually became the Mixtec capital under King Jaguar Claw.

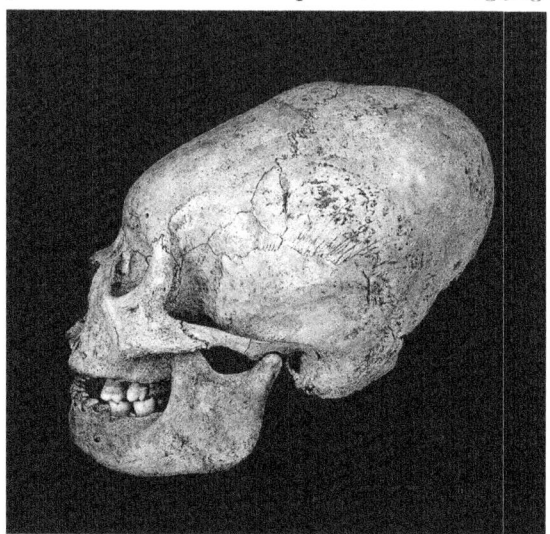

Modified Mixtec skull found in Monte Negro.
Muséum de Toulouse, CC BY-SA 4.0 <https://creativecommons.org/licenses/by-sa/4.0>, via Wikimedia Commons;
https://commons.wikimedia.org/wiki/File:D%C3%A9formation_P%C3%A9ruvienne_MHNT_Noir.jpg

---

[17] J. P. Blomster and Chávez Salazar, "Origins of the Mesoamerican Ballgame: Earliest Ballcourt from the Highlands Found at Etlatongo, Oaxaca, Mexico," *Science Advances* 6, no. 11 (March 13, 2020). doi: 10.1126/sciadv.aay6964. PMID: 32201726; PMCID: PMC7069692.

Around 250 CE, in the early Classic era, the Mixtec began spreading into the valleys of Oaxaca and Puebla, entering into their Ñuiñe cultural phase. Their new proximity to the Zapotecs meant a strong crossover between cultures. For instance, the glyphs in the Ñuiñe writing system were similar to what the Zapotecs were using in Monte Albán, but the Mixtecs had a distinct way of combining symbols. The Mixtecs' trade with the metropolis of Teotihuacan led to cultural exchange, especially in ceramics and artwork.

As time passed, the Mixtecs formed kingdoms that were established on political and marriage alliances among royal dynasties. As the Zapotec culture declined around 800 CE, the Mixtecs reached the apex of their civilization. The Mixtec were as likely to fight each other as they were to fight other civilizations. However, they began expanding farther south, aggressively assimilating Zapotec territory and gaining control of the Oaxaca Valley. The Mixtecs didn't eliminate the Zapotecs, but they forced them to pay tribute and sometimes lived with them in the same cities. The Mixtecs took possession of the mostly abandoned Zapotec capital of Monte Albán around 1350, considering it a sacred place where they buried their own royalty.

The Mixtecs occasionally had female rulers; perhaps the most notable was Queen Six Monkey of Huachino. As archaeologist Daniel Hipolito noted in his article "Art of War," Queen Six Monkey sallied forth into battle wearing her quechquémitl (a poncho-like garment) with a snake design.[18] After she conquered the enemy, the Codex Seldon shows her wearing a garment decorated with seven black, red, and white arrows, a sign of elevated sociopolitical status. Hipolito also remarked that the Mixtec Codex Zouche-Nuttall recorded female warriors defeating mythological creatures.[19]

For centuries before the Spaniards arrived, ancient Mixtecs created pictorial books recording their genealogies, history, mythology, and religious beliefs. Like the Maya, they used deerskin or paper from tree bark, forming fold-out books called codices (singular: codex). The Aztecs

---

[18] Daniel Santos Hipolito and Jose Antonio Casanova Meneses, "Armas Mixtecas Acercan al Público al Arte de la Guerra entre los Mixtecos durante el Posclásico," *Instituto Nacional de Antropología e Historia* 36 (February 2018). https://inah.academia.edu/DanielSantosHipolito

[19] Daniel Santos Hipolito and Jose Antonio Casanova Meneses, "Armas Mixtecas Acercan al Público al Arte de la Guerra entre los Mixtecos durante el Posclásico," *Instituto Nacional de Antropología e Historia* 36 (February 2018). https://inah.academia.edu/DanielSantosHipolito

also produced codices, but they burned most of theirs during a revisionist history phase and lost many more when the Spaniards burned their cities. Most of the surviving pre-Hispanic codices are Mixtec.

The Codex Bodley was twenty-two feet long when completely unfolded. It recorded some royal lineages, which were integral since the Mixtecs believed their nobility descended from the gods. The Mixtecs considered their kings and queens as intermediaries between the gods and people; thus, preserving the bloodlines by only marrying other royals with divine ancestors was imperative. The Codex Bodley also included creation stories and exploits of their legendary monarchs.

Although the royal families of the various city-states intermarried, the Mixtec city-states often vied for power with each other. Their codices recorded pivotal wars between the major players: Jaltepec, Suchixtlan, Tilantongo, Tlaxiaco, Tututepec, and Yanhuitlan. The artist/scribes who painted the codices employed bright colors and minute details, using red lines to divide the page and guide the reader through a maze of unfolding stories. The style of writing varied among the Mixtec regions.

A revered Mixtec tale found in the Codex Bodley and the Codex Zouche-Nuttall recorded the feats of the renowned 11th-century king Eight Deer Jaguar Claw of Tilantongo. "Eight Deer" was the day and month of his birth, a typical naming practice among the Mixtec. He ruled from 1084 to 1115 CE and became the only king to unite the Mixtecs of the mountains, valley, and coast, creating a formidable empire.

His city of Tilantongo was one of the oldest Mixtec cities, but it was still a leading city in the Postclassic era (900–1521 CE). In his first year as king, Jaguar Claw made a pilgrimage to the mountain city of Chalcatongo to pay homage to the goddess of death and elicit her backing in his empire-building schemes. His first target was the mighty city of Tututepec, about two hundred miles south of Tilantongo near the Pacific Ocean.

At this time, Oaxaca's Pacific coast region had a small population but fertile land for growing cotton. Valuable resources from the ocean included fish, salt, and seashells (with which the elite loved to decorate their clothing). The area also had rainforests where the Theobroma cacao trees grew. The Mesoamericans made chocolate from cacao beans; they even used them as currency. The brilliant red and green quetzal birds also lived in the rainforest, and the elite Mesoamericans coveted their feathers for elaborate headdresses and clothing.

Jaguar Claw and his brother, Twelve Earthquake, successfully conquered Tututepec. In a grand ritual with the high priests and nobles, Jaguar Claw moved the goddess of death to a temple on Bird Hill in Tututepec. Controlling the coast brought unimaginable wealth to Jaguar Claw and his empire, as they traded priceless resources throughout Mexico. Beginning in 1095, Jaguar Claw and Twelve Earthquake resumed their expansion campaign. In two years, they conquered twenty-five cities, mainly of the Chatinos, a branch of the Zapotecs. At the end of their campaign, the goddess (or priestess) Lady Nine Grass proclaimed Jaguar Claw the *yaha yahui* or high priest of the Mixtec, giving him the power to shapeshift into an animal or the wind.

The Toltecs, who ruled from Tollan three hundred miles north, colonized Cholula in Puebla. Cholula's Toltec king was Jaguar Four, Face-of-the-Night, and in 1097, he sent four ambassadors to Jaguar Claw, proposing an alliance. The Mixtecs and Toltecs played a ritual ball game to celebrate their union, which Jaguar Claw's team won. After Jaguar Claw helped to expand Toltec territory in Puebla, he traveled to Cholula for a grand ceremony. The Toltecs rewarded him with a turquoise nose ring, symbolizing his position as the Mixtec emperor.

Face-of-the-Night and Jaguar Claw from the Codex Zouche-Nuttall.
https://commons.wikimedia.org/wiki/File:Oaxaca_ocho_venado.png

Jaguar Claw's half-sister, Jade Fan, was his lover until she was married to his mortal enemy, King Bloody Jaguar. When Jaguar Claw was forty, he married Jade Fan's daughter, Thirteen Serpent. In 1101 CE, he conquered his hated father-in-law's city and killed him and most of Bloody Jaguar's brothers, sparing only the youngest, Four Wind. That was a poor decision, as Four Wind led a coalition army against Jaguar Claw fourteen years later. Four Wind took him prisoner and sacrificed him.

Mixtec artisans were renowned for their gold metalwork and their outstanding expertise in jewelry and intricate mosaics. After they fell to the Aztecs, the Mixtecs paid an annual tribute of gold items and ten decorated human skulls to Aztec Emperor Moctezuma II. The skulls were covered with a mosaic of lignite, turquoise, and sometimes jade, with eyes of fool's gold (iron pyrite) and conch shells. Mixteca codices showed priests and kings wearing the skulls as an ornament hanging down their backs, probably representing the "smoke and mirrors" god, Tezcatlipoca.

A human skull covered with a mosaic of turquoise, jade, and lignite.
Wikipedia Loves Art participant "artifacts," CC BY 2.5
<https://creativecommons.org/licenses/by/2.5>, *via Wikimedia Commons;*
https://commons.wikimedia.org/wiki/File:WLA_lacma_Mosaic_Skull_Mixteca-Puebla_Style.jpg

In 1458 CE, the Aztecs conquered some Mixtec city-states while others maintained independence. In 1486, the Aztecs built a fort at Huaxyácac hill (near today's Oaxaca City), where they administered tribute payments from the Zapotecs and Mixtecs. The Mixtecs sent so much of their artistic work in tribute payments that it's difficult to discern whether Aztecs or Mixtecs made pieces found in Aztec cities.

Three decades after the Aztecs built the Huaxyácac hill fort, word spread throughout the Mixtec territory of the arrival of ships carrying men with beards. In 1521, they heard the Aztecs had fallen to the red-headed Hernán Cortés and his soldiers. Francisco de Orozco marched into the Oaxaca Valley the following month, representing the Spanish Crown. The Mixtecs submitted, mostly peacefully, having heard of the atrocities the Aztecs suffered.

Zealous Catholic priests arrived, determined to eliminate Mixtec polytheism. New diseases, such as influenza, measles, and smallpox, reduced the estimated 1.5 million Mixtecs to 150,000 by 1650. However, once the Mixtecs acquired immunity, the population bounced back. Today, about 800,000 Mixtecs live in Mexico and 500,000 in the United States, with 530,000 still speaking the Mixtec languages.

Key Takeaways:
- Nusabi (cloud people); Mixtecatl in the Aztec language
    - Kinsmen of Zapotecs in language and culture
    - Rose to power as Zapotec civilization peaked
- Development of their civilization
    - First cities around 500 BCE
    - Impacted by Zapotecs and Teotihuacanos
- Vied for control with other cultures
    - Gained supremacy over Zapotecs
    - Queen Six Monkey and other women warriors
- Mixtec culture
    - Language and writing
    - Legend of Jaguar Claw from codices
    - Exquisite turquoise and gold jewelry
- Conquest by Aztecs and Spaniards

Chapter 5: The Toltecs

The Toltecs migrated from the harsh northwestern deserts into central Mexico in the 7th century CE and built a mighty city in the Tula Valley, seventy miles north of today's Mexico City. Their capital of Tollan grew to about sixty thousand people, and its fierce warriors conquered territories until it ruled an empire of colonies stretching into southern Mexico. Although their civilization collapsed in the mid-12th century, the Toltecs left an enduring cultural legacy for the Aztecs, Maya, and other central and southern Mexican people.

Their name meant "artisan" due to their legendary skill in artistry and architecture. They were ardent followers of the feathered serpent god Quetzalcoatl; their famous king Cē Ācatl Topiltzin even took the name of this deity. Toward the end of the Toltec rule, they became notorious for frequently sacrificing people and displaying their skulls on a rack in their temple complex.

How do we know what we know about the Toltecs? Their priest Huematzin reportedly chronicled their history, including their arduous journey south to the Tula Valley, in the *Teoamoxtli* (*Things of the Divine*). The Aztecs said the book contained Toltec proverbs, laws, sacrificial rites, astrology, calendar, and philosophy. If the book really existed, it was lost. Only a few scattered glyphs in the Toltec ruins at Tollan indicate the Toltecs knew how to write, although the Aztecs said the book was pictorial. Glyphs that are central Mexican in nature appear in the Toltec section of Chichén Itzá in the Yucatán Peninsula, a city apparently built by both the Maya and Toltecs.[20]

The Aztecs either copied the book or recorded what must have been a robust oral tradition. The Mexica tribe of the Aztecs also migrated from the northwestern deserts, arriving in Tollan shortly after it collapsed. The Mexica lived in the mostly abandoned city for twenty years, absorbing its culture. They arranged marriages with the remnants of the Toltec nobility, thus claiming descent from the Toltec aristocracy. The Aztecs wrote the Codex Chimalpopoca shortly after the Spaniards arrived; it was probably a copy of an older version providing some details of Toltec history.[21]

The Acolhua-Aztecs arrived in the Valley of Mexico earlier than the Mexica-Aztecs and coexisted with the Toltecs for at least a half-century. Fernando de Alva Cortés Ixtlilxóchitl, a descendant of the Acolhua-Aztec kings, wrote *Relación Histórica de la Nación Tulteca* around 1600. He consulted the ancient codices (more might have existed at that point) and interviewed the elderly Aztec scholars, who remembered the old songs and traditions.

Diego Durán, a Dominican friar who grew up in Mexico and was fluent in Nahuatl, collected accounts from the Aztecs and read their codices. He wrote the *History of the Indies of New Spain* in the late 1500s, a record of the Aztecs and other indigenous people of central Mexico. Some scholars scoff at the Aztec accounts as mythological, and some even suggest the Toltec Empire was a baseless legend. Although parts of the Aztec accounts are fanciful, the archaeological evidence of an enormous city in the Tula Valley with distinctive architectural features is unquestionable. Moreover, the Mixtecs interacted with the Toltecs and recorded details of the empire's royalty and colonization in their codices.

---

[20] Ross Hassig, *War and Society in Ancient Mesoamerica* (Berkeley: University of California Press, 1992), 125.

[21] *History and Mythology of the Aztecs: The Codex Chimalpopoca*, trans. John Bierhorst (Tucson: The University of Arizona Press, 1992).

Pyramid B at Tula with the Atlanteans at top and colonnades at bottom.
AlejandroLinaresGarcia, CC BY-SA 3.0 <https://creativecommons.org/licenses/by-sa/3.0>, via Wikimedia Commons; https://commons.wikimedia.org/wiki/File:TulaSite104.JPG

The Toltecs were a Chichimeca tribe, the Nahuatl-speaking hunters and gatherers of northwestern Mexico's barren wastelands. According to the Aztecs, the Toltecs abandoned their nomadic lifestyle to establish the city of Huehue-Tlapallan. Eventually, two Toltec chiefs attempted to usurp power, leading to thirteen years of civil war. After losing, the two chiefs and their supporters went into exile between the mid-400s and mid-500s CE (depending on how one interprets the dates in the codices).

They traveled almost two hundred miles until they came to a land called Tlapallanconco, where they regrouped and settled for several years. Their long-lived and insightful astrologer-priest Huematzin reminded them that prosperity and power always follow persecution. He cautioned them not to stay so close to their enemies and shared his vision of a large, fertile land with few people.

The Toltecs left their older folk and young children in Tlapallanconco and set out to find that new land. They vowed to abstain from sexual relations for twenty-three years so that pregnancies and small children wouldn't impede their migration. After reaching Xalisco, which was near the ocean, they settled for eight years. Then they continued their migration, moving from one place to another until twenty-three years had elapsed. Celebrating the end of their abstinence with a big party, they resumed lovemaking and started having babies again. They continued to move on every few years but left some families behind to establish colonies.

After over a century of moving from one temporary settlement to another, they came to their final destination of Tula (or Tollan) in today's state of Hidalgo. Arriving between the mid-500s and mid-600s, the Toltecs weren't Tula's first inhabitants. The massive city of Teotihuacan, sixty miles southeast, had colonized the area for centuries. But Teotihuacan was in its final throes and was in no position to challenge the newcomers.

The high priest Huematzin was reportedly still alive, although he would have been well into his second century of life. He suggested they strike a deal with the nearby Chichimeca tribe, a different branch from the Toltecs and a potential threat. They asked the Chichimeca tribal chief to give one of his sons to be their king in exchange for leaving the Toltecs in peace. Thus, their first king was the Chichimeca prince Chalchiuhtlanetzin, who ruled for fifty-two years.

The next king was Ixtlilcuechahua, who was either Chalchiuhtlanetzin's son or the son of a Toltec chieftain, depending on the account. By this point, Teotihuacan, the one-time powerhouse of central Mexico, had collapsed, and Ixtlilcuechahua expanded Toltec dominion over the former Teotihuacan colonies. The Toltec architectural style and artifacts have been found from the Pacific to the Gulf of Mexico and into the Yucatán Peninsula, where the Toltecs migrated in several waves.

The Atlantean warriors stand sentry atop Pyramid B at Tollan.
H. Grobe, CC BY 3.0 <https://creativecommons.org/licenses/by/3.0>, via Wikimedia Commons; https://commons.wikimedia.org/wiki/File:Mexico1980-170_hg_1.jpg

Next to the old settlement of Tula Chica, the Toltecs built Tula Grande, a stunning city gleaming with jade, gold, and eye-catching sculptures and architecture. At the center of Tula Grande, also known as Tollan, stands the remarkable ruins of its ceremonial plaza, complete with a ballcourt and striking pyramids and temples. The five-tiered Pyramid B is an impressive example of the Toltecs' incredible architecture. At its top stand the nearly fifteen-foot-high Los Atlantes or Atlanteans: pillars carved in the shape of warriors holding atlatl spear-throwers that once supported the roof of a temple. In front of the pyramid are the remains of a colonnaded walkway. Rows of carvings of jaguars alternating with coyotes and eagles decorate the pyramid.

The most prominent Toltec leader was the semi-mythological Cē Ācatl Topiltzin, who ruled in the 10th century. His father was Mixcoatl, a great Toltec chieftain who was later elevated to deity status as the Aztec god of the hunt. Mixcoatl was hunting one day when he encountered a naked woman named Chimalma. For some reason, he started shooting arrows at her, but she had the power to deflect his arrows, which aroused his admiration and passion. Mixcoatl married Chimalma, who became pregnant when she swallowed a jade stone.

Mixcoatl was assassinated by his brother, and Chimalma died in childbirth, leaving the newborn Cē Ācatl Topiltzin an orphan. Chimalma's parents raised him, teaching him about the feathered serpent deity Quetzalcoatl, who was worshiped in the nearby megacity of Teotihuacan. Cē Ācatl Topiltzin was so devoted to the god that he took his name; however, he detested the human sacrifices the Teotihuacanos offered to Quetzalcoatl.

When Cē Ācatl Topiltzin Quetzalcoatl grew up, he killed his father's assassin and became the king of Tollan, encouraging the worship of Quetzalcoatl but forbidding human sacrifice. His reign was the Toltec Golden Age, a time of prosperity and peace. The city surged ahead in agricultural technology and became famous for its artistry. Migrants poured into the wealthy city, seeking a better life. For over fifty years, Cē Ācatl Topiltzin served as their king and priest. He was a wise and merciful ruler.

But then, the smoke and mirrors god, Tezcatlipoca, deceived Cē Ācatl Topiltzin with black magic by giving him a mirror. When the king looked at it, his face was distorted. Tezcatlipoca reassured him, saying, "Don't worry, just drink this potion, and you'll look normal again. Look! Here's your sister. Why don't you share the drink with her?"

The king and his sister were unaware that the drink contained hallucinogens. The following day, Topiltzin's attendants found him lying next to his sister, both naked. The king wasn't sure what had happened, but he was humiliated and horrified. He left Tollan and wandered through Mexico, cutting himself until his blood ran in a wretched attempt to purge his sin. Eventually, he reached the Gulf of Mexico.

His story has several endings. One is that Topiltzin immolated himself on a funeral pyre. As thousands of red and green quetzal birds flew out of the flames, his spirit rose into the sky to become Venus, the morning star. Another version is that he sailed on a serpent raft into the Gulf of Mexico, promising to return in a "one-reed" year, the beginning of the fifty-two-year cycle of the Mesoamerican calendar.[22] Centuries later, when Hernán Cortés arrived by ship in a one-reed year, some Aztecs thought he might be the returning Topiltzin Quetzalcoatl.

Cē Ācatl Topiltzin on his serpent raft from Fray Durán's Codex.
https://commons.wikimedia.org/wiki/File:Quetzalcoatl_on_his_raft_of_serpents.jpg

---

[22] *The Codex Chimalpopoca*, 26.

Topiltzin's abdication left a power vacuum in Tollan. Most of the city's migrant population came from cultures where human sacrifice was considered a necessary evil to maintain the balance of the cosmos. The Toltecs had rarely practiced human sacrifice, and Topiltzin tried to eradicate it. Yet, once he was out of the picture, the new ruling class surged ahead with the gory practice. In the central ceremonial plaza stood a skull rack holding the heads of sacrificial victims whose beating hearts had been cut from their bodies. Archaeologists unearthed the skeletons of twenty-four children, ages five to fifteen, who had been decapitated in a mass sacrifice to Tlaloc, the god of rain. In another mass grave, they found forty-nine more child sacrificial victims.

The city was divided into two groups. On one side were the pro-Quetzalcoatl Toltecs, who were against human sacrifice and favored a theocracy led by a priest-king. The other side favored a military dictatorship and frequent human sacrifice to ensure success in war and protection from calamities. For centuries, internecine strife continued, flaring up and then dying down. Some Toltecs left for other places, such as the Yucatán Peninsula.

Amid the chaos, a young woman named Xóchitl caught the eye of King Tecpancaltzin when she visited the palace with her family. Her father, Papantzin, wanted to introduce the king to a beverage he'd invented called pulque, which was made from fermented agave (maguey) sap. The king enjoyed the drink and asked Papantzin to send Xóchitl with more. When Xóchitl returned with the pulque, the king detained Xóchitl and made her his concubine. Papantzin came to the palace, sputtering in rage, but Tecpancaltzin granted him lands and titles to keep him quiet. Xóchitl had a child named Meconetzin, "child of maguey," who became the crown prince since the king's wife had no sons. When Queen Maxio died, Tecpancaltzin made Xóchitl his queen.

As the palace intrigue played out, ethnoreligious conflict rocked the city over the issue of human sacrifice and whether Quetzalcoatl or the smoke and mirrors god Tezcatlipoca should be the chief deity. After decades, the schism finally reached a boiling point with a great battle in which the Tezcatlipoca faction prevailed. Xóchitl led a female battalion into combat in a desperate attempt to turn the tide of the war, but she and King Tecpancaltzin died on the battlefield.

Meconetzin, whom Ixtlilxóchitl said was also called Topiltzin, ascended the throne and apparently managed to quell the conflict. Many

Quetzalcoatl followers migrated to the Yucatán, joining a thriving Toltec community there. During Meconetzin's reign, eerie omens appeared, heralding impending disaster. These omens included a deformed rabbit with what looked like deer antlers, which was followed by an epidemic that killed nine hundred people.

The last Toltec king was Huemac, who inherited a kingdom on the brink of collapse. A megadrought almost wiped out the Maya civilization of the Yucatán Peninsula and might have also impacted Tollan. The Toltecs suffered a seven-year famine, and Huemac sacrificed his children in a frantic attempt to regain the rain god Tlaloc's favor. Around 1115 CE, the Chichimeca invaded and burned the pyramids and temples.

Eventually, Huemac led most of the remaining Toltecs out of the city, and they wandered for seven years, with some of the group dispersing to the Yucatán and Puebla. Finally, they settled in the Teotihuacan settlement of Chapultepec Hill, located on the southern end of Lake Texcoco (in today's Mexico City). The Toltecs continued on in the colonies they had established in the Valley of Mexico, Puebla, and the Yucatán, but they were no longer a united empire.

Key Takeaways:
- Sources for Toltec history
    - Aztec codices, supposedly based on Teoamoxtli (Things of the Divine)
    - Fernando de Alva Cortés Ixtlilxóchitl (Relación Histórica de la Nación Tulteca)
    - Durán's History of the Indies of New Spain
- Early settlements and civilization
    - A Chichimeca tribe that migrated south
    - Arrived in Tollan (Tula) in the 6th or 7th century CE
    - King Ixtlilcuechahua expanded Toltec territory
    - Pyramid B and Los Atlantes
- Cē Ācatl Topiltzin
    - Mythical parents Mixcoatl and Chimalma
    - Reigned over a peaceful kingdom; eradicated human sacrifice
    - Abdicated throne; swore to return in a one-reed year
- Empress Xóchitl
    - From concubine to queen
    - Rode out to battle with women of Tollan

- Emperor Huemac and Toltec collapse
    - Civil war, drought, and Chichimeca attack
    - Huemac led remnants to Chapultepec

Chapter 6: The Aztecs

From their island in a swamp, the extraordinary Aztecs built an incredible empire covering eighty thousand square miles, with six million people living in around five hundred city-states. Although the Aztecs were latecomers to the Valley of Mexico, they were empowered by a strong self-identity and a vision for greatness. The Aztecs' canny ability to assimilate other cultures and adapt to rapid change catapulted them to the top. Yet their cruelty and disregard for their disgruntled provinces opened the door for their cataclysmic fall to the Spanish conquistadors.

The Aztecs were infamous for bloody and frequent human sacrifices and even cannibalism. Yet they had schools in every neighborhood, with mandatory education for all teenage boys and girls. The Mexica-Aztecs lived in a pristine city with a remarkably advanced waste-management system. They had a law code and a social welfare system for orphans, widows, the poor, the elderly, and wounded warriors. An aqueduct piped in drinking water for Tenochtitlan's population of 200,000, with dikes and dams providing ingenious floodwater control. Lacking arable land, they built floating islands to grow food for their massive population.

The Aztec origin myth began with seven tribes on the idyllic island of Aztlán. They were all Aztecs, named after their island, but the tribes were the Xochimilca, Tlahuica, Acolhua, Tlaxcalteca, Tepaneca, Chalca, and Mexica. One by one, the Nahuatl-speaking tribes left their island paradise and migrated south to the Valley of Mexico.[23] The last to go was the

---

[23]Elzey, "A Hill on a Land," 110-11.

Mexica, whose codices say they left Aztlán around 1168 CE.

When they crossed to the mainland, the hummingbird god Huitzilopochtli sang to them from the shore, telling them they were now his people. He gave them the necessary tools for their journey and made them a powerful and wealthy people, but they had to do one thing: sacrifice humans to him. So, they captured a woman and two men of the Chicomóztoc-Mimixcoa tribe and offered them to Huitzilopochtli as their first human sacrifices.

Following their new god, the Mexica-Aztecs journeyed south through the searing desert. Finally, they arrived in the densely populated Valley of Anahuac surrounding Lake Texcoco, a region with dependable rainfall and good soil. The Mexica encountered the other Aztlán tribes, but their kinsmen were unwelcoming. They had already carved out their new city-states and didn't want power struggles over resources and land.

For almost a century, the Mexica-Aztecs lived in slave-like subservience as mercenary soldiers and construction workers for their kinsmen tribes. They intermarried in an attempt to build alliances and eventually captured the island of Chapultepec from the Tepanecs. Considering the island sacred because they revered its previous Teotihuacan and Toltec inhabitants, the Mexica lived there for twenty years until the Tepanecs wrested it back. Then, they found refuge with the Colhuacan people, descendants of the Toltecs, and allied with them in a war against the Xochimilca, another Aztec tribe.

After killing thousands of the Xochimilca warriors on behalf of their overlords, the Mexica asked for the Colhuacan king's daughter, telling him they wanted to worship her as a goddess. Their idea of "worship" was bizarre and macabre: they killed and flayed her, and the Mexica high priest wore her skin. Furious, the Colhuacans came after them, determined to destroy every last man. The Mexica fled into the swamp, and while hiding out in the cattails, their god Huitzilopochtli told them to look for an eagle perched on a prickly pear cactus. They were to build their new city at that location and subjugate the surrounding tribes and cities.

The following day, they saw it. An eagle with a snake in its talons was sitting on a prickly pear cactus on an island in the marshy southwestern end of Lake Texcoco. The land belonged to the Tepanec-Aztecs, their former enemies, but they forged a new alliance: they would fight as mercenaries for the Tepanecs in exchange for the island. The Mexica built Tenochtitlan in the swamp. They connected the island with causeways to the mainland and scratched their way to the top against their rival tribes.

Diego Rivera's mural depicting the causeway leading to Tenochtitlan.
https://commons.wikimedia.org/wiki/File:El_templo_mayor_en_Tenochtitlan.png

Their first houses were reed structures, but as their wealth grew, the Mexica built homes of stone and wood. A grand ceremonial complex with a high pyramid (the Templo Mayor) topped by two temples stood in the middle of Tenochtitlan, surrounded by four districts. Around the central temple complex stood the gleaming palaces of the city's aristocrats. Tenochtitlan grew to about 200,000 people, larger than most European cities of its day. Canals intersected their island city through which the Mexica traveled by canoe.

Itzcoatl, the fourth Mexica *tlatoani*, or king, broke Tenochtitlan free of Tepanec rule and formed an empire with two other city-states. His name meant obsidian snake, and he had been quietly waiting for the right opportunity to strike. His father was the first king of Tenochtitlan, then his older half-brother, and then his brother's son, Chimalpopoca. Meanwhile, Itzcoatl formed astute alliances for his ultimate goal of throwing off the Tepanec overlordship.

By this point, the Mexica had risen in power to become the overlords of two other Aztec tribes: the Xochimilca and Tlahuica. Yet they were still technically under Tepanec overlordship. Then, the powerful Tepanec *huey tlatoani* (emperor) Tezozomoc died, and a younger son, Maxtla, staged a coup d'état and stole the throne from his half-brother, Tayatzin. Mexica King Chimalpopoca came to the aid of Tayatzin, his mother's brother, but Maxtla's men captured Chimalpopoca. They put him in a cage, where he died of strangulation, either by his own hand or by the Tepanecs.

This sudden shift in affairs thrust Itzcoatl to the Mexica throne; however, he faced an immediate crisis. Emperor Maxtla wasn't finished punishing Tenochtitlan. He blockaded the Mexica city and cut the aqueduct bringing fresh water to the citizens. He also planned to kill Nezahualcoyotl, Itzcoatl's friend and the Acolhua king of Texcoco, which was just across the lake from Teotihuacan. Nezahualcoyotl fled east to Huexotzinco, an ancient Toltec city close to Puebla, and rallied support from its king, who happened to be another friend of Itzcoatl.

Itzcoatl also asked the city of Tlacopan for help. Tlacopan was actually a Tepanec city but had fought against the usurper Maxtla and lost. They knew Maxtla would wreak his revenge, so they allied with Tenochtitlan and Texcoco for survival. King Nezahualcoyotl of Texcoco negotiated a 100,000-man, 5-city alliance against Emperor Maxtla. These city-states included Tenochtitlan, Texcoco, Tlacopan, Huexotzinco, and Tlatelolco, another Mexica city.

The Battle of Azcapotzalco from the 16th-century Tovar Codex.
https://commons.wikimedia.org/wiki/File:The_Battle_of_Azcapotzalco_WDL6746.png

In 1428, the coalition army conquered the hostile Tepanec cities and then laid siege to the Tepanec capital of Azcapotzalco. The army burned the capital down and sacrificed Maxtla. The military from Huexotzinco headed back home, leaving the Mexica and Acolhua cities in power, along with the Tepanecs of Tlacopan. Tenochtitlan, Texcoco, and Tlacopan formed the Triple Alliance of the three Aztec cities, agreeing to continue conquering together until they ruled all of central Mexico. Tenochtitlan and Texcoco would each get two-fifths of the tribute payments from subjugated cities, and Tlacopan would get one-fifth.[24]

And thus, the Aztec Empire was born. The original agreement was to take turns ruling the empire, but after a few years, Tenochtitlan rose to become the supreme military and political head. Texcoco developed into a brilliant cultural center, as Nezahualcoyotl gathered philosophers and scholars into his city and wrote its first law code. The king was an architect and engineer and assisted Tenochtitlan with a dike and dam system for flood control. He also designed magnificent temples and his clifftop palace in Texcoco. Tlacopan, the minor partner of the Triple Alliance, receded into the background.

Culturally, the Aztecs tended to be assimilators rather than inventors, taking some customs to grotesque extremes. They followed the Mesoamerican 365-day solar calendar, which they called xiuhpōhualli, and the 260-day ritual calendar, tōnalpōhualli. The ritual calendar was divided into twenty-day units, each with a festival dedicated to a specific deity. In the Festival of Atlcahualo, they sacrificed children from elite Aztec families to Tlaloc, the rain god. The next festival was Tlacaxipehualiztli when the priests wore the skins of sacrificial victims.

The solar and ritual calendars lined up every fifty-two years, an event that was celebrated with the New Fire Ceremony. The Aztecs enlarged their pyramids and temples, and people thoroughly cleaned their homes and tossed out old cooking pots and clothing in this time of renewal. On the night before the first day of the new fifty-two-year cycle, they would quench all the fires in the hearths and temples around the city. At the top of Mount Huizachtecatl, a high mountain that could be seen from the towns around Lake Texcoco, they sacrificed a victim and lit a bonfire. From that fire, torches were brought down the mountain to the cities,

---

[24] Richard F. Townsend, *The Aztecs* (3rd, revised ed.) (London: Thames & Hudson, 2009), 74-5.

relighting the fires in each home and temple.[25]

The role of religion affected all classes of Aztec society, and as a theocratic state, religion integrated with politics. The king was also a priest; his duty was to maintain balance and harmony in his city-state and the cosmos. Under the king was a hierarchy of priests, priestesses, monks, and nuns who tended the great temples in the city center and ministered in the neighborhood shrines. Most people began their days by visiting the local temples to pray to the gods.

Huitzilopochtli from the 16th-century Codex Telleriano-Remensis.
https://commons.wikimedia.org/wiki/File:Huitzilopochtli_telleriano.jpg#file

The chief Aztec deity was Huitzilopochtli, the bloodthirsty hummingbird god of war and the sun. Huitzilopochtli demanded human sacrifice in ever-increasing numbers. His worship sometimes included

---

[25]Ross Hassig, *Time, History, and Belief in Aztec and Colonial Mexico* (Austin: University of Texas Press, 2001), 7-19.

cannibalism of the arms and thighs of sacrificial victims. This god was specific to the Mexica-Aztecs. Other cultures did not worship Huitzilopochtli until the Aztecs gained power. As they conquered new cities and towns, they let the people worship whatever gods they wanted as long as they added Huitzilopochtli into the mix as the head of their pantheon.

Another important deity was Tezcatlipoca, the cunning smoke and mirrors god of the night. The brother and nemesis of the feathered serpent deity Quetzalcóatl, Tezcatlipoca, tricked Toltec King Cē Ācatl Topiltzin with his black magic. Worship of this god led to a horrific increase in human sacrifice. For one year before the Toxcatl festival, a handsome and strong young soldier impersonated the god. Then, the Aztecs sacrificed him as drums beat and dancers spun about and cut themselves with knives. The young man's head adorned the skull rack that could hold thousands of the grisly relics, a custom picked up from the Toltecs.

Tlaloc, the rain deity, had been worshiped by the Teotihuacanos, the Toltecs, and numerous other Mesoamerican civilizations. Like most cultures in ancient Mexico, the Aztecs portrayed him with goggle eyes and fangs. At the top of Tenochtitlan's highest pyramid, the Templo Mayor, stood two temples: one for Huitzilopochtli and one for Tlaloc, who demanded child sacrifice in exchange for rain. Elite families gave their baby boys to be drowned, with 20 percent of Tenochtitlan's children feeding the god, especially in times of drought.

Children who survived the five annual festivals involving child sacrifice would be schooled at home from ages three to thirteen. Then, teenagers of both genders attended neighborhood schools; the Mexica-Aztecs were among the first in the world to mandate education for young people. Younger children learned practical skills from their parents. Mothers taught their little girls to weave cotton and to cook. Boys went to work with their fathers to learn a trade. Their fathers also taught them how to fish and make baskets from reeds.

Around the age of fourteen, boys from the nobility attended a *calmecac* school, where they lived in dormitories and studied astronomy, reading, writing, history, religion, and war. Their training focused on positions as administrators, codex painters, medical professionals, priests, and teachers. Boys from non-elite families also lived in dorms at the *telpochcalli* schools, where they received instruction in military skills and religion. They continued training in a trade, such as craftsmanship or agriculture. Teen girls lived at home but attended day school to learn theology, dancing, and singing. Some girls received training in midwifery and other medical work.

Tenochtitlan needed a way to feed its 200,000 people living on two connected islands, so it demanded tributes of corn and other food from the provinces. For fresh vegetables, the city relied on the floating gardens, called chinampas, surrounding the city. More extensive floating gardens grew on Lake Xochimilco, which connected to Lake Texcoco's southern end. The Xochimilca sent food to Tenochtitlan by raft in tribute payments.

The lake agriculturalists built underwater supports of wooden stakes and woven reeds to form a platform on which they would pile mud dredged from the shallow lake bottom. In the mild climate, the farmers grew seven crops a year in the fertile floating gardens. When they harvested one crop, they immediately planted a new one from seedlings started on rafts. The farmers traveled by canoe around the canals that connected the floating gardens.

The Aztecs entered the Valley of Mexico as a ragtag band of nomads, but they quickly adapted to the more civilized cultures while steadily fighting their way to the top. They broke free from their overlords through canny alliances and formed a great empire. And yet, it came crashing down only a century later when the Spaniards arrived. Perhaps it would have imploded anyway, even if the Europeans hadn't invaded.

The Aztecs drained the provinces they ruled of resources without giving much in return. They drafted their warriors to fight for them and took their children as slaves and sacrificial victims. They attacked their neighbors to acquire more victims to feed their bloodthirsty gods. They also failed to realize that leadership must always look to the future, guarding its resources and stewarding its people to meet the challenges ahead.

Key Takeaways:
- Five hundred city-states and six million people
- It had a law code, waste management system, and social welfare system.
    - History overview
    - Aztlán: island of origin
    - Led by hummingbird god Huitzilopochtli

- o   Subservience to other tribes for about a century
- o   Formed Triple Alliance with Texcoco and Tlacopan
- Calendar System
    - o   365-day solar calendar (xiuhpōhualli) and 260-day ritual calendar (tōnalpōhualli)
    - o   New Fire Ceremony launched a new fifty-two-year cycle
- Role of religion
    - o   Theocracy, where kings were also priests
    - o   Chief god Huitzilopochtli, the hummingbird god of war and the sun
    - o   Second in rank was Tlaloc, the god of rain, who demanded child sacrifice
    - o   Tezcatlipoca and Quetzalcoatl were other important gods.
    - o   Worship involved human sacrifice and sometimes cannibalism
- Mandatory education for all teen boys and girls
- Floating chinampas fed the large population

Section Two: Historical Periods

Chapter 7: Preclassic Mexico (1900 BCE–250 CE)

Humans lived in ancient Mexico from the days when fourteen-foot-tall Columbian mammoths roamed the Valley of Mexico. Over time, the ancient humans developed from nomadic hunters and gatherers into farmers who lived in permanent or semi-permanent villages. Some civilizations advanced faster than others, especially in fertile, well-watered areas suitable for agriculture.

The Guilá Naquitz Cave enters the base of a cliff three miles from Mitla in the Oaxaca Valley. It holds seeds dating as far back as 6000 BCE and is the oldest evidence of domesticated crops in Mexico. What were the earliest plants grown in Mexico? Squash was first, followed by maize (corn) and beans. These three plants formed the "Three Sisters" companion planting, which spread from Mexico throughout North America. The indigenous people planted beans around the corn stalks, which acted as a trellis, while the beans put nitrogen into the soil. In between the corn stalks, the people grew squash, which shaded the ground, keeping it moist.

Archaeologists divide pre-Hispanic Mesoamerican history into three major eras: Preclassic, Classic, and Postclassic. Scholars don't quite agree on exactly when each period and sub-period began and ended, but they are roughly the same. The Preclassic period extended from about 1900 BCE to 250 CE, the Classic period from 250 to 900 CE, and the Postclassic from 900 to 1521 CE.

This chapter explores the Preclassic period, also known as the Formative era, when people began making pottery, forming ceremonial centers, and building cities. The Formative period is marked by the emergence of more sophisticated agricultural methods, developing arts, and hierarchal societies. It is called "Preclassic," as the Classic period marks the beginning of megacities, such as Teotihuacan, with elaborate art and architecture.

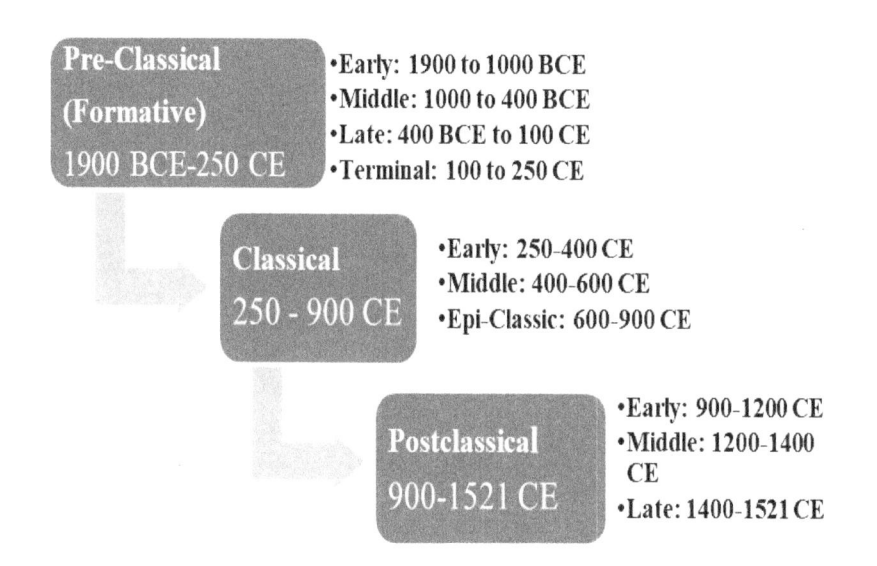

Pre-Classical (Formative) 1900 BCE-250 CE
- Early: 1900 to 1000 BCE
- Middle: 1000 to 400 BCE
- Late: 400 BCE to 100 CE
- Terminal: 100 to 250 CE

Classical 250 - 900 CE
- Early: 250-400 CE
- Middle: 400-600 CE
- Epi-Classic: 600-900 CE

Postclassical 900-1521 CE
- Early: 900-1200 CE
- Middle: 1200-1400 CE
- Late: 1400-1521 CE

A handy guide to the Mesoamerican eras.

The Preclassic era has four sub-divisions: the Early Formative (1900-1000 BCE), the Middle Formative (1000-400 BCE), the Late Formative (400 BCE-100 CE), and the Terminal Formative (100-250 CE). The ancient people of Mexico learned to form clay into pots and fire them in pits or open bonfires at the beginning of the Early Formative era. Scholars analyze the distinctive types of pottery to identify the historical periods and the civilizations that made them.

Puerto Marqués and La Zanja, south of Acapulco Bay in Guerrero, could be the sites of Mexico's earliest known pottery. Archaeologist Charles Brush called it "Pox Pottery" because small pits marked the inside of the vessels, possibly caused by wiping the interior as the clay dried. Using radiocarbon analysis, he dated the Puerto Marqués ceramics to

2400 BCE. However, a recent excavation dated similar pottery from Puerto Marqués to between 1820 and 1400 BCE.

Nine hundred miles down the Pacific coast from Puerto Marqués is Paso de la Amada in the state of Chiapas in the Mazatán region near Guatemala's border. Beginning in about 1900 BCE, the Mokaya people settled in this area, producing round, neckless *tecomate* pottery jars. The Mokaya entered their Locona phase around 1650, with more variety in their ceramics, including figurines.

The Locona phase also marked the beginning of chiefdoms and large-scale architecture and when Paso de la Amada became a regional ceremonial center. The Mokaya built Mexico's first known ballcourt with a sunken compacted earthen floor around 1650 BCE. It had rows of earthen benches on each side of the narrow alley-like playing field, which was about 250 feet long, 22 feet wide, and open at each end.[26]

Two hundred miles south of Paso de la Amada is Chiapa de Corzo on the Pacific coast. The Zoque people settled here around 1400 BCE, developing sophisticated hieroglyphic writing at about the same time as the Maya. From 1200 to 600 BCE, Chiapa de Corzo was one of Mexico's largest urban centers, with a strong connection to the Olmecs, judging by pyramids and pottery styles. The local Zoque people might have been vital trade partners or colonized by the Olmecs, whose core area was 160 miles north.

Based on La Venta's alignment, archaeologists believe the Olmecs used the 260-day ritual calendar by 800 BCE. The first written date, corresponding to December 36 BCE in our calendar, was in Chiapa de Corzo on "Stela Two," apparently inscribed by the Epi-Olmecs. The Olmec Cascajal Block found close to San Lorenzo demonstrated that the Olmecs were using simple glyphs by the late 10th century BCE. The Epi-Olmecs developed the more sophisticated Isthmian script. A potsherd found in Chiapa de Corzo dating to approximately 300 BCE is the earliest example of the Epi-Olmec text and parallels the emergence of the Mayan logo-syllabic script.

Chiapa de Corzo has the oldest pyramid tomb, dating between 700 to 500 BCE. A priest or king around fifty years old lay in state in a stone chamber inside the pyramid with a one-year-old baby on his chest. Another male, around eighteen years old, was unceremoniously tossed

---

[26] Blomster and Salazar, "Origins of the Mesoamerican Ballgame."

into the tomb. He was likely a servant sacrificed to serve his master in the afterlife. On a landing outside the tomb lay a middle-aged woman, probably his wife. The man and woman wore jade collars, their bodies were draped with pearl, jade, and amber ornaments, and their mouths were filled with precious jewels. Olmec-type ceramics were in the tomb, but the stone walls and wooden roof were a Zoque innovation.

While the Mokaya, Olmecs, and Zoque flourished in the south, Tlatilco emerged as an early chiefdom center in the Valley of Mexico around 1250 BCE, about thirty miles north of today's Mexico City. Its sister city of Tlapacoya, southeast of Mexico City, was founded earlier, around 1500 BCE. The Tlatilco were prosperous trade partners with the Olmecs and were known for their peculiar terracotta figurines.

The Tlatilco "pretty-lady" figurines had thin waists, broad hips, balloon-like thighs, and usually no feet or hands. The ceramic statuettes were about six inches tall and sometimes wore ballerina-type skirts. They had slanted eyes. Some wore hoop earrings, and most had a braided coif or a cap. Some were pregnant or holding a child, suggesting a fertility cult, and a few figurines had two or three faces. The Tlatilco culture faded away by 800 BCE for unclear reasons.

Tlatilco figurines dating from 1300 to 1000 BCE.
Madman2001, CC BY-SA 4.0 <https://creativecommons.org/licenses/by-sa/4.0>, via Wikimedia Commons; https://commons.wikimedia.org/wiki/File:Tlatilco_culture_figurines.jpg

About 250 miles south of the Valley of Mexico, the Zapotec civilization emerged about the same time as the Tlatilco civilization. The Zapotecs erected their first ceremonial buildings in San José Mogote about 1300 BCE, which eventually grew into a city-state of one thousand people ruling over forty nearby villages and towns. The Zapotecs used glyphs by 650 BCE and developed sophisticated hieroglyphics by 500 BCE.

Although the Maya culture emerged by at least 1900 BCE, their first-known ceremonial centers were Ceibal in Guatemala and Aguada Félix in Tabasco, Mexico, which were built between 1000 and 800 BCE. Their first city-state was Kaminaljuyú on the western side of today's Guatemala City, which grew into a large city around 800 BCE. The Maya carved glyphs in stone stelae by 900 BCE and developed their logo-syllabic script, which had picture symbols and phonetic symbols, by 300 BCE.

The Valley of Mexico's first city-state with a social hierarchy was Cuicuilco on Lake Texcoco's southern shore. It was settled by 1200 BCE. The city of twenty thousand people ruled over several large towns by 800 BCE. Cuicuilco had an aqueduct piping fresh water into the city, as well as irrigation canals and pyramids. The city's population began declining around 100 BCE, probably due to volcanic activity and competition with the rapidly growing metropolis of Teotihuacan, which was forty-five miles northeast. In the late 3rd century, a massive eruption of the Xitle volcano buried Cuicuilco under a thick layer of lava and ash.

The Mixtec culture emerged to the north of the Zapotecs around 1500 BCE. The highland Mixtec "Alta" built their earliest cities of several thousand residents at Etlatongo and Monte Negro in 500 BCE. Around 300 BCE, they constructed Tilantongo, which later became the Mixtec capital. The Mixtec did not develop into a more sophisticated civilization with writing until the Classic era when they moved into the Oaxaca Valley, close to the Zapotecs.

Teotihuacan formed into an urban center in the northeastern Valley of Mexico by at least 200 BCE. Its population eventually grew to a massive size, yet it collapsed around 650 CE, leaving few clues as to who built this metropolis and how it was governed. The Aztecs thought the gods or maybe giants created the city. The Totonac people of Puebla and Veracruz claimed to have been the original builders who then migrated south after the city fell. The Totonacs did have cultural and trade links to Teotihuacan, so they might have been among its early inhabitants.

Archaeologists Tatsuya Murakami and George Cowgill suggested that several civilizations cooperated in establishing the city in what they called *synoikism*. The goal might have been forming a united front against Cuicuilco, the Valley of Mexico's powerhouse at the time.[27] The valley's scattered, decentralized settlements might have united with the Totonacs, the remnants of the Olmecs, and the Zapotecs.

Cowgill, who spent most of his career excavating and studying Teotihuacan, said that by 1 BCE, the city's population reached forty thousand. The Teotihuacanos had not yet built their three great pyramids or their apartment compounds, but it might have been the largest city in Mexico at the beginning of the Common Era, certainly the largest in the Valley of Mexico. By 100 CE, Teotihuacan had grown to eighty thousand people, and the initial construction of the Pyramid of the Moon was completed, although it would be enlarged several times.

A flurry of energetic building projects transformed Teotihuacan in the Terminal Formative era, perhaps under the leadership of a potent dictator or a series of ambitious monarchs. From 150 to 200 CE, the Teotihuacanos built the ornate Feathered Serpent Temple and the thirty-eight-acre Ciudadela courtyard surrounding it. A row of feathered serpent heads projected out from each layer of the pyramid, alternating with a fanged, goggle-eyed creature, perhaps a crocodile deity or the rain god. Construction of the Pyramid of the Sun, which towered over the city as Mexico's highest pyramid at the time, might have begun around 200 CE.

Vista of Teotihuacan from the Moon Pyramid, with small temples in the foreground, the Avenue of the Dead, and the Sun Pyramid in the background.
Johannes Kruse, CC BY 2.0 <https://creativecommons.org/licenses/by/2.0>, via Wikimedia Commons; https://commons.wikimedia.org/wiki/File:Teotihuacan_(cropped).jpg

---

[27] Matthew Robb, ed, *Teotihuacan: City of Water, City of Fire* (Berkeley: University of California Press, 2017), 21.

Most of the Valley of Mexico's population migrated into Teotihuacan after 100 CE. By 200 CE, Teotihuacan's population reached its apex of 125,000 to 200,000 people. The surrounding region, extending out twenty miles from the city, tripled in population. Migrants also came from outside the Valley of Mexico, as the Maya, Mixtecs, and more Zapotecs were drawn to the flourishing economic hub. The various ethnic groups formed barrios, which housed workshops producing their specialties in ceramics, obsidian crafts, jewelry, clothing, and more.[28]

The many distinct civilizations of the Preclassic age shared several religious ideologies. All primary Mesoamerican cultures of the Formative era worshiped the jaguar, the largest feline in the Americas. As a creature of the night, the jaguar was the god of the underworld but also the god of water and fertility. The Teotihuacanos kept captive jaguars, which they sacrificed at the dedication of their pyramids. The Olmecs had carvings of "were-jaguars," creatures with cleft heads and grimacing mouths, often with partial human child characteristics. The Maya believed the jaguar god protected people.

Most civilizations in central and southern Mexico worshiped the sun, moon, and a feathered serpent, which the Yucatán Maya called Kukulkan. The Preclassic Cuicuilco, Maya, and Teotihuacan cultures worshiped an old man deity, who is often depicted sitting cross-legged and balancing a brazier on his head. He is thought to have been a fire god. The storm, rain, and war god, which the Aztecs later called Tlaloc, pervaded Preclassic cultures. He was the benevolent god of rain and fertility yet the destructive god of hurricanes, lightning, and hail. He also demanded child sacrifices. Most ancient Mesoamericans practiced animal and human sacrifice.

Although religious beliefs in the various cultures of ancient Mexico evolved as the centuries passed, they shared a common worldview and many similar deities. The core Mesoamerican belief system of the Preclassic era continued through the Classic and Postclassic periods until the Spaniards arrived. Many ancient Mexican cities were aligned with where the sun rose on specific days in the shared ritual calendar. Pyramids and other temples in the middle of cities were worship centers where priests and kings offered sacrifices. The ancient people believed that deities influenced every aspect of their lives. Thus, keeping the gods happy

---

[28] Cowgill, "State and Society,"129.

was a driving force in their everyday traditions and monthly festivals.

Key Takeaways:
- Early civilizations
    - Guilá Naquitz Cave: first domesticated crops in Mexico, circa 6000 BCE
    - Puerto Marqués and La Zanja: first ceramics in Mexico, circa 2400 BCE, maybe later
    - Paso de la Amada: Mesoamerica's first ballcourt, circa 1650 BCE
    - Chiapa de Corzo: first written date (36 BCE), first pyramid tomb (700 BCE)
    - Tlatilco culture: Valley of Mexico's first chiefdom; known for ceramic figurines
- Zapotecs
    - Established San José Mogote in 1300 BCE, grew to one thousand people and ruled forty towns
    - Using glyphs by 650 BCE and logo-syllabic hieroglyphics by 500 BCE
- Maya
    - First ceremonial center in Mexico, Aguada Félix in Tabasco, 1000-800 BCE
    - First used simple glyphs by 900 BCE, sophisticated hieroglyphics by 300 BCE
- Cuicuilco, the first city-state with a social hierarchy in the Valley of Mexico: 1200 BCE
    - Population of twenty thousand by 800 BCE with aqueduct, irrigation, and pyramids
    - Covered by lava flow from Xitle volcano in 3rd century CE
- Teotihuacan, established between 400 and 200 BCE
    - Multiethnic city probably from the outset
    - Population of forty thousand by 1 BCE, probably the largest city in Mexico at the time
    - 100 CE: population up to eighty thousand; Moon Pyramid built
    - Feathered Serpent Pyramid was built between 150 and 200 BCE
    - 200 BCE: population at least 125,000; Sun Pyramid possibly begun

- Common religious ideologies of Preclassic Mexico
  - Jaguar deity
  - Sun, moon, feathered serpent, old man/fire god, rain god

Chapter 8: Mexico in the Classic Period (250–900 CE)

The Teotihuacan megacity dominated the Valley of Mexico in the Classic era, while Monte Albán ruled the Oaxaca Valley and Cholula the Puebla region. Several Maya city-states in the Yucatán and Mexico's southern border were at their zenith, such as Palenque in Chiapas, Edzna in Campeche, and the nearby "Snake Kingdom" of Calakmul. The collapse of Teotihuacan, Cholula, and Monte Albán in the Epi-Classic (Late Classic) age left a power vacuum for other cities to fill, including Xochicalco in Morelos, Cacaxtla in Tlaxcala, and El Tajín in Veracruz.

At the onset of the Classic period, Teotihuacan grew into the largest city in the Western Hemisphere, with the sixth-highest population in the world. Through thriving coast-to-coast trade and sometimes conquest, it was the powerhouse of Mesoamerica from 300 to 600 CE. Majestic pyramids, palaces, and temples with spectacular murals and sculptures lined its magnificent Avenue of the Dead, which ran on a north-south axis through the megacity's core. Teotihuacan was a commercial hub, with over six hundred workshops producing highly prized ceramics, jewelry, weaponry, and clothing.

Teotihuacan launched an incredible construction project in the early Classic era, erecting about 2,300 one-story apartment complexes for its massive population. Each walled compound housed up to one hundred people, with a large courtyard at its entrance featuring a small temple for worship and brilliant murals on the walls. The people living within each compound were usually kinsmen or shared the same ethnicity. The compounds were like a series of enclosed villages within the metropolis, providing a safe place for children to play and a sense of belonging.

Teotihuacan had distinct neighborhoods for its various ethnicities. For instance, the Maya lived in the city's center, just west of the Avenue of the Dead. People from the Gulf Coast lived in the Teopancazco barrio southwest of the urban center, and a large Zapotec population lived on the far western side. Each of these barrios had workshops producing regional specialties. The Zapotecs created Gray Ware pottery, while the Gulf Coast population sewed cotton clothing decorated with bright feathers and shells for the elite. Other barrios produced knives and spearheads from razor-sharp volcanic obsidian glass, exquisite jewelry, and various goods, which were traded throughout central and southern Mexico, Guatemala, Belize, and Honduras.

The old man god sits in a shrine with brilliantly painted murals.
Gary Todd, CC0, via Wikimedia Commons;
https://commons.wikimedia.org/wiki/File:Teotihuacan_Mural_%26_Stone_Brazier.jpg

Between 250 and 400 CE, the Teotihuacanos enlarged the Moon Pyramid at the northern end of the Avenue of the Dead three times. Anthropologists Ruben Cabrera and Saburo Sugiyama discovered a vault in the pyramid's core in 2004, where they found fifty sacrificed animals, including eagles, jaguars, pumas, wolves, and rattlesnakes. They also uncovered the skeletons of twelve humans, ten of whom were decapitated. They had been sacrificed at the dedication of the third layer of the pyramid. More renovations of the Moon Pyramid continued about every fifty years until 400 CE, when it reached its final height of 140 feet.

The Pyramid of the Moon stood at the northern end of the Avenue of the Dead, the city's central boulevard, and the Feathered Serpent Pyramid stood at the southern end. The 216-foot Pyramid of the Sun, built around 250 CE, towered in the middle and was visible from all points of the metropolis. The Aztecs misnamed it; the pyramid probably wasn't dedicated to the sun but more likely to the goggled-eyed rain god to whom children were sacrificed. Archaeologists found the remains of sacrificed babies and young children with images of the rain god in a vault under the pyramid. They found more child skeletons on all four corners of each of the pyramid's layers.[29]

Teotihuacan had friendly trade and diplomatic relations with the Zapotec city of Monte Albán, which was three hundred miles southeast. Hundreds of Zapotecs lived in the Oaxacan barrio in Teotihuacan, and some Teotihuacanos lived in Monte Albán. Stone stelae inscriptions in Monte Albán document diplomatic visits from Teotihuacan. Both cities reached their apex and then collapsed at about the same time.

By 500 CE, Teotihuacan's population declined, and the city ultimately collapsed around 650. The causes of the city's downfall are unclear; however, centuries earlier, civil unrest of unknown origins rocked the megacity. Around 350 CE, some craftsmen abruptly abandoned their workshops, leaving their tools behind. At about the same time, the Teopancazco barrio experienced massive human sacrifice or violent struggle. One-third of the buried men had been decapitated.

Anthropologist Linda Manzanilla spent eight years unearthing the Teopancazco neighborhood and believes tension and competition between the city's multiple ethnicities led to unrest. She thinks the workshop craftsmen clashed with the wealthy businessmen who were the liaison between the government and the workers. Between 550 and 650 CE, another riot erupted. Unruly crowds burned and vandalized the palaces, temples, and administrative centers along the Avenue of the Dead but left the living quarters unharmed.[30]

---

[29] Nawa Sugiyama, et al., "Inside the Sun Pyramid at Teotihuacan, Mexico: 2008–2011 Excavations and Preliminary Results," *Latin American Antiquity* 24, no. 4 (2013): 403–16. http://www.jstor.org/stable/23645621.

[30] Linda R. Manzanilla, "Cooperation and Tensions in Multi-ethnic Corporate Societies Using Teotihuacan, Central Mexico, as a Case Study," *Proceedings of the National Academy of Sciences*,

Another probable cause for tensions in the city was drought caused by global cooling, which led to food shortages. Global climate change entered an acute phase in the Northern Hemisphere in 536 CE, and temperatures remained abnormally low for about a century. Cooler temperatures meant less rain, and the springs that Teotihuacan depended on for irrigation dried up, creating an agricultural crisis and food shortages. In this period, a high rate of stillborn babies and child mortality in Teotihuacan underscored the near-famine conditions. Analysis of burials in one barrio showed almost one-third were stillborn or newborn babies. Less than 40 percent of children reached their teens, and most adults died by their mid-forties.

The world's largest pyramid by volume, bigger than anything in Egypt, lies in Cholula, thirty miles southeast of the rumbling 3.37-mile-high El Popocatépetl volcano. Today, the Tlachihualtepetl pyramid is overgrown with vegetation, looking like a small mountain with a colonial-era multi-domed church perched on top. But at one time, it was a massive adobe brick structure measuring 984 feet wide by 1,033 feet long at its base.

Just outside today's city of Puebla, Cholula was established around 200 BCE or earlier, about the same time as Teotihuacan, seventy miles north. Cholula's original inhabitants were probably related to the Zapotecs and Mixtecs, but the remnant of the Olmecs had a considerable influence. Regular summer rain and runoff from the snowy mountains meant the inhabitants of Cholula enjoyed flourishing agriculture. Its alluvial soil had a high clay content, and the region became renowned for its pottery.

Cholula was a trade hub between the Valley of Mexico and the Yucatán Peninsula. At the end of the Formative era, the city surged in population while the surrounding areas emptied, similar to how Teotihuacan simultaneously attracted a migrant population. This period was when Cholula's people began the first phase of their great pyramid and continued enlarging it in four major stages over the next six centuries.

Cholula entered the Classic era as the dominant force in the Puebla region, building the second pyramid structure, called the Pyramid of the Painted Skulls, between 250 and 300 CE. It had the talud-tablero architecture associated with Teotihuacan, indicating a strong influence from the megacity. This talud-tablero pyramid layer featured murals of red and yellow skulls with insect-like bodies. The first and second pyramids,

---

112, no. 30 (March 2015): 9214-15. https://doi.org/10.1073/pnas.1419881112

which were adjacent to each other, were eventually encompassed by much larger pyramid layers that covered them both.

Connected to the pyramid is a mausoleum with the remains of a man and woman buried with lavish grave offerings and the jawbone of a Xoloitzcuintle (Mexican hairless) dog. Twenty-four tunnels, totaling five miles, wind through and under the pyramid, where archaeologists found a sculpture of the goggle-eyed, fanged rain god called Tlaloc by the Aztecs. Child sacrifices indicate the rain god was worshiped at the pyramid, although it is also associated with the feathered serpent deity. In the Postclassic era, some Toltecs migrated here when Tula fell and buried their royalty in the pyramid.

The Maya of Mexico reached the pinnacle of their civilization in the early Classic period and then experienced a hiatus followed by another wave of growth in population and culture. By the late 200s, the Maya extensively used their logo-syllabic script and included dates on their inscriptions on stone pillars and slabs (stelae). Vaulted or arched architectural features are a hallmark of Maya architecture in the Classic era.

The Palenque palace tower with a corbel arch at the lower left.
Bernard DUPONT, CC BY-SA 2.0 <https://creativecommons.org/licenses/by-sa/2.0>, via Wikimedia Commons; https://commons.wikimedia.org/wiki/File:The_Observation_Tower_-_Palenque_Maya_Site,_Feb_2020.jpg

A stunning example of this architectural feature is the A-shaped corbel arches in Lakamha (called Palenque by the Spanish) in Chiapas. Under K'inich Janaab' Pakal, who became king at age twelve in 615 CE and ruled until his death at eighty, the city attained staggering prosperity. Despite ongoing warfare with Calakmul, he initiated an ambitious building project of temples and palaces. One palace had a four-storied tower and corbel arches, which were novel architectural features in Mexico.

Palenque's great rival Calakmul was about two hundred miles northeast in the rainforests at the base of the Yucatán Peninsula. The kings of both city-states claimed divine ancestry and called on the nobility of the towns and cities over which they ruled to provide warriors for their military clashes. Calakmul's "Snake Kingdom" dynasty persisted for one thousand years, and some of the richest royal Maya tombs are in this resplendent city.

In 562 CE, Calakmul conquered the mighty Maya city of Tikal in Guatemala, which the Teotihuacanos had previously invaded in 378 CE and ruled for several generations. Calakmul ascended as the Maya superpower under the leadership of King Sky Witness (r. 561–572). In 599, his son, Scroll Serpent, attacked Palenque, sparking an ongoing war between the Calakmul Snake Kingdom and the Palenque Bone dynasty, with Palenque losing most of the battles. Within a century, Calakmul's mini-empire stretched southeast to Belize, with unimaginable wealth flowing into the city from its lucrative trade routes. Breathtaking murals covered the Chiik Nahb pyramid depicting trade exchanges and consumption of luxury goods.

A mural from Calakmul's Chiik Nahb pyramid.
Elelicht, CC BY-SA 3.0 <https://creativecommons.org/licenses/by-sa/3.0>, via Wikimedia Commons; https://commons.wikimedia.org/wiki/File:Calakmul_Fresken.JPG

The megacity of Teotihuacan in the Valley of Mexico collapsed in the Epi-Classic era (600-900 CE), leaving a power vacuum that enabled other cities to rise in power. Cacaxtla in Tlaxcala and Xochicalco in Morelos apparently allied in this period to snatch the trade routes that Teotihuacan once controlled. The Olmeca-Xicalanca founded both cities. They were a people with strong Maya influence who originally lived in the Olmec Gulf Coast areas and eventually migrated north.

Brilliantly painted in scarlet, blue, green, and gold, well-preserved murals from Cacaxtla depict battle scenes between Maya and highland people. The Gulf Coast Maya are shown with flat foreheads from cranial modification and feathered headdresses, and they fight against warriors wearing jaguar skins and long nose plugs. One figure representing the Eagle Lord has a blue face mostly covered by a bird mask and rides on a feathered-serpent raft as a quetzal bird flies upward.[31]

The Eagle Lord rides the Feathered Serpent in this Cacaxtla mural.
HJPD, CC BY-SA 3.0 <https://creativecommons.org/licenses/by-sa/3.0>, via Wikimedia Commons; https://commons.wikimedia.org/wiki/File:Cacaxtla2.jpg

New regions rose to dominance in the Epi-Classic or Terminal Classic age as the Zapotecs, Teotihuacanos, and some Maya cities faded. This

---

[31] Donald McVicker, "The 'Mayanized' Mexicans." *American Antiquity* 50, no. 1 (1985): 82-101. https://doi.org/10.2307/280635.

period's vibrant art and architecture reflect an eclectic cultural blending on a grand scale. New population centers emerged, trade routes changed, and innovation surged in this time of migration and shifting political landscapes.

Key Takeaways:
- Teotihuacan: the powerhouse of Mesoamerica in the Classic period
    o The largest city in the Americas, sixth largest in the world
    o 2,300 one-story apartment compounds and over 600 workshops
    o The moon pyramid enlarged multiple times with human and animal sacrifices
    o 216-foot Pyramid of Sun dedicated to the rain god
    o Global cooling, reduced rainfall, food shortages, rioting, and collapse by 650 CE
- Cholula: largest pyramid in the world; close connection to Teotihuacan
- Classic age Maya: pinnacle in Classic era with a hiatus in the middle
    o Palenque in Chiapas: corbel arches, high tower, rival of Calakmul
    o Calakmul in Campeche: conquered Tikal in Guatemala and extended to Belize
- Xochicalco and Cacaxtla
    o Rose to power as Teotihuacan collapsed
    o Settled by the Olmeca-Xicalanca

Chapter 9: Postclassic Mexico (900–1521 CE)

Chaos, warfare, and the decline of many prominent city-states marred Postclassic Mexico. And yet, it was a time of dynamic technological advances in engineering, architecture, and weaponry. The population grew exponentially, and in many ways, life was better than ever before in ancient Mexico. But at the end of the era, Mexico was fractured, suffering from oppressive overlords and unbridled human sacrifice. The city-states were unprepared to unite against the Spanish invaders.

As the Maya of the Yucatán Peninsula rose in power during the Postclassic era, they had to find reliable fresh water for their growing cities. The peninsula's northern half has no above-ground rivers, and the lakes' saline content makes the water unsuitable for drinking or watering crops. The Yucatán does have an underground freshwater aquifer accessible by numerous sinkholes throughout the region. These sinkholes are called cenotes. Some of these cenotes form a large half-circle as part of the Chicxulub crater created by a prehistoric asteroid; the rest of the crater is in the Gulf of Mexico.

Chichén Itza exploded into power in the Postclassic era, ruling most of the Yucatán Peninsula. It had four cenotes with plentiful fresh water. One of the sinkholes, the Sacred Cenote, had steep limestone walls, making it difficult to climb out if a person was thrown in. This cenote was a sacrificial place where men and boys were fed to the rain god Chaac. In recent years, divers have found a treasure trove of gold and jade objects at the bottom of the sinkhole, as well as human skeletons.

Several migrations of Toltecs from Tula between 900 and 1200 CE are reflected in Chichén Itza's architecture, particularly its El Castillo Pyramid. It was dedicated to Kukulkan, the Maya name for the feathered serpent deity whom the Aztecs called Quetzalcoatl. Archaeologists recently found a fifth cenote under this pyramid. It was full of sacrificial items, including human remains. The pyramid is aligned with the sun, so the setting sun on the spring and fall equinoxes casts a shadow leading to a sculpture of the Feathered Serpent's head at the bottom. It seems as if the serpent's shadow is slithering down the pyramid on those two evenings of the year.

Temple of Kukulkan (El Castillo) in Chichén Itza.
Carlos Delgado, CC BY-SA 3.0 <https://creativecommons.org/licenses/by-sa/3.0>, via Wikimedia Commons; https://commons.wikimedia.org/wiki/File:Chich%C3%A9n_Itz%C3%A1_-_17.jpg

Maya cities in the Yucatán that didn't have the advantage of cenotes connected to the underground aquifer had to find other ways to control and contain water. They carved enormous underground cisterns out of the underlying rock, which they covered with stucco to keep the water from seeping into the porous limestone. They arranged their cities so that water flowed from the higher areas into the cistern during the six months of heavy rain, keeping an adequate water supply for the six dry months.

But once they had a steady water supply, the Yucatán Maya had a new problem. They liked painting their buildings with red paint, but the rain gradually washed the paint off the buildings and into the cisterns. The mercury in the paint caused grave health issues, brain damage, and sometimes death. The Yucatán Maya made an engineering breakthrough when they discovered that the negatively charged mineral zeolite was like a magnet for the positively charged mercury. It could draw mercury out of the body and out of the water. So, they built a water filtration system with zeolite gravel and quartz sand wrapped in reed mats through which the water flowed as it entered the cistern. They wouldn't have known about negatively charged and positively charged minerals, but they discovered that zeolite purified the water and used it as a filter.

The island city of Xaltocan at the center of Lake Xaltocan in the Valley of Mexico, which was established around 800 CE, grew in power as the capital of the Otomi people from 1200 to 1395 CE. Some of the Toltec survivors of Tollan fled to Xaltocan. Together with the Otomi people, they launched an energetic engineering project to dredge the lakebed sediment to expand their island and construct the floating chinampas gardens. Centuries later, the Mexica-Aztecs adopted this system for their island capital of Tenochtitlan. The Codex Chimalpopoca tells of a violent conflict between Xaltocan and the Tepanec-Aztec city-state of Cuautitlán, which the people of Xaltocan eventually lost in 1395. They were forced to abandon their island.

By this point, metallurgy was developing in Mexico, which wasn't the game-changer for Mesoamerican weaponry that one would expect. Metalwork with copper, silver, and gold reached western Mexico from South America between 600 and 800 CE, especially among the Mixtecs. As the Mixtec and other metalsmiths developed innovative technologies and alloys, they achieved greater strength in metals. By 900 CE, they were blending copper and tin to make bronze.

Their initial interest was the beauty and colors of various metals in artwork, but metal's practical use in everyday implements like axes, fishhooks, and needles soon became apparent. Curiously, most of the ancient Mexican civilizations delayed applying metals to weaponry. The two exceptions were the Maya, who used copper knives and axe heads by the late Classic era, and the Purépecha (called Tarascans by the Spaniards) of the Pacific coast, who used copper shields and spearheads.

Most Mesoamericans used stone, jade, flint, and obsidian for knives, arrowheads, and spearheads up until the Spanish arrived. Obsidian glass was sharper than razor blades and highly lethal, although easily breakable. Non-metal blades were deadly enough when pitted against the quilted armor and wicker shields of Mexico's indigenous people, but they were not deadly against the Spaniards' steel armor.

One well-known Postclassic weapon used by the Aztecs was the macuahuitl, a three-foot wooden club with rows of embedded obsidian blades. The Aztecs have the most notoriety for using this weapon, but the Mixtecs, Maya, and Toltecs brandished the macuahuitl before the Aztecs even arrived in the Valley of Mexico. The sharp obsidian blades could slice off a man's head or disembowel a horse, a strategy the Aztecs later learned when fighting against Spanish cavalry.

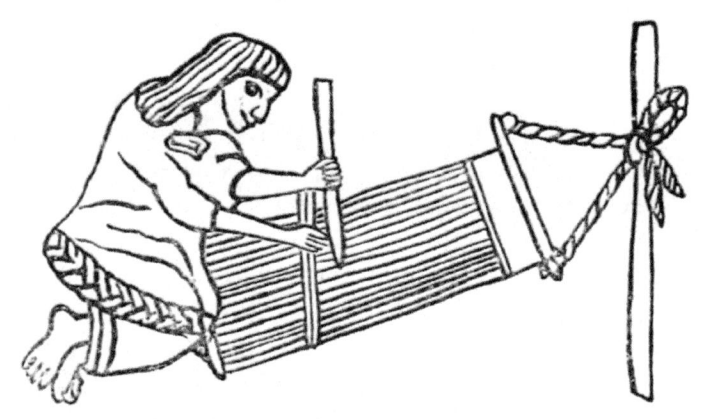

Drawing of a woman weaver from the Codex Mendoza (circa 1541).
https://commons.wikimedia.org/wiki/File:A_glimpse_of_Guatemala_-_A_Woman_Weaving.png

Cotton cloth may not seem remarkable, but it played a vital role in ancient Mexico's economy. Cotton spinning and weaving technology took off in Mexico's Postclassic age. Ancient indigenous people began spinning cotton into thread with simple spindle whorls: disks with a hole in the middle. A weaver inserted a thin wooden rod called a spindle into the hole and then pulled out a bit of fiber from a wad of cotton and attached it to the spindle. Holding on to the fiber, the weaver spun the whorl, which twisted the cotton into thread that was then woven into cloth on a backstrap loom.

The region of Morelos in the Puebla area was well known for growing and spinning cotton. Several important new devices made cotton spinning easier and faster, which increased production levels. Excavations at Xochicalco in Morelos show the Epi-Classic weavers used a more sophisticated spindle whorl beginning around 1100 CE. Spindle whorls found in Tula are similar to what the indigenous Huastec people on the Gulf Coast still use today. Around 1200 CE, weavers began using a small ceramic bowl into which they inserted the spindle, increasing the spinning speed.[32]

In the Classic era, weavers only needed to produce enough cloth for their families and to sell for profit. However, once the Aztecs rose to power and their empire swallowed up Morelos, they demanded a large quantity of woven cotton cloth as tribute payments. The women spent most of their days weaving to meet the quota, so advanced technology that could speed up the time required to spin cotton eased their burden.

The ruins of the ancient city of El Tajín lay hidden away in the Veracruz rainforest for five centuries before being rediscovered in 1785. While other urban centers collapsed, El Tajín reached its peak at the beginning of the Postclassic period, covering four square miles with a population of about twenty thousand. The city introduced novel architecture to Mesoamerica, such as key-pattern decorations, columns with intricate reliefs, windows in homes, and a poured cement roof almost one meter thick.

El Tajín's dramatic Pyramid of the Niches introduced two architectural features: window-like niches lining each of its seven stories capped by triangular flying cornice overhangs. Originally painted crimson with black niches, the 365 niches represented the days of the solar year. The Totonac people, who claim to have built Teotihuacan, currently live in the El Tajín region and might have constructed the city. However, some scholars believe the Huastec people might have been the city's founders. While most Mesoamerican cities had ballcourts, El Tajín had seventeen, more than any other.

---

[32] Michael E. Smith and Kenneth G. Hirth, "The Development of Prehispanic Cotton-Spinning Technology in Western Morelos, Mexico," *Journal of Field Archaeology* 15 (1988): 349-355.

El Tajín's Pyramid of the Niches.

Irvin ulises, CC BY-SA 3.0 <https://creativecommons.org/licenses/by-sa/3.0>, via Wikimedia Commons https://commons.wikimedia.org/wiki/File:Piramide_de_los_nichos.jpg

The hallmarks of Postclassic Mexico were population migrations and growth, most notably in the Valley of Mexico, where the population grew to an estimated one million. Waves of Chichimeca people migrated from the northwestern deserts, while the populations of collapsed cities moved to the still thriving urban centers, forming blended ethnicities. The Maya abandoned many of their majestic cities in southern Mexico and Central America, partly due to a drought between 800 and 900 CE, which shifted their power to the Yucatán.

The Postclassic era also appears to have been a time of political experimentation. In the Classic era, the Yucatán Maya had a theocratic priest-king governance, but in the Postclassic period, models of dual rulership or rule by a council (oligarchy) might have emerged. Some archaeologists believe that Chichén Itza had a "multepal" council of elite rulers; however, this theory lacks firm evidence. The Postclassic Maya stopped recording details about their kings on stone stelae, which hints that they didn't have single monarchs but decentralized leadership.

As anthropologists Jeremy Sabloff and William Rathje noted, without a dominant dynastic elite, energy was no longer expended on building towering monuments to glorify their kings. They believe that growth in trade and productivity led to collective wealth and a higher standard of living for everyone in a thriving economy. Their field research of Cozumel, an island off the Yucatán coast, provided valuable information about the Postclassic Maya. It was an important trading center and reached its peak growth in the Postclassic era through the influence of merchants rising in power and influence.[33]

The Postclassic Yucatán Maya carried out long-distance trading via large canoes along the Gulf Coast. Christopher Columbus reported spotting such a canoe off the Honduras coast in 1502. The Maya produced a high quantity of salt in the Yucatán, which was in high demand as far away as the Aztec capital of Tenochtitlan in the Valley of Mexico. Cacao beans for making chocolate were another sought-after trade item.

This flourishing trade reached from the Valley of Mexico down the Gulf and Pacific coasts into Central America, creating an interconnectedness between the various cultures. Sabloff and Rathje believe this was the highest volume and most extraordinary trade diversification ever seen in Mesoamerica up to that point. The massive trade of luxury goods throughout Mexico was no longer for the elite. The working class now had access to chocolate, obsidian, and fine goods, which led to a more egalitarian society.[34]

Key Takeaways:
- Technological advances
    - Aligning the pyramid with the sun to cast a "slithering snake" shadow
    - Underground cisterns with water purification systems
    - Development of metallurgy
    - Deadly macuahuitl war club
    - Sophisticated cotton spinning spindle and bowl
    - El Tajín novel architecture: niches, flying cornices, poured cement roof
- Possible new administrative models: dual rulership and oligarchic councils
- Trade improved life from the Classic to Postclassic periods

---

[33] Jeremy A. Sabloff, "It Depends on How We Look at Things: New Perspectives on the Postclassic Period in the Northern Maya Lowlands," *Proceedings of the American Philosophical Society* 151, no. 1 (2007): 11–20. http://www.jstor.org/stable/4599041.

[34] Sabloff, "New Perspectives on the Postclassic," 20–26.

Section Three:
The Fight for Ancient Mexico

Chapter 10: Preparing for Battle

For thousands of years, the Mesoamericans fought for power, access to valuable resources, and victims to sacrifice to their gods. As the 16th century dawned, they would have to fight for their survival when the Spaniards set foot in Mexico, determined to reap the gold and other wealth the land offered. Several momentous battles before and after the Spanish arrived changed the course of Mexico's history. Certain rituals revolved around warfare, and ambassadors, messengers, and spies contributed to how the battles played out. The "Flower Wars," military societies like the Eagle and Jaguar warriors, and the weaponry of ancient Mexico all played a part in warfare as well.

Since all able-bodied Aztec men were warriors, a special ritual celebrated a newborn boy's future role. Four days after his birth, the midwife bathed the baby in the early morning sun, and the infant received his name. The midwife placed a small arrow in the baby's right hand and a miniature shield in his left. An elite warrior would then take the arrow, shield, and the child's umbilical cord and bury it next to a deceased warrior who was a fearless fighter.

Aztec warriors could achieve high social status regardless of their family background if they were courageous, skillful, and adept at capturing the enemy alive. All Aztec boys attended mandatory schools where military training was paramount. Superior warriors won admission to one of the warrior societies and could work their way up in rank and honor. The critical factor was successfully capturing enemy soldiers for slaves and human sacrifices.

When a soldier captured his first enemy fighter, he became part of the Tlamani warrior society. He received a shield, a macuahuitl war club, two capes, and a red loincloth to mark his new status. Like all elite warriors, he tied his hair into a bun with a red ribbon. Capturing two enemy fighters took him to the next level, the Cuextecatl society. Then, he wore a bodysuit and a conical hat and carried a round shield, all in scarlet with black parallel lines.

Three captured warriors elevated him to the Papalotl or Butterfly warrior status. Although it seems strange to equate butterflies with war, the Aztec goddess of war was Ītzpāpālōtl, or "Obsidian Butterfly." Aztec warriors believed if they died in battle, they would be reincarnated as butterflies or hummingbirds. The Butterfly warriors wore a white tunic, carried a yellow shield, and wore the honorable butterfly banner on their backs.

A jaguar knight in the Codex Magliabechiano brandishes a macuahuitl club.
https://commons.wikimedia.org/wiki/File:Jaguar_warrior.jpg

When a warrior captured four or more enemy soldiers, he became a Cuauhocelotl fighter, joining the ranks of the Jaguar and Eagle knights. The Jaguar knights stood out with a bodysuit of jaguar or ocelot skin and a "helmet" of the big cat's head. Feathered bodysuits clothed the eagle warriors, and they wore a helmet shaped like an eagle's head. The elite Jaguar and Eagle knights carried atlatl spear-throwers, macuahuitl war clubs, spears, and colorful shields. A commoner automatically joined the nobility and was awarded land if he achieved this rank. He also received the right to drink the alcoholic pulque, wear flashy jewelry, and keep concubines in addition to his wife.

The top-notch military ranks were the Otomi and the Shorn Ones. These warriors were the special forces with the highest training. The Otomi warriors, named after the fierce Otomi ethnic group, wore bright emerald green bodysuits and "claw" banners on their backs topped with brilliant green feathers. The Shorn Ones were the highest level. They shaved their heads except for a long braid hanging down the left side of their heads. They wore a yellow bodysuit and a white shell necklace. The Shorn Ones carried a yellow and green shield and a red and white striped back banner topped with green feathers.

The Aztecs had a system of relay runners posted about every two and a half miles on the empire's main roads. The runners ran full speed to the next runner, delivering messages between cities or military stations. The Aztecs also used two types of spies. The *quimichtin* spies wore the clothing and spoke the language of a targeted region. Before invading, these Aztec spies scoped out the kinds of defense, military strength, and other factors of a region. The *naualoztomeca* spies were tradesmen who traveled abroad, selling and buying goods while picking up valuable information in the marketplaces.[35]

When the Aztecs targeted a city, they sent ambassadors offering peaceful admission into the Aztec Empire. The city had twenty days to decide. If they were still wavering, a second entourage of delegates visited, warning of the horrors the city faced if they resisted. If the city didn't surrender after another twenty days, the Aztecs ruthlessly pounced, demolishing the city and taking the people as slaves and sacrificial victims.[36]

The Maya, Teotihuacanos, Toltecs, and Aztecs used the atlatl spear-thrower or dart-thrower. The Aztecs only permitted royalty and the elite warriors to use this tool that flung *tlacochtli* (small spears or darts) at a high velocity toward the enemy. The *Tequihua,* the Aztec archers,

---

[35] Hassig, *War and Society*, 51-52, 165.
[36] Hassig, *War and Society*, 160.

fashioned five-foot-long simple bows called *tlahhuītōlli* out of one piece of wood from Buddleja butterfly bushes, with animal sinew for string. Another weapon was the *tēmātlatl* sling, which was woven from maguey fiber and shot rocks or clay balls at the enemy.

These drawings from the Codex Mendoza show warriors of various ranks taking prisoners by grabbing their buns.

https://commons.wikimedia.org/wiki/File:Codex_Mendoza_folio_65r-3.jpg

To protect themselves from flying rocks, spears, and arrows, the Maya, Aztecs, and other soldiers of ancient Mexico carried wood or wicker shields, which the Aztecs called *Chīmalli*. They were brightly painted in geometric designs, with colorful feathers hanging down. The Maya and Aztecs wore quilted cotton armor, about one-half to one inch thick, which was soaked in brine to form a stiff surface.

The Aztecs believed that when they sacrificed humans, the energy released from the slain victims fed the gods. In return, the gods provided rain, power, protection, and other benefits. In the decades before the Spaniards arrived, the Aztec Empire was unraveling at the edges, with disgruntled populations rising up. When they faced conflict, drought, or other challenges, the Aztecs ramped up the human sacrifices, killing up to twenty thousand people annually. Some scholars believe the number was much higher, perhaps up to a quarter million, but that rate would have quickly wiped ancient Mexico's population out.

With over one thousand sacrifices a month, the Aztecs desperately needed victims. They mostly sacrificed prisoners of war; however, once they conquered the surrounding regions, they no longer had thousands of prisoners to feed the gods. In their minds, failure to sacrifice to the gods would lead to apocalyptic disasters like epidemics, hurricanes, starvation, and invasion by their enemies.

So, they devised ritual warfare called Flower Wars, where the objective was not to kill or conquer but to capture prisoners to sacrifice. The Tlaxcalan people, who lived west of the Aztec heartland, were often the opponents in the Flower Wars, along with the city of Cholula to the south. In a Flower War, the battle ended when both sides captured their quota of sacrificial victims. The Aztecs' perceived need for human sacrifice was so horrific that they staged these battles every twenty days. Of course, it meant losing their own warriors to the opposing side.

Illustration from the Durán Codex of a Flower War against Huexotzinco in Puebla that did not end well for the Aztecs (on the right side of the painting).
https://commons.wikimedia.org/wiki/File:La_derrota_en_la_batalla_de_Atlixco_contra_los_Huejot zingas,_en_el_folio_168v.png

One humorous battle was a fake confrontation to settle the Triple Alliance's leadership question. The original 1428 agreement was for the kings of Tenochtitlan, Texcoco, and Tlacopan to take turns leading the empire. However, when the Mexica-Aztec Moctezuma I became king of Tenochtitlan in 1440, he demanded the other two cities recognize him as supreme emperor (*huey tlatoani*).

To save face, King Nezahualcoyotl of Texcoco proposed a choreographed "battle" to cede ascendency to Tenochtitlan. The warriors from Texcoco lined up facing the Mexica from Tenochtitlan, and each side yelled taunts at the other. The Texcoco warriors abruptly spun around and dashed back to their city with the Mexica in hot pursuit. The battle ended without bloodshed when Nezahualcoyotl lit a gigantic bonfire on Texcoco's highest pyramid in "surrender." From that point on, the Tenochtitlan king ruled the Aztec Empire.

In 1478, the Aztecs suffered a humiliating defeat to the Pacific-Coast Purépecha-Tarascan Empire, located northwest of the Aztec Empire. Despite decades of warfare, the Aztecs could never defeat the Purépecha. King Axayacatl marched with thirty-two thousand Aztec warriors to Taximaroa (today's Hidalgo). But the Purépecha met him with fifty thousand soldiers armed with copper shields and spearheads. The Aztecs' wooden or wicker shields were no match for metal spearheads, and the Purépecha spears were too long for the Aztec warriors to get within striking range with their war clubs. Outnumbered and with inferior weaponry, the Aztecs lost twenty thousand men in one day.

Before this battle, the Aztecs and Purépecha had built garrisons along their borders to discourage attempts to cross into the other's territory. After defeating the Aztecs, the Purépecha increased their fortifications and also took advantage of the Otomi people, who had lost their homeland to the Aztecs. The Otomi people were fierce fighters and among the original inhabitants of the Valley of Mexico. They had formed part of Teotihuacan's multiethnic population in the Classic era, and when that city collapsed, they built their island city of Xaltocan. They lost a brutal war and their island kingdom to the Tepanec-Aztecs in 1395 and migrated south and west to Hidalgo, Puebla, and Tlaxcala.

The Purépecha invited the Otomi to settle in their territory along the Aztec border. All they needed to do was help defend against Aztec incursions. The Otomi were willing to fight their bitter rivals and were grateful for land to settle. After beating the Aztec invasion in 1478, the Purépecha marched southeast later that year in a counterattack, coming within fifty miles of Tenochtitlan. To prevent further catastrophe, the Aztecs negotiated a demilitarized zone between the two empires, and a ceasefire ensued for over three decades.

In 1516, the Aztecs captured Tlahuicole, a legendary Tlaxcalan war hero, the most vicious fighter among his people. The Aztec emperor, Moctezuma II, was so awed by Tlahuicole's gutsiness and prowess that he offered the Tlaxcalan captive his freedom. But Tlahuicole refused, feeling it would be humiliating to return home after being captured. He demanded the usual captive warrior's death of human sacrifice. Instead, Moctezuma made him commander-in-chief of the Aztec warriors and sent him to fight the Purépecha, who had invaded again.

After Tlahuicole crushed the Purépecha army and returned with hundreds of captives, Moctezuma again offered him freedom or a permanent army command. Once again, Tlahuicole refused, feeling that release was dishonorable and fighting for the enemy was treason, especially since he would have to fight his own people. So, Moctezuma chained him to a huge stone disk called a *temalacatl* in a human sacrificial ritual where two captive warriors fought to the death. Tlahuicole killed the first eight elite warriors who battled him one-on-one but finally fell to the ninth contestant.

In addition to garrisons and using the Otomi people in a buffer zone, the Purépecha maintained cordial relations with their tributary cities on their borders. While the Aztecs demanded oppressive tribute from the city-states they conquered, the Purépecha exchanged resources for tribute. It was more of an equal trade situation that didn't bleed their conquered territories dry. The Purépecha ruled fairly and harmoniously, encouraging loyalty from their far-flung provinces and the willingness to fight against common enemies.

By contrast, the Aztecs ruled their conquered territories harshly, demanding not only commodities as tribute payments but also people. They drafted men for the military and enslaved the children. They frequently raided their unconquered neighbors for sacrificial victims, believing they needed to increase their gory rituals to maintain power. This cruelty cultivated hatred in the surrounding territories, ultimately leading to the Aztec defeat when the Spanish arrived, as several tribes allied with the Europeans.

Key Takeaways:
- Birth ritual for boys with shield and arrow
- Prominent warrior societies based on how many captives were taken in battle
    - Tlamani, Cuextecatl, and Butterfly Warriors
    - Eagle and Jaguar warriors
    - Otomi and Shorn Ones, the highest-ranking warriors
- Ambassadors invited cities to join the Aztec Empire and warned against refusing
    - Relay runners carried messages at high speed

- Spies disguised themselves to fit in and gather information
  - Weaponry: war clubs, spears, dart-throwers, bows and arrows
  - Flower Wars for sacrificial victims
  - Important battles
  - A fake battle to cede supremacy to Tenochtitlan's dominance
  - A decisive struggle lost against the Purépecha, who had metal spearheads and shields
  - The capture of the mighty warrior Tlahuicole of Tlaxcala
- Fortifications: garrisons, demilitarized zone, settling allies on border

Chapter 11: The Spanish Conquest and Its Aftermath

On March 4th, 1517, Francisco Hernández de Córdoba sighted the northern tip of the Yucatán Peninsula after a storm blew his three ships off course on their expedition from Cuba. Sailing along the coast, he was astonished to see the tall and elaborate buildings of a Maya city; the Spaniards had yet to encounter such sophisticated architecture in the New World. The pyramid reminded the conquistadors of Egypt, so they dubbed the city "El Gran Cairo."

The Maya feigned friendliness as they paddled their canoes up to the ships. But when the Spaniards came ashore the next day, the Maya attacked, killing two of their men. Rowing quickly back to their ships, the Spaniards set sail, traveling along the coast, searching for a river or stream as they were desperate for drinking water. But the rivers of the northern Yucatán run underground.

After three weeks, they finally spotted a river, but their landing was disastrous. The Maya attacked, killing over half their men and wounding the rest, with twelve arrows piercing Córdoba's body. He clung to life on the voyage back to Cuba but died on arrival. Yet Governor Velázquez of Cuba was intrigued by the tales of an advanced civilization and people draped in gold and jade ornaments.

Two years later, eleven more ships arrived at Cozumel in the Yucatán, this time commanded by Hernán Cortés. Through sign language, the Maya communicated that two Spaniards had lived nearby for eight years after being shipwrecked. One was Jerónimo de Aguilar, a Franciscan friar, who gratefully joined Cortés as a translator, having learned the Mayan language. The other, a sailor named Gonzalo Guerrero, was covered with piercings and tattoos and had married a Maya noblewoman. He had achieved a high status with his fighting skills, and he was happy to continue in his new life.

Cortés sailed north to Tabasco, where twelve thousand Potonchán-Maya attacked twice, but the Spaniards had cannons, crossbows, muskets, and steel armor and swords. What really terrified the Maya were the horses, which they had never seen before. The Potonchán surrendered with gifts of gold and twenty slave women. One woman, Doña Marina or La Malinche, was an Aztec who had been captured or purchased as a child. She could speak both the Mayan language and the Aztec Nahuatl. Cortés made her one of his translators and his mistress.

A few days later, Moctezuma II stood in his palace in Tenochtitlan, his brow furling at the news that the men with shining armor were building a village at Veracruz. He called several ambassadors, telling them, "Go greet these strangers and give them gifts. Give them gold! The Maya say they like gold. But tell them to stay on the coast. Warn them to stay away from Tenochtitlan! And paint pictures of these strangers and their armor and weapons. Bring those back to me."

The ambassadors greeted Cortés with figurines of gold, and he gave them glass beads and a helmet, which he asked them to bring back filled with gold dust. The ambassadors returned a few days later with the gold dust and polite greetings from Moctezuma. But they repeated Moctezuma's strict warnings to remain on the coast and not to come to Tenochtitlan. Yet the gold was like a siren's call, and Cortés promptly marched inland with his men, horses, fifteen cannons, and translators.

Twenty-five miles from Veracruz, they received a warm welcome from the Totonac people, who assured them they would fight against the Aztecs. But when Cortés reached Tlaxcala, the fierce warriors fought him for three days. Cortés won them over by returning his Tlaxcalan prisoners of war each day instead of sacrificing them as the Aztecs and Tlaxcalans did. His translators instructed the released prisoners to tell the Tlaxcalan chiefs he wished to ally with them against the Aztecs. This was an offer the Tlaxcalans couldn't refuse, so they joined Cortés's entourage.

The Spaniards and Tlaxcalans marched along to Cholula, a long-time ally of Tlaxcala. But the Aztecs had conquered Cholula two years earlier, forcing them to break their alliance with the Tlaxcalans. When Cortés entered the city, everyone was on edge. Bernal Díaz, one of the conquistadors, wrote they found wooden cages "full of men and boys who were being fattened for the sacrifice at which their flesh would be eaten."[37] The Tlaxcalans warned Cortés the warriors of Cholula might attack.

The Cholula people were trying to decide whether to obey Moctezuma's orders to kill the Spaniards or ally with the Spaniards and their old friends, the Tlaxcalans. Doña Marina overheard the local women discussing a planned attack on the Spaniards while they slept, spurring Cortés to launch a preemptive strike. The Spaniards slaughtered three thousand Cholula warriors and nobility in three hours and burned the ancient city.

On November 8th, 1519, Cortés boldly marched across the causeway leading over Lake Texcoco to the island city of Tenochtitlan. Cortés looked around in awe at the resplendent city of 200,000 people. As Tenochtitlan's people looked on, Moctezuma met him on the causeway, regally attired in gold, jewels, and feathers. It was the one-reed year, and whispers swept through the crowd, "Could this be Cē Ācatl Topiltzin Quetzalcoatl? Is the great Toltec king returning as he prophesized he would in a one-reed year?"

With Doña Marina translating, Cortés meets Moctezuma II in this Tlaxcalan illustration from the Lienzo de Tlaxcala Codex.
https://commons.wikimedia.org/wiki/File:Cortez_%26_La_Malinche.jpg

---

[37]Bernal Díaz del Castillo, *The Conquest of New Spain*, trans. J. M. Cohen (Harmondsworth, England: Penguin Books, 1963 [1632]), 150.

Moctezuma greeted Cortés by placing a chain of gold and a garland of flowers around his neck and hosting Cortés and his officers in the palace of Axayacatl, who was his deceased father. But a week later, Cortés learned that the Aztecs had attacked the men he'd left behind in Veracruz. He swept into Moctezuma's palace with several captains, hissing, "Come with us now! If you call for help, we'll run you through."

He hustled Moctezuma into Axayacatl's palace, where Moctezuma lived under house arrest until his death. The Tenochtitlan Aztecs were unnerved by the move and by the Tlaxcalans roaming their city. The city's restlessness continued for five months until Cortés learned that 19 Spanish warships had arrived with 1,400 soldiers. Governor Velázquez of Cuba had commanded Cortés only to explore Mexico, not establish a colony. But Cortés had founded a settlement in Veracruz, so the governor sent men to arrest him.

Appointing his officer Pedro de Alvarado to take charge in Tenochtitlan, Cortés rushed back to the coast, snuck into the camp by night, and captured the Spanish commander. He then set to work wooing the rest of the Spanish forces. "Come back to Tenochtitlan with me! There are storerooms full of gold there. You'll be richer than your wildest dreams."

The newly arrived conquistadors switched sides and marched with Cortés back to Tenochtitlan with ninety-six horses. Two thousand more Tlaxcalans joined them on the way back. Meanwhile, murder and mayhem rocked Tenochtitlan. In Cortés's absence, King Moctezuma had requested and received permission from Alvarado for the nobility to celebrate a beloved Aztec festival. One thousand Aztec aristocrats gathered in the courtyard of the city's ritual center, dancing and singing as drums played.

Suddenly, Alvarado and the Spanish soldiers charged into the courtyard and blocked the exits. They began brutally slaying the revelers, stripping them of any valuables in what is known as the Massacre in the Great Temple. Frantically, the Aztec nobles rushed to find a way out. Some managed to scale the high wall, yelling to the people in the city to come and defend them. A hail of javelins sailed toward the Spaniards, who hurried back to the palace, where the Aztecs blockaded them.

Cortés arrived to find that the Aztecs had made Moctezuma's brother, Cuitláhuac, the new emperor while Moctezuma was still under house arrest. The Aztecs permitted Cortés and his new army to pass through the city, but Cortés knew that fighting could break out at any moment. He ordered Moctezuma to go out on the balcony, calm the people down, and tell them to grant safe passage for the Spaniards out of the city and back to the coast. But the Aztecs considered Moctezuma a puppet for the Spaniards and jeered, flinging rocks and darts at the balcony.

What happened next depended on who was telling the story. The conquistadors reported that three stones struck Moctezuma, and he sustained a head wound and died three days later. However, the Aztecs accused the Spaniards of strangling the emperor. At any rate, the Aztecs already had a new emperor, and Moctezuma was no longer useful to anyone. The crucial matter for the Aztecs was what to do about the Spaniards holed up in the palace of Axayacatl.

Their supplies of gunpowder, food, and water were running out, so Cortés negotiated a one-week ceasefire, telling the Aztecs, "We will return the gold and other treasures we took and leave your city in peace."

Instead, Cortés and his men snuck out of the city that night, hauling as much gold and other treasure as possible. But the causeway connecting the city to the mainland had gaps with portable bridges that the Aztecs removed each night to safeguard the city. The Spaniards brought one movable bridge with them but didn't think about how hundreds of soldiers would need to cross one span before they could move the bridge to the next gap.

It was pouring rain, which kept the Aztecs inside, and no one noticed the men surreptitiously moving through the city. The Spaniards got out to the causeway and crossed the first gap with their movable bridge when an Aztec priest at the peak of the great pyramid sounded the alarm. The Spaniards' portable bridge became stuck, trapping them on the causeway.

Cortés and the cavalry charged ahead down the causeway, with their steeds leaping over the gaps, unaware of the chaos behind them. They reached the shore and whirled their mounts to see a ghastly scene unfolding. The Aztec warriors charged out of the city, sending a hail of arrows toward the soldiers on the causeway. Hundreds of canoes poured out of the city's canals and attacked the Spaniards and Tlaxcalans from the water. The Spaniards who fell into the water were weighed down by the gold they were carrying and drowned.

The Spaniards flee the Aztecs on La Noche Triste or Sad Night. Florentine Codex drawings by Fray Bernardino de Sahagún.
https://commons.wikimedia.org/wiki/File:Spanish_Conquistadors_in_retreat_from_Aztec_Warriors_after_La_Noche_Triste.jpg

Cortés raced back to the causeway to help fight and was wounded in the head. The men got the portable bridge loose, and the survivors finally reached the mainland. On La Noche Triste, or Sad Night, about one thousand Spaniards and two thousand Tlaxcalans perished. They lost all of their artillery and gold, and most of the men were wounded. In a series of letters Cortés wrote to King Charles V, he recorded the horror of the fateful night and the events before and after.[38]

The conquistadors had no time to grieve their lost comrades or tend to their wounds, as thousands of angry Aztecs were closing in. The Tlaxcalans led them north around the connected lakes as they fought off attacks from bands of Aztecs. When the Aztecs killed one of their horses, the Spaniards were so hungry they ate the entire animal, including its skin. About forty thousand Aztecs launched a full-scale attack when they reached Otumba on the northeastern side of the lake system.

Two tactics saved the Spaniards that day. The Castilian cavalry put their horsemanship skills into play, charging the Aztecs, who had never battled horses, and breaking through their lines repeatedly. Cortés told his men to focus their attacks on the Aztec chiefs. After killing the Aztec commander-in-chief, the Aztecs fell back, and the Spaniards and Tlaxcalans chased

---

[38] Hernán Cortés, *Cartas y Relaciones de Hernán Cortés al Emperador Carlos V*, ed. Pascual de Gayangos (Paris: A. Chaix, 1866). https://www.cervantesvirtual.com/nd/ark:/59851/bmc0974782

them off. It was a bittersweet victory. Only 440 Spanish soldiers survived, and all of them were wounded, as were many of the Tlaxcalans.

The soldiers finally stumbled into safety in the mountainous Tlaxcalan territory, and Cortés renewed the terms of an alliance with the Tlaxcalans. He awarded them the city of Cholula, freedom from tribute, and an equal share of the loot from their future forays together. His Veracruz settlement sent reinforcements, and supply ships with more soldiers and horses arrived from Cuba and Spain. Neither of these places realized Cortés was still in power.

Cortés worked his way around the eastern side of Lake Texcoco, solidifying alliances with the Acolhua-Aztecs, the Tepanec-Aztecs, the Otomi, and other tribes against the Mexica-Aztecs. In September 1520, smallpox struck Tenochtitlan, decimating the number of warriors and killing the new emperor, Cuitláhuac. His cousin, Cuauhtémoc, succeeded him as the last Aztec emperor.

Cortés's ingenious battle plan for attacking the island city of Tenochtitlan was to build thirteen small, shallow ships called brigantines, which were propelled by oars and sails and armed with cannons. Using the expertise of Martín López, a carpenter in his entourage with shipbuilding experience, and eight thousand indigenous workers to cut timber, the shipbuilding began. North America's first shipyard was miles from the lake, 7,500 feet above sea level, and in Tlaxcalan territory, where it would be safe from Aztec intrusion. They built a secret canal to the lake and hauled unassembled sections of the ships a mile down to the channel, where they put the ships together and launched them. The Spaniards and Tlaxcalans carried out this impressive feat in only fifty days.[39]

On April 28th, 1521, the ships sailed down the canal and into the lake. At this point, the Spaniards had eighty-six cavalrymen, about one thousand infantrymen, and about twenty thousand indigenous allies fighting with them. One battalion marched to the island of Chapultepec to cut the aqueduct that piped fresh water into Tenochtitlan, which was surrounded by brackish water. From the Chapultepec hilltop, the Spaniards cheered as they watched the ships navigating across the lake to the city of Iztapalapa on the other end of the causeway leading to Tenochtitlan.

---

[39] Robert F. Carter, "North America's First Shipyard," *The Military Engineer* 57, no. 379 (1965): 338–40. http://www.jstor.org/stable/44571688.

Five hundred canoes poured out of Tenochtitlan but stopped short when they drew close to the ships. While the Aztecs silently floated, scrutinizing the vessels, the wind arose, and Cortés ordered the ships to attack. With the wind behind their sails, the brigantines cut through the water toward the canoes, crushing any that did not move fast enough. The Spanish land army rushed down the causeway while the brigantines prevented the Aztec canoes from getting closer. When Aztecs from other cities launched a rear attack, ten thousand Tlaxcalans blocked their way.

The brigantines attacked by water and the land army from the causeways.
Fray Bernardino de Sahagún, Florentine Codex.
https://commons.wikimedia.org/wiki/File:Brigantines_in_the_Siege_of_Tenochtitlan.jpg

The Spaniards had complete control of the causeways, but rooftop archers in the city prevented them from getting close. The brigantines and foot soldiers launched cannon fire and shot fiery arrows to burn and destroy the structures on the city's perimeter. The small ships even sailed into the canals interlacing the metropolis, firing cannonballs along the way. Cortés's land forces reached the city's center and set fire to the temple complex.

But the sun was setting, so the Spaniards retreated to the causeway for the night. The Mexica-Aztecs used this moment to counterattack from the rear, killing more than a thousand Tlaxcalans and capturing some Spaniards. They hauled these men to the top of the highest pyramid and cut their beating hearts out of their chests.

The Spaniards set up camp on the causeways, and months of fighting ensued. The Spaniards gradually gained control of sections of the city and burned those neighborhoods down, forcing the population into an ever-dwindling remnant of the city. At first, the Aztecs outside the city smuggled in water and food by canoe, but the brigantines ended that. With the aquifer cut off, the city had no fresh water, and the people began drinking the saline water in the canals, dying from dysentery and dehydration as a result. Most other Aztec cities around the lake surrendered.

Finally, thousands of men, women, and children spilled out of the one-eighth section of the city still standing. Despite their surrender, the Tlaxcalans immediately attacked against Cortés's orders, killing over fifteen thousand citizens. Then, a fleet of canoes launched into the lake, which the Spanish brigantines intercepted. In one canoe, they saw the emperor, Cuauhtémoc, with his family. They captured him on August 13th, 1521, ending the siege. The Aztec Empire had fallen.

Most of the other civilizations in Mexico surrendered within a year with little or no fighting, hoping to avoid the devastation visited on the Aztecs. The Maya continued fighting fiercely; it took 170 years for the Spaniards to conquer all the Maya city-states. Despite eleven years of warfare, northwestern Mexico's fierce, nomadic Chichimeca remained undefeated. Finally, the Spanish friars demanded an end to the gory warfare and instituted a new program of colonizing Christianized Tlaxcalans in northwestern Mexico. They befriended the nomadic Chichimeca and helped "tame" them, teaching the Chichimeca to be ranchers and farmers. Spanish friars lived among them, introducing the Chichimeca to Catholicism.

Key Takeaways:
- 1517: Francisco Hernández de Córdoba discovers Mexico
- 1519: Hernán Cortés arrives and heads inland
    - Acquired Fray Jerónimo de Aguilar and Doña Marina (La Malinche) as translators
    - Allied with the Totonacs and Tlaxcalans
    - Destroyed Cholula
- Arrival in Tenochtitlan
    - Placed Moctezuma II under house arrest
    - Massacre of noblemen in the temple
    - Moctezuma killed
- La Noche Triste
    - Spaniards attempted to sneak out of Tenochtitlan
    - Aztecs killed or wounded most Spaniards and many Tlaxcalans
- Cortés regrouped and planned siege
    - Formed alliances with many cities
    - Built small ships and a canal to Lake Texcoco
    - Smallpox hit Tenochtitlan
- Siege of Tenochtitlan
    - Spaniards attacked by ships and land army
    - Tenochtitlan fell after five months; the emperor captured
- Aftermath
    - Most civilizations in Mexico surrendered with little resistance
    - Maya fought for 170 years
    - Chichimeca undefeated; enticed to join a settlement program

Section Four:
An Unforgettable Legacy

Chapter 12: Legendary Figures

The history of ancient Mexico is the stories of its people, from the farmers in the fields to the rulers in the palaces. We have little surviving information for most of its people other than what can be gleaned from archaeological analysis. But the tales of some legendary figures have been preserved through oral traditions and written accounts. Let's take a look at some of them.

Itzamná and Kukulkan

Zamná (or Kukulkan) was a priest who legend says arrived in the Yucatán from Tula. He founded (or renovated) Chichén Itzá and other cities in the Yucatán and invented writing. For his contributions to civilization, he became Itzamná, the god of the sky, one of the most prominent deities of the Maya. The paradox is that the Maya believed the god Itzamná created the world from chaos and created human beings, so how could Zamná become Itzamná if humans already existed? Not to mention the Maya had been writing for centuries before Tula was founded (which did not have an advanced writing system). Apparently, both a god and a person had the same name, and their stories got mixed up. Some scholars believe that Zamná was Cē Ācatl Topiltzin since he came from the Toltec city of Tula.

The deity Itzamná and his wife, the moon goddess Ixchel, were the parents of the other gods. From Itzamná flowed the sky and earth, day and night, sun and moon, birth and death, male and female, and the heavens and the underworld. Itzamná invented the sciences, astrology, medicine, agriculture, the calendar, and writing and taught them to the

Maya. His images are often of a stern older man sitting on a throne with a long, pointed nose. He is sometimes portrayed as a crocodile or as the Bird of Heaven (Itzam Yeh) perched on the World Tree (Ceiba), holding a two-headed snake in its beak.

Itzamná, Maya creation god.
Salvador alc, CC BY-SA 3.0 <https://creativecommons.org/licenses/by-sa/3.0>, via Wikimedia Commons; https://commons.wikimedia.org/wiki/File:Itzamna_sculpture.JPG

Sometimes, Itzamná is equated with Kukulkan, the feathered serpent deity, who is part rattlesnake and part quetzal bird. The Olmecs, Teotihuacanos, Zapotecs, Mixtecs, Toltecs, and Aztecs also worshiped the Feathered Serpent as the creator god of the sky and bringer of the wind and rain. The Toltecs and Aztecs knew him as Quetzalcoatl, the god of agriculture, arts, and science and the inventor of the calendar. He gifted corn to humans and was associated with Venus, the morning star.

Spearthrower Owl (Atlatl Cauac or Jatz'om Kuy)

The Teotihuacanos did not keep records of their monarchs, but Mayan inscriptions named Spearthrower Owl as king of Teotihuacan from 374 to 439 CE. His reign coincided with an uprising when Teotihuacan's Feathered Serpent Temple was burned and partly obscured by the construction of the Adosada platform. Why would the Maya of Tikal in Guatemala write about the king of Teotihuacan, who was located almost eight hundred miles northwest? The inscriptions say that a warlord of Spearthrower Owl, called Siyaj K'ak' (Fire-is-Born), invaded Tikal in 378 CE, killing the Maya king Jaguar Paw (Chak Tok Ich'aak I). General Fire-is-Born made Spearthrower Owl's son, First Crocodile (Yax Nuun Ayiin), the new king of Tikal.[40]

The Maya said that General Fire-is-Born went on to conquer Uaxactun, just south of Tikal, and he and his descendants ruled that city for generations. First Crocodile ruled Tikal until he died in 404 and was succeeded by his son Storm Sky (Sihyaj Chan K'awiil), who ruled for fifty-two years until his death in 456. Teotihuacan also installed Great Sun, Quetzal Bird the First (K'inich Yax K'uk' Mo') as the king of Copan, over two hundred miles south of Tikal in Honduras.

Curiously, First Crocodile might not have been the Teotihuacan prince the Maya believed him to be. A pyramid in Tikal supposedly houses his tomb, as an inscription on a cup beside his skeleton reads, "The cup of Spearthrower Owl's son." But isotype analysis of the remains, which shows the person's lifelong diet, indicates he grew up around Tikal. He might have been passing himself off as Teotihuacan royalty, or perhaps he was a Teotihuacan prince who grew up in the Yucatán for some reason.

Nezahualcoyotl

Nezahualcoyotl (1402–1472 CE) was king of Texcoco after masterminding and commanding the coalition army that brought the Aztec Empire into being. He was a poet, prophet, and engineer, and after the Triple Alliance was established, he ruled the Alcoa-Aztecs. However, before that happened, when he was still a teenage prince, he fled to the mountainous Tlaxcala territory after the invading Tepanecs killed his father. While in exile, he experienced a sudden spiritual perception, which was written down by his great-grandson:

---

[40] Michael D. Coe, *The Maya (Ancient Peoples and Places Series)* (London and New York: Thames & Hudson, 1999), 90.

"Some immensely powerful and unknown god is the creator of the whole universe. He is the only one that can console me in my affliction and help me in such anguish as my heart feels; I want him to be my helper and protection."[41]

Nezahualcoyotl's painting in the Codex Ixtlilxóchitl.
https://commons.wikimedia.org/wiki/File:Nezahualcoyotl.jpg

Once he trounced the Tepanecs and became king of Texcoco, Nezahualcoyotl built a pyramid to Tloque Nahuaque, "the unknown yet always near, self-existing creator."[42] Tloque Nahuaque was unusual in that he did not require human sacrifice. Nezahualcoyotl only offered incense and flowers to his god.

Nezahualcoyotl had 110 children with his wives and concubines, yet he fell in love with the wife of a minor king under him. He sent that king to

---

[41] Juan Bautista de Pomar. "Relación de Tezcoco," in *Relaciones de la Nueva España*, ed. Vázquez Chamorro. (Madrid: Historia 16, 1991).
[42] Pomar, "Relación de Tezcoco."

fight the Tlaxcalans, where he was killed, and Nezahualcoyotl then made the beautiful Queen Azcalxochitzin his wife. Soon after, swarms of locusts struck Texcoco, stripping the fields bare of corn, tomatoes, and peppers. The crops that survived shriveled from drought. Nezahualcoyotl's people were starving, and he felt his sin had caused the famine. He opened the treasury to buy food for his citizens and paid the school fees of children who had lost their parents in the disaster.

Xicotencatl the Elder

Xicotencatl was the long-lived Tlaxcalan ruler of Tizatlan who cautioned the Council of Tlaxcala when considering Cortés's proposed alliance. In the debate over whether to join forces with the Spaniards, a Tlaxcalan noble named Maxixcatzin encouraged the coalition. He said the gods and ancestors ordained this opportunity to break the Aztec yoke.

Xicotencatl the Elder in the Lienzo de Tlaxcala Codex.
https://commons.wikimedia.org/wiki/File:Xicotencatl_the_elder.jpg

Yet Xicotencatl warned, "Cortés might be our friend now, but would he still be once Tenochtitlan falls? Would he become the enemy within? Are the Spaniards gods? Or are they ravenous monsters gorging themselves on gold? Would we spill our blood only to become enslaved to them?"

Although the aged Xicotencatl pointed out that defeating the Mexica-Aztecs would come at a price, the Council of Tlaxcala voted to ally with

Cortés. The Lienzo de Tlaxcala Codex says that Xicotencatl was 120 years old and had over five hundred wives and children when he first met Cortés.

Apoxpalon (Paxbolonacha)

Apoxpalon was a Chontal Maya of Tabasco, a group that claimed lineage from the Olmecs. In 1525 CE, he rose from the position of merchant to become king of Itzamkanac, the capital of the Chontal Maya city-state. These Maya didn't have royal dynasties but elected their kings based on their abilities, usually merchants who acquired a knowledge base through their travels. Apoxpalon's specific abilities included an astute understanding of arithmetic, and he had broad experience in farming, fishing, and hunting.

Apoxpalon became king shortly after Cortés crushed the Aztec Empire and was nervous about what would happen to him when Cortés traveled to his region. His son met Cortés with gifts of gold, telling him that his father had died. Cortés expressed his sympathy but suspected it was all subterfuge, as he knew King Apoxpalon had been alive just four days before. Nevertheless, Cortés gave the young prince the bead necklace he was wearing as a gift and continued on his way.

Cortés arrived in Teoticaccac, about eighteen miles from Itzamkanac, where the city's leader graciously welcomed him. Teoticaccac's ruler disclosed that Apoxpalon was alive and well but afraid that Cortés would kill him and take his wealth. Cortés then interrogated Apoxpalon's son, who admitted his father was alive. Two days later, Apoxpalon arrived, apologetically explaining his fear of foreigners and horses. He invited Cortés to Itzamkanac, where the Spaniards stayed in his palace and enjoyed a night of feasting and celebration. When Cortés left the next day, he gave the king a horse as a gift, and Apoxpalon overcame his fear of the animal and learned how to ride[43]

Hernán Cortés

Hernán Cortés's overriding ambition and charismatic personality launched a stellar career, yet his disregard for authority and ruthlessness sometimes derailed his goals. In his mid-twenties, he caught the eye of Cuba's governor, Diego Velázquez, who elevated him in rank. Yet the

---

[43] Susan Schroeder, ed., *Chimalpahin's Conquest: A Nahua Historian's Rewriting of Francisco Lopez de Gomara's La conquista de Mexico* (Redwood City: Stanford University Press, 2010), 386-9. https://doi.org/10.1515/9780804775069-184

governor was displeased when Cortés became romantically involved with Velázquez's sister-in-law Catalina while flirting with her sister. Cortés married Catalina mainly to further his career.

In 1518, Velázquez commissioned Cortés to lead an expedition to Mexico but changed his mind at the last minute. Cortés set sail anyway, an act of mutiny, which was then exacerbated by Cortés establishing a colony in Veracruz against the governor's strict orders. He declared himself independent of Cuba and presented his new town as a colony of Charles V, King of Spain and the Holy Roman Emperor. Cortés sent a ship full of gold with letters to Charles, telling him about his explorations and why he had separated from Velázquez.

Once Cortés conquered Tenochtitlan, he eliminated indigenous leaders he considered a threat by accusing them of conspiracy and hanging them. He did this with Xicotencatl the Elder's son, fulfilling the ancient leader's prophecy. Cortés allowed the last Aztec emperor, Cuauhtémoc, to live for four years but then took him on an expedition into Maya territory and hanged him for alleged conspiracy. To rein in Cortés and other conquistadors, King Charles established the Council of the Indies to govern all of Spain's new colonies in the Americas and the Pacific.

Hernán Cortés, Naval Museum of Madrid.
https://commons.wikimedia.org/wiki/File:Hern%C3%A1n_Cort%C3%A9s_an%C3%B3nimo.jpg

A year after Tenochtitlan fell, Catalina came to Mexico, unhappy to find her husband's pregnant translator and mistress, Doña Marina, living in his palace. At a dinner party, she lashed out at Cortés and then stormed out of the room. Hours later, she was found dead in her room. Cortés was charged with murder by strangulation, but the charges were dropped, perhaps due to lavish bribes. He acknowledged Doña Marina's son, Martín, as his own, eventually making him legitimate.

In 1529, Cortés married Doña Juana de Zúñiga, a Spanish noblewoman, and Charles V made him marquess of the Valley of Oaxaca. A year earlier, Cortés violated Moctezuma II's daughter Doña Isabel and got her pregnant. At around age twelve, Isabel became the child bride of her uncle Cuitláhuac, who became emperor after Cortés put her father under house arrest. Months later, Cuitláhuac died of smallpox, and she married her cousin Cuauhtémoc, the last Aztec emperor. Cortés executed Cuauhtémoc several years later and took the seventeen-year-old Isabel into his home. When she got pregnant, he quickly married Isabel to a friend, and a baby girl was born several months later. Isabel refused to have anything to do with the infant, so Cortés sent his daughter to a relative to raise.

Cortés accumulated breathtaking wealth through his landholdings, the treasures he acquired in his conquests, and his thirty-five silver mines. Yet he spent most of his money on more expeditions and was heavily in debt when he died of dysentery. However, he did acknowledge and provide for his eleven children from his second wife and multiple mistresses.

Key Takeaways:
- Itzamná and Kukulkan
  - Itzamná was the god of the sky and creation
  - Sometimes equated with Kukulkan, the feathered serpent deity
- Spearthrower Owl
  - According to the Maya, king of Teotihuacan from 374 to 439 CE
  - His general invaded Tikal in 378; his descendants ruled several Maya cities
- Apoxpalon
  - Chontal Maya merchant who became king
  - Faked his death to Cortés

- Nezahualcoyotl
    - King of Texcoco, commander of coalition Aztec army
    - Poet, prophet, engineer, and one of the Triple Alliance founders
    - Worshiped the omniscient, uncreated creator
- Xicotencatl the Elder: aged Tlaxcalan ruler who argued against allying with Spaniards
- Hernán Cortés
    - Extremely ambitious, ruthless, disregarded authority, yet persuasive and charming
    - Began career in Cuba, then conquered much of Mexico and part of Central America

Chapter 13: Art, Architecture, and Artifacts

Palaces, pyramids, brilliant murals, painted pottery, and ornaments of jade and gold all contributed to ancient Mexico's rich assortment of architecture and art. Some themes pervaded the various cultures, but each civilization had distinctive features. The art and architecture of ancient Mexico mirrored the political ideals, religious beliefs, worldviews, and lifestyles of its people. Viewing these artifacts gives us a portrait of what life was like and how people viewed the spiritual and physical worlds.

The Olmecs

In addition to Mesoamerica's first known pyramid and their unique colossal heads, the Olmecs left a legacy of art and architecture that impacted future cultures. Using the Coatzacoalcos River system, they imported jadeite and obsidian from Guatemala, from which they carved weaponry and images of supernatural creatures. Their expansive trade network, which spread from the Gulf Coast to the Pacific Ocean, meant that the Olmecs influenced other civilizations far from their heartland.

Their images featured the were-jaguar, a part-jaguar and part-human creature, perhaps an Olmec deity. These carvings had a cleft head, almond eyes, and a downturned gaping mouth. Most were-jaguar images were babies held out in the arms of a man, as if in sacrifice. The Olmecs also carved jade jaguar masks. Olmec paintings discovered deep within the Juxtlahuaca Cave in Guerrero, dating from 1200 to 900 BCE, depict a leaping jaguar and a feathered serpent. A fascinating image of a bearded man with a tail and spots on his arms and legs appears to be either a half-jaguar and half-man creature or a man wearing a jaguar skin.

The Las Limas figure is a twenty-two-inch-high greenstone carving of a man holding a limp were-jaguar baby, dating from 1000 to 600 BCE.
Mag2017, CC BY-SA 4.0 <https://creativecommons.org/licenses/by-sa/4.0>, via Wikimedia Commons; https://commons.wikimedia.org/wiki/File:Se%C3%B1or_de_las_limas_2.jpg

The Maya

Maya art was partly for visual pleasure, partly to depict historical events, but mainly to express their polytheistic religious beliefs. It featured dragon and serpent motifs as a link between the underworld and the land of the living. Images of deities often had jaguar features, representing courage and strength. They believed their most powerful priests and kings could shapeshift into jaguars; thus, some images have faces that are jaguar on one side and human on the other.

The Maya demonstrated an understanding of chemistry in their brightly colored pigments. They blended clay with indigo leaves, creating a chemical reaction that turned yellow or turquoise, depending on what they added to the mixture. Their murals usually reflected war or religious festivals but occasionally the everyday life of non-royal people. The Maya also carved stone, jade, and wood. They cut enormous boulders into the shape of crocodiles, jaguars, and snakes. Death masks of jade, gold, or shells covered the faces of deceased royalty.

Captive warriors plead for mercy from King Yajaw Chan Muwaan in this mural from Bonampak.
https://commons.wikimedia.org/wiki/File:01-maya-lidar-mapping.jpg

Maya architecture featured a network of causeways spreading from the ceremonial centers, often acting as dams in the lowland cities. They built trios of pyramids, with two smaller pyramids facing a giant one. Sometimes, they had pyramid quads, with three small pyramids across from the larger one, and occasionally, they built identical pyramids side by side. The Maya constructed some cities according to a pattern that reflected certain glyphs when viewed from above.

Maya jade death mask from the city of Calakmul.
Estela Parra, CC BY-SA 4.0 <https://creativecommons.org/licenses/by-sa/4.0>, via Wikimedia Commons; https://commons.wikimedia.org/wiki/File:Mascara_de_calakmul.jpg

The Zapotecs

Some of the Zapotecs' most distinctive artwork revolved around burials. They formed elaborate clay urns, which were buried close to the bodies, representing hybrid bat creatures and jaguars (the Maya and Zapotecs worshiped both animals). The funerary urns also featured various deities sitting cross-legged with elaborate headdresses. Sometimes, they were realistic human figures, perhaps representing the deceased person.

Zapotec tombs for illustrious citizens had cement floors, stone or adobe walls, and a doorway. Once the person was buried, a high mound of dirt covered the vault. The funerary urns were placed in groups of five just outside the tomb, usually on the door lintel. It's a mystery what the hollow urns held, if anything, as no residue remains. Like the Maya and Mixtecs, the Zapotecs carved death masks and were among the first in Mexico to work with metals.

A Zapotec funerary urn from the Classic era.
Simon Burchell, CC BY-SA 3.0 <https://creativecommons.org/licenses/by-sa/3.0>, via Wikimedia Commons; https://commons.wikimedia.org/wiki/File:Zapotec_funerary_urn_1,_Museo_de_Am%C3%A9rica.jpg

One especially intriguing example of Zapotec architecture was the arrowhead-shaped Building J, which was built in Monte Albán around 100 BCE. It pointed to the Capella (or Goat) star, the sixth-brightest star in the sky. The Capella is actually a group of four stars that are exceptionally brilliant when close to the horizon on winter nights. The arrowhead building is dedicated to military conquests, with the heads of conquered kings carved upside-down around the exterior.

Teotihuacan

Archaeologists believe that Teotihuacan was ruled by a council rather than one powerful king for at least part of its existence. The artwork for this multiethnic city doesn't glorify its rulers, only deities and primordial creation mythology. Humans are often depicted wearing similar clothing with no distinguishing characteristics. Art historian Esther Pasztory believed the impersonal repetitive artwork might have been mandated to promote an egalitarian society where collective values trumped individualism.[44]

A Teotihuacan priest wearing a dragon mask.
UNESCO / Dominique Roger, CC BY-SA 3.0 IGO <https://creativecommons.org/licenses/by-sa/3.0/igo/deed.en>, via Wikimedia Commons; https://commons.wikimedia.org/wiki/File:Painting,_Mexico_-_UNESCO_-_PHOTO0000001337_0001.tiff

Brilliant murals in crimson, green, and gold covered the palace and temple walls, as well as the exterior walls of the apartment compounds. They featured priests offering sacrifices, jaguars, and deities like the Feathered Serpent and the Great Goddess (called Spider Woman because

---

[44] Esther Pasztory, *Teotihuacan: An Experiment in Living* (Norman: University of Oklahoma Press, 1997), xv-xvi.

of the spiders dangling from her headdress). People are usually depicted with short, squat bodies that are almost eclipsed by enormous masks and headdresses.

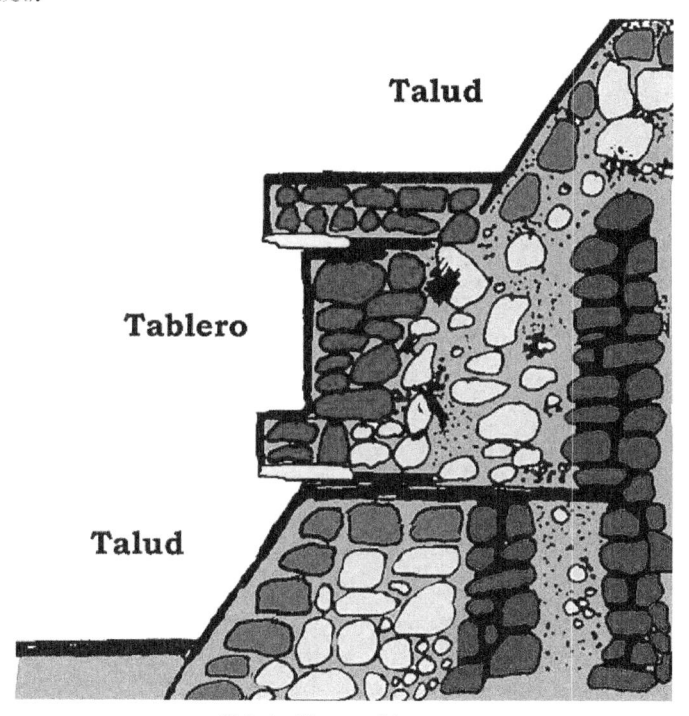

Talud-tablero architecture.
HJPD, CC BY-SA 3.0 <https://creativecommons.org/licenses/by-sa/3.0>, via Wikimedia Commons; https://commons.wikimedia.org/wiki/File:TableroTalud.jpg

At 216 feet, Teotihuacan's Sun Pyramid was the highest in Mexico when it was built and is the seventh-largest pyramid in the world today by volume. The Sun Pyramid and Cholula's Great Pyramid (the largest in the world by volume) were built using the talud-tablero architecture, a Teotihuacan hallmark. Cholula had a close relationship with Teotihuacan, as well as a similar culture. A talud-tablero pyramid has a steep slope (talud) with a ledge sticking out like a table (tablero).

The Mixtecs

The Mixtecs were the premier artisans of Mexico's Postclassic era and were especially renowned for their exquisite gold work. They were masters of elaborate mosaics of turquoise, jade, obsidian, and coral, and their delicate carvings on jaguar bones and wood were highly prized throughout Mexico. Their codices or complex pictorial stories written on deerskin were far more detailed and stylistic than those of the Maya or Aztecs.

An intricate Mixtec golden serpent labret (lip plug) ornament.
Sailko, CC BY 3.0 <https://creativecommons.org/licenses/by/3.0>, via Wikimedia Commons;
https://commons.wikimedia.org/wiki/File:Messico,_mixtechi-aztechi,_labret_(orecchino_per_sotto_il_labbro_inferiore)_a_forma_di_serpente,_IX-XI_sec,_oro_sbalzato_01.JPG

Mixtec pottery displayed unparalleled diversity and form, with striking scenes in precise detail. One beautiful example of Mixtec polychrome ceramics is a pedestal bowl with a brightly polished orange and red surface. Three snarling jaguars were painted white, grey, black, and brown. Feather-like blades jut out from a feline's rump and claw, possibly representing obsidian blades used in sacrifice.

A Mixtec ceramic pedestal bowl.
Metropolitan Museum of Art, CC0, via Wikimedia Commons;
https://commons.wikimedia.org/wiki/File:Pedestal_Bowl_MET_DP102174.jpg

The Toltecs

The Toltecs' name meant craftsmen, and their fame in stunning architecture and crafted objects especially impressed the Aztecs, who sought to emulate their culture. The Aztecs spent twenty years living and studying the culture when they arrived in Tula, which had become a ghost town. When they left, they took artifacts and returned later to take more. The Toltecs specialized in sculptures, including reliefs, pillars carved in the shape of warriors, and smaller carved pieces.

One type of small sculpture, the chacmool, originated with the Toltecs, who introduced them to the Maya of Chichén Itza. The Aztecs also adopted this art form. The chacmool were small stone statues carved to look like a human man lying on his back propped up on his elbows and balancing a bowl on his chest. The head is turned to the side and looking up. The bowl on the figurine's chest held a sacrificial offering; in the case of the Aztecs, it held a human heart cut from a sacrificial victim. The Toltecs likely used it for the same purpose.

This chacmool is from Chichén Itza, which had a strong Toltec influence.
Luis Alberto Lecuna/Melograna, CC BY-SA 2.0 <https://creativecommons.org/licenses/by-sa/2.0>, via Wikimedia Commons;
https://commons.wikimedia.org/wiki/File:Maya_Chac_Mool_by_Luis_Alberto_Melograna.jpg

The Toltecs carved mesmerizing reliefs on walls, such as the "wall of serpents" in Tula, which was over one hundred feet long and depicted human skeletons and slithering snakes. The serpents appear to be eating the human bones, or the skeletons are emerging from their mouths. The skeletons might have represented revered ancestors, especially since the wall is just next to Pyramid B, which was dedicated to the city's rulers.

Skeletons, skulls, and human hearts seemed to pervade Toltec culture, with depictions of jaguars and eagles feeding on human hearts and skull racks of sacrificial victims.

The Aztecs

The Aztecs' flashy art and architecture were used as propaganda to exert political and cultural dominance over conquered regions. The Aztec myths depict them as wandering nomads from the northwestern deserts who entered the Valley of Mexico as a cultural blank slate. Descriptions of Aztlán, their mythical island of origin, talk about its natural beauty, not its architecture or art. The Aztec art and architecture were a hodgepodge of influences, mainly from the Toltecs, Teotihuacanos, and Mixtecs. They brought Mixtec and Zapotec artisans into Tenochtitlan and appropriated styles from other Mesoamericans. The city's sculptures, murals, and architecture were an incongruous mixture of styles.

Like the Mixtecs, the Aztecs built libraries of codices or pictorial books about history, religion, and administrative matters, such as tribute payments. They used amate paper made from the Ficus tree, with 480,000 sheets of paper provided as an annual tribute payment from forty towns in the Morelos area. The art in the codices was not as complex as the Mixteca codices, but both had artwork that was more representative than realistic.

The Mixtec artist community in Tenochtitlan produced exquisite pendants, earrings, and other jade, turquoise, amethyst, and gold jewelry. They also created stunning mosaic sculptures, such as a double-headed serpent carved from cedar and covered in "scales" of turquoise with a scarlet mouth and nose from the Spondylus spiny oyster. Its gleaming white fangs were cut from conch shells. The Aztecs had several serpent gods, such as the Fire Serpent, Feathered Serpent, and Cloud Serpent. This sculpture was probably Xiuhcoatl, the Fire Serpent (or Turquoise Snake).

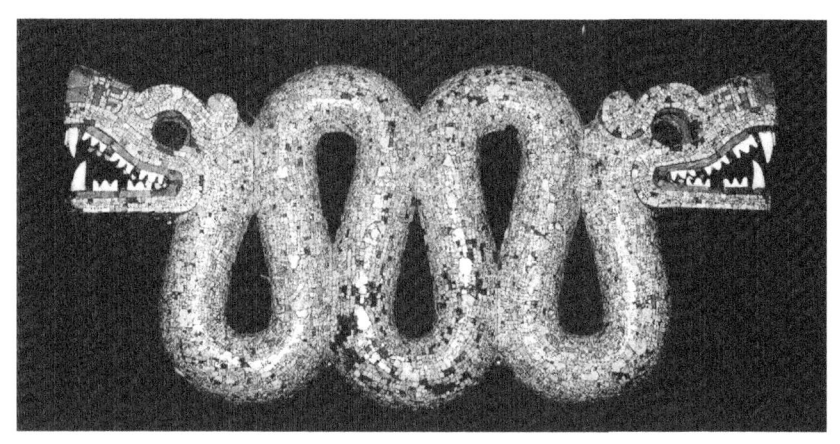

Double-headed serpent turquoise mosaic
British Museum, CC BY-SA 4.0 <https://creativecommons.org/licenses/by-sa/4.0>, via Wikimedia Commons; https://commons.wikimedia.org/wiki/File:Double_headed_turquoise_serpentAztecbritish_museum.jpg

The Aztec nobility and priests loved to drape themselves in featherwork clothing and headdresses. Their favorite feathers were from the emerald green and red quetzal birds of the rainforest. Moctezuma II had a zoo and botanical gardens just outside Tenochtitlan, where flamingos and other brilliantly colored birds produced feathers. Featherwork artisans, who had a designated neighborhood in Tenochtitlan, also created eye-catching mosaics from feather pieces.

Key Takeaways:
- Olmecs: Colossal heads, were-jaguar, jaguar masks, cave paintings
- Maya
    - Bright pigment for paint formed by chemical reaction
    - Architecture: causeways, pyramid grouping, cities portraying glyphs from above
- Zapotecs
    - Elaborate tombs with groups of funerary masks
    - Arrowhead building pointing to the Capella star
- Teotihuacan
    - Artwork impersonal and repetitive, promoting egalitarianism
    - Talud-tablero architecture in pyramids
- Mixtecs: master goldsmiths renowned for exquisite artistry
- Toltecs: chacmool and wall relief of serpents devouring human skeletons

- Aztecs
    - Appropriated styles from other cultures, especially Toltec and Mixtec
    - Used 480,000 sheets of paper from Morelos for pictorial codices and records
    - Featherwork clothing and mosaics

Chapter 14: Ancient Cities

Spectacular reminders of once-great civilizations cover Mexico's landscape, and lidar technology continues to locate the ruins of grand cities in the southern rainforests. Most of these archaeological sites are still being excavated and analyzed, with intriguing new secrets coming to light. Mexico has a diverse collection of stunning ancient cities, so let's explore several remarkable Maya cities and the multiethnic city of Teotihuacan.

Ek' Balam

One of Mexico's earliest cities, Ek' Balam, was founded about 300 BCE near the top of the Yucatán Peninsula. Its name means Black Jaguar or Jaguar Star. The city had a long history, but it dramatically declined in the Postclassic age. At the height of its power in the late Classic era, it was the capital of the Talol Kingdom, receiving tribute from the surrounding region, with roads leading out in all directions.

The city covered about ten square miles, with defensive walls surrounding over forty structures of temples and elite residences in the city's center. The religious and administrative centers were in two plazas on a north-south axis. Over forty inscriptions were carved or painted on the walls, giving historical information on its rulers in the 8th and 9th centuries. The enormous "Oval Palace" has rounded walls, a unique feature of three Maya cities in the Yucatán Peninsula (the other two are Tulum and Chichén Itza). Since only a fraction of the city has been excavated, new discoveries will shed more light on the city's history.

"Angels" or winged warriors on Ukit Kan Le'k Tok's ornate tomb.
Photo modified: zoomed in. Credit: Dennis Jarvis from Halifax, Canada, CC BY-SA 2.0 <https://creativecommons.org/licenses/by-sa/2.0>, via Wikimedia Commons; https://commons.wikimedia.org/wiki/File:Mexico-6147_-_Mayan_Angels_-_I_don%27t_think_so..._(4669701256).jpg

Ek' Balam's first king mentioned in inscriptions was Ukit Kan Le'k Tok, who ruled from 770 to 801 CE. He built the extravagant "acropolis," which was 90 feet high and 480 feet long, with stairways leading up its six stories. Within its fourth level is his well-preserved tomb behind an intricate frieze, sitting inside the colossal fangs of a gaping jaguar mouth. The elaborate stucco façade features geometrical motifs and unique angel-like winged warriors. Scholars debate the mystery of these winged men, which are not seen elsewhere in Mesoamerica. What do they represent?

Teotihuacan

A stupendous political and commercial empire, Teotihuacan was established about the same time as Ek' Balam and reached its zenith in the early Classic era. Its stunning ruins captured the imagination of the Aztecs and still amaze tourists today. Teotihuacan was the capital of the entire Valley of Mexico and controlled trade from the Gulf Coast to the Pacific Ocean and well into Central America. Its culture impacted most of central and southern Mexico, with its distinct architecture and artistry seen in Guatemala, Honduras, and Belize.

As a cosmopolitan metropolis with multiple ethnicities housed in over two thousand apartment compounds, Teotihuacan had unparalleled cultural and social diversity. The archaeological record shows that the Gulf Coast people, Maya, Oaxacan, and other immigrants sustained their cultural identity, albeit with some adjustments. The various ethnicities maintained strong links with their homelands, which bolstered Teotihuacan's trade monopoly.

Teotihuacan passed through several phases of religious and political upheaval. No archaeological evidence of human sacrifice exists for its first several centuries, at least not on a large scale or as a state ritual. The first known human sacrifice was at the dedication of the Feathered Serpent Pyramid, where about two hundred people were sacrificed between 150 and 200 CE.

The early layers of the Moon Pyramid did not show human sacrifice, but small numbers of humans were sacrificed during the renovations, which took place around 250 CE. At about the same time, child sacrificial victims were buried under the Sun Pyramid at each level. A large-scale massacre or human sacrifice of Maya immigrants occurred in the central Plaza of Columns around 350 CE. After this, human sacrifice seems to have diminished or ended at the state level, as no further sacrificial victims have been found in the archaeological record.

Teotihuacan pottery warrior.
Gary Todd, CC0, via Wikimedia Commons;
https://commons.wikimedia.org/wiki/File:Teotihuacan_Pottery_Warrior_Figure.jpg

In addition to the three great pyramids lining the main corridor, which the Aztecs called the Avenue of the Dead, the Xalla palace had a large pyramid encircled by four smaller pyramids. The smaller pyramids were dedicated to the rain god, the mountain god, the water goddess, and the fire god. Brilliant murals adorned the palace walls; however, it burned down around 550 CE in the revolt that spelled the beginning of Teotihuacan's collapse.

Chichén Itza

As Teotihuacan declined, the Maya city of Chichén Itza sprang up in the Yucatán Peninsula about forty miles southwest of Ek' Balam. Its variety of architectural styles suggests a multicultural population, similar to Teotihuacan. It might have received migrants from Teotihuacan and Maya cities once they declined in the late Classic era. Its archaeological record and legend of the priest Zamná point to a definite Toltec influence via several waves of immigrants.

Chichén Itza reached its zenith from 900 to 1000 CE as the political capital of the central and northern Yucatán. Its vast trade empire stretched into central Mexico and down to southern Central America via its Isla Cerritos port on the Yucatán's northern coast. Chichén Itza experienced two distinct periods of growth. The first was mainly Maya architecture from 800 to 1000, followed by a partial collapse due to a severe one-hundred-year drought. As rainfall resumed and the Toltecs migrated in, a second wave of construction continued, lasting from 1100 to 1200.

In 1527, Spain attempted to conquer the Yucatán. The Maya brutally defeated and destroyed most Spanish forces in the first campaign. In 1532, the Spaniards tried to gain control of the central Yucatán by defeating Chichén Itza. They were initially successful, but the Maya launched a counterattack within months, driving most Spaniards from the peninsula in 1535. It would take another fifty years for the Spaniards to gain a shaky hold on the Yucatán, and only then because three epidemics had killed half the Maya population.[45]

Xochicalco

Sixty miles southwest of today's Mexico City, Xochicalco rose to power as Teotihuacan faded, growing to a population of about twenty thousand. Although a settlement had existed for centuries, it grew into a city when the Maya Olmeca-Xicalanca from Campeche arrived around 650 CE. Some Teotihuacanos probably migrated to Xochicalco since its architecture features a Maya and Teotihuacan blend with a bit of Zapotec and Gulf Coast influence.

The Xochicalco people maintained their calendar's accuracy by cutting a hole in a cave in the hillside through which the sun shone directly to the floor twice a year in mid-May and late July. The Pyramid of the Plumed Serpents featured gently sloping talud-tablero walls surrounding an open-air courtyard rather than reaching a peak. The entire outer surface of the walls is covered with mesmerizing carvings of writhing feathered serpents coiling around the cross-legged "Lords of Time" priests.

---

[45] Georges Frey, "The Endless Conquest of Yucatán," *Popular Archaeology*, January 14, 2022.

Priests sit inside the Plumed Serpent's undulating coils on Xochicalco's pyramid.
Arian Zwegers from Brussels, Belgium, CC BY 2.0 <https://creativecommons.org/licenses/by/2.0>, via Wikimedia Commons; https://commons.wikimedia.org/wiki/File:Xochicalco,_Temple_of_the_Feathered_Serpent,_Maya_ruler_(20498593528).jpg

The hilltop city was an architectural masterpiece with retaining walls and terraces creating platforms linked by staircases and ramps. Defensive walls encircled the lower residential area, while the middle level featured a marketplace, ballcourt, palace, and elite residences. At the top of the hill were temples, pyramids, another ballcourt, and a large rainwater cistern. Raiders sacked and burned Xochicalco around 900 CE despite its formidable defense system. Three centuries later, the Tlahuica-Aztecs resettled the city as a lucrative cotton-growing and paper-producing center.

Uxmal

Uxmal (meaning "built three times") was another Maya Yucatán city in the Puuc ("hill") region about one hundred miles west of its sister city, Chichén Itza. It was built in 500 CE by the long-lived Xiu dynasty and was the western Yucatán's most powerful city by 850, which was when most of its monumental buildings were erected. Conflict with the Toltecs who migrated to the region, compounded by the great drought, resulted in Uxmal's decline around 1100. The Xiu dynasty relocated to Maní, about twenty-five miles east.

The Maya built Uxmal to align with the rising and setting of Venus on auspicious calendar dates. Like Xochicalco, the city's architects had to contend with hilly terrain. The main ceremonial buildings had two stories. The first layer was punctuated by doorways with sculptures of the rain god Chaac over them. Lavish carvings and stone mosaics covered the second layer, with more images of Chaac at the corners.

Uxmal's ceremonial center has survived in good condition for over a millennium thanks to its expertly cut stones mortared with concrete. Uxmal's Pyramid of the Magician has rounded sides rather than sharp corners and was probably the earliest ceremonial building, built around 500 CE and expanded through the years. How did it get its name? One legend says that the magician god Itzamná erected it in one night. Another story is that a dwarf who hatched from an egg built the pyramid overnight through his mother's sorcery and became Uxmal's new king.

Tulum

Tulum sits on a bluff overlooking the Caribbean Sea in today's state of Quintana Roo. It was the last city built by the Yucatán Maya, with the surviving buildings constructed between 1200 and 1400 CE, although one stela and Building Fifty-nine date to the Classic era. Building Fifty-nine, the Temple of Nauyaca, is a modest one-story shrine outside the city's walls and close to the shore. It might have served as the ceremonial center for villages in the region before the city's construction.

The people of Tulum worshiped Ah Muzen Cab, the descending or diving god (or the bee god). Its image is carved into many of the city's ceremonial buildings. Tulum's seaside location made it a powerful contender in sea trade, especially with obsidian. Towering forty feet above the sea, this was one of the cities that astonished the early Spanish explorers who had not yet seen large buildings and complex cities in the New World.

El Castillo in Tulum.
Amber Funderburk Vyn, CC BY-SA 4.0 <https://creativecommons.org/licenses/by-sa/4.0>, via Wikimedia Commons; https://commons.wikimedia.org/wiki/File:CastilloTulum.jpg

The parts of Tulum not protected by the sheer cliffs dropping to the sea were encircled by a twelve-foot-high, two-foot-thick defensive wall with watchtowers on the western corners. A cenote sinkhole provided drinking water. The El Castillo structure served as a temple to the Feathered Serpent, with carvings of the deity adorning the lintels. It also served as a navigational guide to incoming canoes at its busy trade port, marking a break in the reef and a spot where a gentle slope led up to the city between the steep cliffs. Small fires in the windows on the side facing the sea lit the way for maritime traders arriving by night.

Key Takeaways:
- Ek' Balam
    - Long-lived Maya city near the top of the Yucatán Peninsula; capital of Talol Kingdom
    - Known for exquisite stucco relief carvings (including winged warriors) on a tomb
- Teotihuacan
    - Political empire over Valley of Mexico; trade empire extending to Central America
    - Human sacrifice at the state level from 150 to 350 CE
- Chichén Itza
    - Multicultural population and vast trade empire
    - Engaged in a long war against Spaniards
- Xochicalco
    - A blend of Maya and Teotihuacan architectural influence on the hilltop city
    - Fell to raiders around 900 CE, resettled in 1200 by Aztecs
- Uxmal
    - Built and ruled by the Xiu dynasty; it declined after Toltecs' arrival
    - Legend says the rounded Pyramid of the Magician was built in one night
- Tulum
    - Last city built by Yucatán Maya (between 1200 and 1400 CE)
    - Seaside trade center, with the El Castillo temple serving as a navigational guide

Chapter 15: Ancient Mythology and Cosmology

How did ancient Mexico's mythology and cosmology impact its history, art, and architecture? This chapter will explore the Mesoamerican understanding of the nature of the universe and how that influenced their belief system. The people of ancient Mexico believed the gods and other supernatural beings were intertwined with their everyday lives. Let's explore their myths, what their emblems revealed about their cosmology, some important rituals, and their understanding of the stars, planets, and eclipses.

Ancient Mexicans believed in mythological creatures that lived alongside humans and could bring good or evil their way. For example, the Yucatán Maya believed in leprechaun-like sprites called Aluxo'ob. They were usually invisible, but if people saw them, they looked like miniature Maya people about the size of a four-year-old child and wearing a loincloth. If the Maya heard weird noises at night, especially if they had just bought new land or were living in a new house, they said it was an Alux who was disturbed by the changes. The Maya also believed the Aluxo'ob could cause fevers and other health problems.

However, the Maya thought the Aluxo'ob mainly benefited humans because they helped people live in harmony with nature. The creator god, Junab K'uj, gave humans the stewardship of nature as their responsibility. After death, people could only make their way to heaven from the underworld if they had a proper relationship with nature in their lifetime.

The Aluxo'ob protected the fields and also lived in the jungles and caves.

When people respected the Aluxo'ob and gave them offerings, the sprites protected them. If a farmer built a little house in his fields, an Alux would move in and look after his land. It chased off animals or humans that would steal the crops and ensured plentiful rainfall. But at the end of seven years, the Alux would go berserk, causing all sorts of mischief, so the farmer had to seal it inside the little house.

The people of Chiapas believed that gigantic jaguar-like monsters with long, white beards called the Dzulum preyed on women, so they depended on the Balam to protect them. The Balam were shapeshifting, black panthers that guarded the four points of a village. Although magical, the Balam were mortal, as were the Dzulum. Monkeys were also useful in driving off the Dzulum monsters, as they would howl and harass the creatures until they left.

Nahual (or nagual) were humans with the unique ability to shapeshift, although they could only turn into one other animal, not multiple types of creatures. The Mesoamericans believed each person had a "tonal" animal intricately connected to them that could give them special powers (good and evil) and insight into spiritual things. People needed special training to learn how to shapeshift and usually used "magic mushrooms" or other hallucinogens to unlock their powers.

According to the Florentine Codex, the Aztecs believed the atotolin, the white pelican, ruled the rest of the birds. If a person tried to kill a white pelican, it would float in the middle of the lake, giving the person four days to try to shoot it. At sunset on the fourth day, the pelican would cry out, calling the wind, and the water would foam up as all the pelicans squawked and beat their wings. The human's arms froze, so he could not pole his boat, and the water would suck him in, drowning him. If a person managed to shoot a white pelican in the first four days, he would cut open the bird's gut and inspect the gizzard. If the hunter found a jade stone or precious feathers, it meant he would have good fortune, but if he found a piece of charcoal, it meant he would die.

In Aztec mythology, Cipactli was a primordial sea demon, something like a crocodile with multiple mouths, but it was also part fish and part toad. The myth of Cipactli preceded the Aztecs, as the Maya and Olmecs also believed in a crocodilian deity. The gods who created Cipactli realized it would devour the rest of creation with its insatiable appetite, so Tezcatlipoca and Quetzalcoatl caught it, although it ate Tezcatlipoca's foot. They hacked the creature to pieces, forming the heavens from its head, the earth from its midsection, and the underworld from its tail.

Quetzalcoatl and Tezcatlipoca from the Codex Borbonicus.
https://commons.wikimedia.org/wiki/File:Quetzalcoatl_and_Tezcatlipoca.jpg

The Aztecs and most ancient Mesoamericans believed that the world lay in utter darkness in the beginning and was covered by water. The god and goddess Tonacatecuhtli (Sky Father) and Tonacacihuatl (Earth Mother), who held first place in the calendar, created everything else: the stars, mountains, animals, and the other gods. But their first try at creating the earth failed, as the sun was too weak, so the god Tezcatlipoca became the sun. But his brother Quetzalcoatl got jealous and knocked him out of the sky, ending the first world.

In the second creation, Quetzalcoatl was the sun, but Tezcatlipoca got his revenge by blowing all the people off the earth and Quetzalcoatl out of the sky. The third time around, Tlaloc, the rain god, became the sun, but Quetzalcoatl got jealous again and burned up the earth and the sun. The surviving humans became turkeys. Tlaloc's wife, Chalchiuhtlicue, reigned as the sun in the fourth world. Unfortunately, all she knew how to do was make rain, so she drowned all the turkeys and covered the world with a great flood. Even the mountains were underwater.

The gods gathered at Teotihuacan, which the Aztecs believed was where the gods were born. Jealousy and foolishness had destroyed the first four ages: earth, wind, fire, and water. Quetzalcoatl and Tezcatlipoca were ashamed of how they had ruined the world multiple times and promised not to mess things up in the fifth world. They pushed the sky back up, separating it from the earth below. As the gods sat around a great bonfire, they decided that one of them would have to jump into the bonfire to become the next sun. The handsome god Tecciztecatl volunteered but couldn't work up the nerve to jump into the fire. He tried four times but stopped at the last minute.

The smallest and ugliest god, Nanahuatl, looked on in exasperation. He suddenly ran forward and jumped into the flames. After a few minutes, a bright light lit up the sky. It was Nanahuatl, now Tonatiuh, the sun of the fifth world. Tecciztecatl was disgusted with himself for letting the humble god Nanahuatl outshine him. He leaped into the fire, and everyone looked up to see two suns. One of the gods thought this was improper, so he lobbed a rabbit up at Tecciztecatl, dimming his light so that he became the moon with the image of a rabbit on it.

The Codex Chimalpopoca tells of the great flood that covered the mountains in the fourth world when Chalchiuhtlicue was making so much rain. Before it happened, the god Tezcatlipoca warned a man and his wife, Nata (or Tata) and Nena, to hollow out a giant cypress log and go inside it when the waters began to rise. He told them to take some ears of corn but not to eat anything else. But when the waters receded, there were fish everywhere, which Nata and Nena roasted and ate. When Tezcatlipoca smelled the smoke, he came down to see them eating the fish after he told them only to eat corn. He turned the couple into two dogs.

Once the gods successfully began the fifth world with the new sun and moon, they needed to recreate humans. Quetzalcoatl set off to Mictlán, the Aztec underworld, to bring back some of the bones of the earlier humans, many of whom had died because of his diabolical jealousy. The Aztecs considered bones the equivalent of seeds, which meant they could grow new people. He went with his brother Xolotl, the evening star, who knew the way to Mictlán, while Quetzalcoatl, the morning star, knew the way back.

The brothers cautiously approached Mictlantecuhtli, the Lord of the Dead, sitting on his throne surrounded by bones, spiders, and owls. Quetzalcoatl politely asked for some bones, but Mictlantecuhtli was unwilling until Quetzalcoatl explained that he was only borrowing them. Since humans were mortal, the bones would return to the underworld when the people died. The Lord of Death appeared to give permission, but on the way out, Quetzalcoatl fell into a pit that the devious Mictlantecuhtli had prepared to trap him. The bones shattered, but Quetzalcoatl quickly scooped them back into his bag and raced out. He and the other gods stabbed themselves and sprinkled their blood on the bones in penance for their sins that had destroyed the previous worlds. The bones were resurrected, but because they were broken, the new humans came in all shapes and sizes.

A replica of the Sun Stone painted in its original colors.
en:User:Ancheta Wis, CC BY-SA 2.5 <https://creativecommons.org/licenses/by-sa/2.5>, via Wikimedia Commons;
https://commons.wikimedia.org/wiki/File:Aztec_Sun_Stone_Replica_cropped.jpg

The various civilizations of ancient Mexico had key emblems that represented their concept of cosmology. One example is the Aztec Sun Stone, a twelve-foot-wide circular stone with carvings depicting the Mexica-

Aztec cosmology. Sometimes called the Calendar Stone, it has rays like the sun radiating out with a gruesome face with a protruding tongue in the center. Instead of hands, the creature has claws on each side. Although scholars debate who he is, most believe it is the sun god Tonatiuh. The disk represents the Aztec concept of the origin of the cosmos: the five "suns" or eras of the world before the gods finally succeeded. Tonatiuh, the sun of the fifth world, is in the center of the disk, surrounded by four images representing the four earlier worlds.

One implication of the Sun Stone is that the gods Tonatiuh and Tecciztecatl willingly sacrificed themselves to become the sun and the moon. Thus, humans should voluntarily feed the gods by sacrificing themselves. Around Tonatiuh's face and the symbols representing the previous worlds is a band of glyphs representing the twenty days in one month of the Aztec calendar. At the bottom of the disk are two fire serpents facing each other, representing time.

The Maya worshiped many of the same gods (with different names) that the Teotihuacanos, Toltecs, Aztecs, and other civilizations worshiped. They also believed in animism, the concept that animals, plants, and even inanimate things like rocks had a spirit. Thus, everything in nature was sacred to them. The Maya believed the world was a flat square and that four gods on each corner watched over the earth and protected it.

The thirteen layers of heaven were above the earth, and under the earth was Xibalba, nine layers of cold and unhappiness. Dead people had to work their way up through each layer before reaching the heavens. However, women who died in childbirth or people who were human sacrifices went straight to heaven. Everyone else had to follow the roots of the sacred Tree of Life up to its branches that spread out in the heavens. The gods also used the Tree of Life to travel from the heavens to earth and the underworld and back again, representing life's unending cycle.

The Aztecs had a similar concept of the heavens and the underworld, but they believed warriors killed in battle went straight to the eastern paradise, where they rested and recuperated for four years. After that, they were reincarnated as butterflies, eagles, hummingbirds, or owls. They believed that disabled people, lepers, people struck by lightning, and people who drowned went straight to the lowest level of heaven. This might have eased their consciences when they drowned babies as sacrifices to Tlaloc.

Elaborately costumed Maya priests perform rituals in this Bonampak fresco. *Photo zoomed in. Credit: Gary Todd from Xinzheng, China, CC0, via Wikimedia Commons; https://commons.wikimedia.org/wiki/File:Maya_Temple_of_the_Frescoes,_Bonampak,_Murals_Copied_by_Artist_Rina_Lazo_(9758814221).jpg*

The priests dressed in elaborate costumes at religious festivals every twenty days in the sacred calendar of the Maya and other Mesoamericans. Paintings of the festival costumes can be seen in the art of Teotihuacan, in the Mixtec codices, and in the artwork of the Maya, Aztecs, and other groups. Once they were attired in their headdresses, masks, and clothing decorated with feathers, shells, and body plates, their appearance transformed into deities, animals, or famous historical people. They acted out symbolic plays, illustrating the cosmology associated with the festival.

Every twenty years, the Maya observed the K'atun ceremony of inscribing the events of the past two decades, such as the kings and wars, on a stone pillar or slab (stela). This ritual has provided invaluable information that gives us a glimpse into Maya history from centuries ago. Another Maya ritual involved mirrors, which they believed were a portal to the underworld. The especially daring Maya used mirrors to communicate with demons, a risky practice that, according to them, might have ended with them being snatched into the underworld.

The Maya and other Mesoamericans carefully observed the night sky, recording lunar and solar eclipses and the movement of Venus. The Toltecs connected the feathered serpent deity Quetzalcoatl with Venus, and the Mixtecs associated him with Mercury. The Mixtecs associated their flower and crocodile goddesses with eclipses but also connected the crocodile goddess with the moon, as the Maya and Aztecs did. Their understanding of astrology and astronomy guided their decisions and lifestyles.

Key Takeaways:
- Supernatural creatures
  - Aluxo'ob: sprites that helped preserve the balance of nature but could be mischievous
  - Dzulum: bearded jaguar monster; the Balam (panther) and monkeys guarded against them
  - Nahual: humans who could shapeshift into their spirit animal
  - Atotolin: white pelicans; hunters used their gizzards for divination
  - Cipactli: primordial crocodile-like sea demon who threatened to consume everything
- Creation myth
  - World originally in darkness covered by water
  - Gods destroyed the first four suns by jealousy and infighting
  - A humble god jumped into a bonfire, creating the fifth world (today's world)
  - Quetzalcoatl brought bones back from the underworld to make new humans
- Flood myth in Codex Chimalpopoca
  - The flood covered mountains, but Tezcatlipoca warned a man and woman to save themselves in a log
  - They disobeyed him and ate fish, so he turned them into dogs
- Aztec Sun Stone: represented the creation of the first five worlds and time
- Layers of heaven and underworld with the Tree of Life connecting them to earth
- Religious festivals every twenty days; costumed priests acted out cosmological beliefs
- Astronomy and astrology were important as gods were associated with stars and eclipses

Chapter 16: Ancient Mexican Culture and Legacy

Ancient Mexico's culture was a rich array of art, architecture, written language, and religious beliefs. While each civilization had unique contributions, they all shared certain cultural aspects. These shared customs and values flowed from a legacy chain beginning with the Olmecs and other older cultures, subsequently impacting later cultures. Robust trade relations between civilizations led to an interchange of architecture, art, and religion.

How are art and architecture linked to cultural development? In ancient Mexico, art expressed the people's cosmology and understanding of the supernatural. Architecture conveyed religious and political themes, and art and architecture tracked historical events and cultural perspectives. In cities like Teotihuacan, with virtually no literary history, we rely on its art and architecture as a glimpse into its society, politics, religious beliefs, and the changes that shook the city. Even with a written history, such as the Mixtecs or Aztecs, art gives us a deeper understanding of what life was like for ordinary people, not just rulers, priests, and warriors.

Art and architecture can also be used as propaganda to mold public opinion and initiate social, political, and religious change. For instance, we never see artistic depictions of people bowing to their kings in Teotihuacan. The Teotihuacanos didn't glorify their rulers through art. They did paint murals and carved images of their deities, and we see numerous examples of priests offering sacrifices to the gods. But most paintings of warriors or ordinary people show little distinction, almost like repetitive images on wallpaper.

Teotihuacan architecture also seemed to broadcast a message. The city had massive pyramids of several gods in its center, but most of the metropolis consisted of over two thousand apartment complexes, relatively equal in design. From this, archaeologists glean that, for at least part of its history, Teotihuacan promoted a collective society led by a council rather than a hierarchal system ruled by a king. Equality between individuals was promoted in Teotihuacan's art and architecture.

The Aztecs also used architecture for political and religious propaganda. As they conquered new territories, spreading their empire from the Pacific Ocean to the Gulf Coast, they permitted their new subjects to continue worshiping their traditional deities. However, they had to honor the Aztec chief deity, Huitzilopochtli, as the highest deity. To emphasize this, the Aztecs built majestic temples to Huitzilopochtli, god of the sun and war, on mountaintops and in the city centers of their new territories.

Additionally, the Aztecs used art and architecture in their capital of Tenochtitlan to promote the worship of Huitzilopochtli and tell his story. The highest pyramid in Tenochtitlan was the Templo Mayor, which symbolized Mount Coatepec, the hill in the middle of their ancestral island of Aztlán. According to Aztec myth, when Huitzilopochtli's siblings discovered their mother was pregnant with him, his four hundred brothers, led by his sister Coyolxauhqui, attacked her.

Huitzilopochtli spurted out of his mother's belly, fully grown, and sliced his sister's head off. Her body tumbled to the bottom of the hill, breaking into pieces, while Huitzilopochtli killed his brothers and ate their hearts. In 1978, a massive stone was uncovered at the foot of the Templo Mayor's stairs, which depicted Coyolxauhqui with her head and limbs severed from her body. Over ten feet in diameter, the stone's location at the bottom of the model of Mount Coatepec symbolized the story of her gruesome end at the hands of her brother.

Coyolxauhqui's dismembered body on a replica of the Templo Mayor stone.
*Photograph by Mike Peel (www.mikepeel.net)., CC BY-SA 4.0
<https://creativecommons.org/licenses/by-sa/4.0>, via Wikimedia Commons;
https://commons.wikimedia.org/wiki/File:Templo_Mayor_2015_007.jpg*

The civilizations of ancient Mexico didn't arise and develop in a vacuum. They inherited a rich legacy from the cultures that preceded them, and even the oldest complex civilizations interacted with other cultures. This legacy chain began in places like the Guilá Naquitz Cave near Mitla in the Oaxaca Valley, where sophisticated agriculture began in Mexico around 6000 BCE. The cave contained seeds for squash, corn, and beans, which comprised the Three Sisters planting system that spread throughout Mexico and the rest of North America.

Ceramics emerged in ancient Mexico about three hundred miles west of Mitla at Puerto Marqués and La Zanja in Guerrero, possibly dating as early as 2400 BCE. The Mokaya people of Paso de la Amada in the state of Chiapas were the first to build large-scale architecture, including Mexico's first-known ballcourt around 1650 BCE. The ballcourt became an essential feature in most other prominent cultures of ancient Mexico.

The Olmecs began using the 260-day ceremonial calendar by 800 BCE, which the rest of ancient Mexico's advanced civilizations adopted. The earliest known writings in Mexico were simple glyphs carved into the Cascajal Block by the Olmecs in the 10th century BCE. The Maya began using pictorial glyphs about 900 BCE. The Zapotecs of Monte Albán developed hieroglyphics in the logo-syllabic system around 500 BCE, and the Maya started using sophisticated hieroglyphics by 300.

By then, the Epi-Olmecs had developed the Isthmian script as seen on a pottery shard in Chiapa de Corzo on the Pacific coast. Although the Isthmian script had structural similarities to Mayan and Zapotec hieroglyphics, all three writing systems developed independently. They all used pictorial symbols or logograms for nouns and some verbs, and they used phonetic symbols for sounds, but each culture wrote the symbols differently.

Intriguingly, this literary legacy did not spread to other ancient Mexican civilizations as quickly as would be expected. Teotihuacan and the Toltec capital of Tula only show evidence of simple glyphs, despite being influential cities with copious interactions with the literate Maya and Zapotecs. The Mixtecs adopted the logographic system used by the Zapotecs in the Postclassic era, and the Aztecs also copied a variant of the Zapotec script.

The Maya left stunning contributions in art and architecture to the legacy chain passed down to other cultures in Mexico. Some Maya innovations in architecture included extraordinarily steep and high pyramids, pyramids with rounded sides, multi-story buildings, the corbelled arch, and corbelled roofing. A distinguishing feature of Maya architecture is that non-religious buildings were often as ornate as temples. The Maya loved to cover the exterior of buildings with intricate carvings and relief work.

Murals were a favorite of the Maya, a love they adopted from the Olmecs. In Calakmul, at the base of the Yucatán, they had a painted pyramid covered with panels of murals dating to around 600 to 700 CE.

The vivid paintings showed ordinary people rather than the usual kings, priests, or warriors. About one-third of the images were of women, who were rarely depicted in Maya or other Mesoamerican art. Hieroglyphics next to the murals served as captions explaining some of the scenes: preparing corn porridge, offering tamales to eat, and spooning tobacco from a jar. They provide a vivid picture of how non-elite Maya went about their days and what they wore and consumed.

Calakmul's painted pyramid shows maize brew being prepared and served. Bernard DUPONT, CC BY-SA 2.0 <https://creativecommons.org/licenses/by-sa/2.0>, via Wikimedia Commons; https://commons.wikimedia.org/wiki/File:Reproduction_of_Mural_from_Structure_I,_Calakmul.jpg

While the Maya innovated, the Mexica-Aztecs assimilated. As the newcomers to central Mexico, they arrived after wandering the northwestern deserts for decades. They paused in Tula for twenty years to absorb the majestic culture of the nearly abandoned Toltec city. They passed through the ghost town of Teotihuacan, which was even more breathtaking than Tula. They also wandered around the Lake Texcoco system and hired themselves out as workers and soldiers to the other tribes in the area, gathering more cultural information. When they settled Tenochtitlan and established their empire, they imported Mixtec goldsmiths and scribes, the latter of whom wrote the codices that filled their libraries.

The Mexica-Aztecs assimilated Quetzalcoatl, Tlaloc, and other deities from the tribes around them, but they clung to their hummingbird god Huitzilopochtli. They adopted Toltec art and sculptures like the chacmool and the serpent wall in Tula. They learned writing from the Mixtecs and adopted the Mesoamerican calendar. They studied Teotihuacan's architecture and traveled there to offer sacrifices.

Ancient Mexico had several primary language families. Mayan was the language family of the independent Maya city-states scattered throughout southern Mexico and Central America. The Zapotecs, Mixtecs, and Otomi spoke the Otomanguean languages. The people of Veracruz, Puebla, and Hidalgo spoke the Totonacan languages. Nahuatl was the language of the Aztec tribes, the Chichimeca, and probably the Toltecs.

Teotihuacan was a multilingual city, with the Otomanguean languages, Mayan, and Totonacan languages all being spoken. Teotihuacan probably used a northern variant of the Otomanguean language as its dominant administrative language. In the late Classic era, as the Chichimeca tribes migrated south, they brought the Nahuatl language with them. Nahuatl soon became the lingua franca (common language) of the Valley of Mexico.

How did religious belief develop in ancient Mexico? Some scholars believe that central and southern Mexico had one religion expressed in several ways by the Olmecs, Maya, Teotihuacanos, and Zapotecs. This core cosmology was passed on to the Mixtecs, Toltecs, and Aztecs. Other scholars argue that each major civilization had a different belief system yet exchanged ideas with other cultures and developed a syncretism or blend of beliefs.

Clearly, the primary cultures of ancient Mexico shared common religious ideas. They all followed the 260-day sacred calendar and believed the world was originally covered by water and darkness before the present age. They all worshiped the feathered serpent deity and believed he was involved in creation. They also all worshiped the rain deity as a primary god and sacrificed children to him. They all practiced human sacrifice, but the Toltecs and Aztecs remembered a time when they did not sacrifice humans. They believed that people went to one of heaven's levels or to the underworld when they died.

The 260-day sacred calendar, human sacrifice, the Feathered Serpent, and the rain deity all track back to the Olmecs. However, the Olmec rain god was a were-jaguar, not the goggle-eyed fanged creature worshiped by the later cultures of ancient Mexico. The Maya rain god Chaac did not always have goggle eyes, but he did have fangs. He had a human-like body with reptilian scales and a drooping nose that covered his mouth.

Chaak, the Maya rain god.
Gary Todd, CC0, via Wikimedia Commons;
https://commons.wikimedia.org/wiki/File:Chaak_Vessel,_Mayapan,_Post_Classic,_1250-1450_AD.jpg

Despite not having pack animals and sailing technology, long-distance trade flourished in ancient Mexico. In the Classic era, Teotihuacan was a massive market hub with trade networks extending from the Pacific to the Gulf Coast and deep into Central America. Their most vital trade partners were the Maya. Teotihuacan had a near-monopoly on the obsidian trade, which they exchanged for luxury goods, such as exotic feathers, chocolate, and jade.

Hundreds of years later, the Aztecs of Tenochtitlan controlled most of the trade within central and southern Mexico. The *pochteca*, or merchants, even had a god of commerce called Yacatecuhtli. The robust trade networks of ancient Mexico carried technical information, such as farming techniques and metalworking. Religious ideas were shared, and innovative ideas about art and architecture spread. Flourishing trade indelibly impacted ancient Mexico's legacy chain of culture and technology.

Key Takeaways:

- How are art and architecture linked to cultural development?
    - Art and architecture give a glimpse into cultural development within cultures.

- o Art and architecture can be used as propaganda to promote cultural change or impose political and religious ideology.
• A legacy chain of the older and later cultures of ancient Mexico
    - o Sophisticated agriculture, ceramics, and ballcourt developed in western Mexico
    - o Olmecs and Maya used first simple glyphs
    - o Zapotecs used the first sophisticated hieroglyphics, followed by Maya and Epi-Olmecs
    - o Mixtecs and Aztecs adopted the Zapotec writing system
• Factors that influenced the legacy chain or were influenced by it
    - o Maya legacy of art and architecture; Aztec assimilation of multiple cultures
    - o Language development and adoption of different languages
    - o Developments in religious belief
    - o The impact of trade relations between civilizations

Conclusion

The legacies of ancient Mexico endured through the colonial era and continue to shape modern-day Mexico. If not for its ancient civilizations, would Mexico be the nation it is today? Would our world be the same?

The Olmecs introduced many "firsts" to Mexico and the world. By 1700 BCE, the Olmecs were roasting cacao beans to make a chocolate drink, which became wildly popular among the elite in Mexico. The Spaniards introduced chocolate to Europe in the early 1500s, and soon, shipments of cacao beans were traveling from Veracruz to Spain, where hot cocoa became a court delicacy. Today, people consume 7.5 million tons of chocolate products worldwide.

The Olmecs and Maya began using simple pictorial glyphs around 900 BCE, and by 500 BCE, the Zapotecs developed complex hieroglyphics with symbols for nouns and sounds. The Maya, Epi-Olmecs, Mixtecs, and Aztecs subsequently developed written languages. This literacy meant a sizable portion of ancient Mexico's history was preserved.

The Franciscan friars thought the indigenous people would be more open to Christianity if they introduced it in their languages. The friars learned Nahuatl, converted it to the Latin alphabet, then taught the young men to read their language with the alphabet. The Franciscan friars interviewed the indigenous people about their culture and history and read their codices. Fray Bernardino de Sahagún translated the Gospels and the Psalms into Nahuatl and recorded the Aztec culture and history in the Florentine Codex. Fray Diego Durán wrote the Durán Codex or the *Historia de las Indias de Nueva España* in 1581, translating from the

Aztec documents.

The Dominican friars challenged Sahagún and Durán, considering all aspects of the indigenous peoples' culture evil, including their language. The Dominicans destroyed priceless codices and artifacts to impose Spanish culture. But some of Mexico's ancient history was preserved thanks to the Franciscans. The ancient languages survived, with 1.5 million people speaking Nahuatl today and 4.5 million Mexicans speaking other indigenous languages.

Both the Franciscans and Dominicans were pleased when the indigenous people quickly agreed to be baptized as Catholics. They didn't realize that most simply added the Virgin Mary and Jesus to their polytheistic system. The Aztecs had imposed the worship of Huitzilopochtli on the conquered people of Mexico while allowing them to keep their own gods. They were used to this system and merely added Catholicism into the mix. However, they did discard Huitzilopochtli altogether, along with human sacrifice.

Some of the religious practices of ancient Mexico have continued up to the present day in a syncretistic blend with Catholic Christianity. For instance, the Aztec descendants in northern Veracruz worship Ometotiotsij, the ancient Aztec god Ometeotl. Also known as the Sky Father Tonacatecuhtli, he and his wife Tonacacihuatl (Earth Mother) created the universe and the rest of the gods in ancient Mexican cosmology.

The Day of the Dead, celebrated throughout today's Mexico, originated in an Aztec festival celebrating Mictlantecuhtli and Mictecacihuatl, Lord and Lady of the Underworld. Some indigenous people in the Puebla region worship the "Solar Christ," whom they associate with the sun god Tonatiuh. Many Mexicans believe the ancient Aztec mother earth goddess Tonantzin is Our Lady of Guadalupe (the Virgin Mary). The Basilica of Guadalupe was built over a temple to Tonantzin in today's Mexico City.

While inventing chocolate, the Olmecs also mixed sap from the rubber tree and morning glory vines to make rubber balls. This invention led to the game of ulama, which quickly impacted the rest of central and southern Mexico, where over two thousand ancient ballcourts have been unearthed. Ulama is still played today in Sinaloa, Mexico, making it the longest continuously played sport in history. When the Spaniards showed up three thousand years later, they were delighted by the rubber balls and the ulama game. Cortés sent a ball team with bouncy balls to perform for King Charles in 1528.

Over the centuries, the Europeans experimented with rubber, forming erasers in 1770, rubber raincoats in 1824, and shoe soles and bicycle tires in the 1880s. In 1856, Charles Goodyear invented soccer balls made from vulcanized rubber. Before this, teams used pig bladders to play a prototype of soccer (football), similar to the Mexican ulama game. The main difference was that the ball could touch the ground and be kicked with the feet. In ulama, the players hit the ball with their heads, elbows, legs, and hips to keep it in the air and in play. Today, football (or soccer in the US) is Mexico's number one sport and the most popular game globally, thanks to the Olmecs and their bouncy balls.

Many of the Spanish colonists of Mexico were single men, or they left their wives behind. They took indigenous women as their wives or mistresses, who gave birth to *mestizo* children. In today's Mexico, 93 percent of the population are at least partially descended from the ancient people of Mexico, and 15 percent are fully indigenous. The legacy of ancient Mexico lives on through its people.

If you enjoyed this book, a review on Amazon would be greatly appreciated because it would mean a lot to hear from you.

To leave a review:
1. Open your camera app.
2. Point your mobile device at the QR code.
3. The review page will appear in your web browser.

Thanks for your support!

Here's another book by Enthralling History that you might like

Free limited time bonus

Stop for a moment. We have a free bonus set up for you. The problem is this: we forget 90% of everything that we read after 7 days. Crazy fact, right? Here's the solution: we've created a printable, 1-page pdf summary for this book that you're reading now. All you have to do to get your free pdf summary is to go to the following website:

https://livetolearn.lpages.co/enthrallinghistory/

Or, Scan the QR code!

Once you do, it will be intuitive. Enjoy, and thank you!

Works Cited

Anthony, Dani. "Bartolomé de las Casas and 500 Years of Racial Injustice." *Origins: Current Events in Historical Perspective*, https://origins.osu.edu/milestones/july-2015-bartolom-de-las-casas-and-500-years-racial-injustice?language_content_entity=en. Accessed 18 August 2023.

"Aztec Civilization." *National Geographic Society*, 19 May 2022, https://education.nationalgeographic.org/resource/aztec-civilization/. Accessed 30 July 2023.

"Benito Juárez." *New World Encyclopedia*, https://www.newworldencyclopedia.org/entry/Benito_Ju%C3%A1rez. Accessed 18 September 2023.

"Cacao in Olmec Society | Gastronomy Blog." *Boston University*, 20 July 2017, https://sites.bu.edu/gastronomyblog/2017/07/20/cacao-in-olmec-society/. Accessed 21 July 2023.

Cadava, Geraldo. "The Anarchist Who Authored the Mexican Revolution." *The New Yorker*, 5 October 2022, https://www.newyorker.com/books/under-review/the-anarchist-who-authored-the-mexican-revolution. Accessed 1 October 2023.

"The Calendar System." *Living Maya Time*, https://maya.nmai.si.edu/calendar/calendar-system. Accessed 25 July 2023.

Cervantes, Fernando. *Conquistadores: A New History of Spanish Discovery and Conquest*. Penguin Publishing Group, 2021.

Elliott, JH. *Aztec Triple Alliance 1998*, https://people.clas.ufl.edu/sgillesp/files/Aztec-Triple-Alliance-1998.pdf. Accessed 2 August 2023.

Fehrenbach, T. R. *Fire And Blood: A History Of Mexico*. Hachette Books, 1995.

Grove, David C. *Discovering the Olmecs: An Unconventional History*. University of Texas Press, 2014.

Handwerk, Brian. "Discovery in Mexican Cave May Drastically Change the Known Timeline of Humans' Arrival to the Americas." *Smithsonian Magazine*, 22 July 2020, https://www.smithsonianmag.com/science-nature/when-did-humans-reach-america-mexican-mountain-cave-artifacts-raise-new-questions-180975385/. Accessed 9 July 2023.

Jansen, Maarten Evert Reinoud Gerard Nicolaas, and Gabina Aurora Pérez Jiménez. *Time and the Ancestors: Aztec and Mixtec Ritual Art*. Brill, 2017.

"Mexican War of Independence." *New World Encyclopedia*, https://www.newworldencyclopedia.org/entry/Mexican_War_of_Independence. Accessed 26 August 2023.

"Miguel Hidalgo y Costilla (1753-1811)." *Banco de México*, https://www.banxico.org.mx/banknotes-and-coins/miguel-hidalgo-costilla-bankn.html. Accessed 25 August 2023.

"Monumental Mexico – the art and culture of the Olmecs." *Minerva Magazine*, https://minervamagazine.com/monumental-mexico.html. Accessed 19 July 2023.

"Origins of Agriculture." *Archaeological Research in Oaxaca, Mexico*, https://sites.lsa.umich.edu/oaxaca-archaeology/origins-of-agriculture/. Accessed 13 July 2023.

Restall, Matthew. *When Montezuma Met Cortés: The True Story of the Meeting that Changed History*. HarperCollins, 2019.

Reyes, Raul A. "Our Lady of Guadalupe Is a Powerful Symbol of Mexican Identity." *NBC News*, 12 December 2016, https://www.nbcnews.com/news/latino/our-lady-guadalupe-powerful-symbol-mexican-identity-n694216. Accessed 25 August 2023.

Rugeley, Terry. *Epic Mexico: A History from Earliest Times*. University of Oklahoma Press, 2020.

Smith, Michael E. "The Aztecs Paid Taxes, Not Tribute." *Mexicon*, vol. 36, no. 1, 2014, pp. 19-22. *JSTOR*.

Taube, Karl. "Aztec and Maya civilizations are household names — but it's the Olmecs who are the 'mother culture' of ancient Mesoamerica." *University of California*, 9 June 2023, https://www.universityofcalifornia.edu/news/aztec-and-maya-civilizations-are-household-names-its-olmecs-who-are-mother-culture-ancient. Accessed 21 July 2023.

"To James Madison From William Davis Robinson, 28 December 1820." *Founders Online*, https://founders.archives.gov/documents/Madison/04-02-02-0165. Accessed 28 August 2023.

VandeCreek, Drew. "The Mexican-American War." *Northern Illinois University Digital Library*, https://digital.lib.niu.edu/illinois/lincoln/topics/mexicanwar. Accessed 9 September 2023.

"What's happening at the U.S.-Mexico border in 7 charts." *Pew Research Center*, 9 November 2021, https://www.pewresearch.org/short-reads/2021/11/09/whats-happening-at-the-u-s-mexico-border-in-7-charts/. Accessed 20 October 2023.

William, Robinson D. *Memoirs of the Mexican Revolution*. Lackington, Hughes, Harding, Mavor, and Lepard, 1821.

"Zapata Assassinated: April 10, 1919." *Catholic Textbook Project*, 3 April 2020, https://www.catholictextbookproject.com/post/zapata-assassinated-april-10-1919. Accessed 19 October 2023.

Blomster, J.P., and Chávez Salazar. "Origins of the Mesoamerican Ballgame: Earliest Ballcourt from the Highlands Found at Etlatongo, Oaxaca, Mexico." *Science Advances* 6, no. 11 (March 13, 2020). doi: 10.1126/sciadv.aay6964. PMID: 32201726; PMCID: PMC7069692.

Carballo, David M. *Urbanization and Religion in Ancient Central Mexico*. New York: Oxford University Press, 2016.

Carter, Robert F. "North America's First Shipyard." *The Military Engineer* 57, no. 379 (1965): 338-40. http://www.jstor.org/stable/44571688.

Coe, Michael D., Javier Urcid, Rex Koontz. *Mexico: From the Olmecs to the Aztecs*. New York: Thames & Hudson, September 17, 2019.

Coe, Michael D. *The Maya (Ancient Peoples and Places Series)*. London and New York: Thames & Hudson, 1999.

Cortés, Hernán. *Cartas y Relaciones de Hernán Cortés al Emperador Carlos V.* Edited by Pascual de Gayangos. Paris: A. Chaix, 1866.
https://www.cervantesvirtual.com/nd/ark:/59851/bmc0974782

Cowgill, George L. *Ancient Teotihuacan: Early Urbanism in Central Mexico (Case Studies in Early Societies)*. Cambridge: Cambridge University Press, 2015. Cowgill, George L. "State and Society at Teotihuacan, Mexico." *Annual Review of Anthropology* 26 (1997): 129-61. http://www.jstor.org/stable/2952518.

Demarest, Arthur. *Ancient Maya: The Rise and Fall of a Forest Civilization*. Cambridge: Cambridge University Press, 2004. ISBN 978-0-521-53390-4. OCLC 51438896.

Díaz del Castillo, Bernal. *The Conquest of New Spain*. Translated by J. M. Cohen. Harmondsworth, England: Penguin Books, 1963 [1632].

Elzey, Wayne. "A Hill on a Land Surrounded by Water: An Aztec Story of Origin and Destiny." *History of Religions*, 31, no. 2 (1991):105-49.
http://www.jstor.org/stable/1063021.

Evans, Susan T. *Ancient Mexico and Central America: Archaeology and Culture History*. London: Thames and Hudson, 2004.

Flannery, Kent V., and Joyce Marcus. "Las Sociedades Jerárquicas Oaxaqueñas y el Intercambio con los Olmecas." *Arqueología Mexicana*, 87, (2007): 71-76.

Frey, Georges. "The Endless Conquest of Yucatán." *Popular Archaeology*. January 14, 2022.

García-Des Lauriers, Claudia, ed. and Tatsuya Murakami, ed. Teotihuacan and Early Classic Mesoamerica: Multiscalar Perspectives on Power, Identity, and Interregional Relations. Louisville: University Press of Colorado, 2021.

Grennes-Ravitz, Ronald A., and G. H. Coleman. "The Quintessential Role of Olmec in the Central Highlands of Mexico: A Refutation." *American Antiquity* 41, no. 2 (1976): 196-206. https://doi.org/10.2307/279172.

Hassig, Ross. *Time, History, and Belief in Aztec and Colonial Mexico*. Austin: University of Texas Press, 2001.

Hassig, Ross. *War and Society in Ancient Mesoamerica*. Berkeley: University of California Press, 1992.

Headrick, Annabeth. *The Teotihuacan Trinity: The Sociopolitical Structure of an Ancient Mesoamerican City (The William and Bettye Nowlin Series in Art, History, and Culture of the Western Hemisphere)*. Austin: University of Texas Press, 2017.

Hipolito, Daniel Santos, and Jose Antonio Casanova Meneses. "Armas Mixtecas Acercan al Público al Arte de la Guerra entre los Mixtecos durante el Posclásico." *Instituto Nacional de Antropología e Historia* 36 (February 2018).
https://inah.academia.edu/DanielSantosHipolito

History and Mythology of the Aztecs: The Codex Chimalpopoca. Translated by John Bierhorst. Tucson: The University of Arizona Press, 1992.

Hirth, Kenneth G., David M. Carballo, and Barbara Arroyo. *Teotihuacan: The World Beyond the City*. Washington, D.C.: Dumbarton Oaks, 2020.

Holt Mehta, Haley. *Colonial Encounters, Creolization, and the Classic Period Zapotec Diaspora: Questions of Identity from El Tesoro, Hidalgo, Mexico*. PhD diss., Tulane University, 2019.

Hosler, Dorothy, Sandra Burkett, and Michael Tarkanian. "Prehistoric Polymers: Rubber Processing in Ancient Mesoamerica." *Science*. June 18, 1999, 1988-91. doi:10.1126/science.284.5422.1988. OCLC 207960606. PMID 10373117.

Houston, Stephen, and David Stuart. Stuart, David. "Of Gods, Glyphs, and Kings: Divinity and Rulership among the Classic Maya." *Antiquity* 70, no. 268 (1996): 289-312. doi:10.1017/S0003598X00083289.

Inomata, T, D., F. Triadan, F. Pinzón, and K. Aoyama. "Artificial Plateau Construction during the Preclassic Period at the Maya Site of Ceibal, Guatemala." *PLoS One*. 2019 Aug 30;14(8):e0221943. doi: 10.1371/journal.pone.0221943. PMID: 31469887; PMCID: PMC6716660

Joyce, Arthur A. "Interregional Interaction and Social Development on the Oaxaca Coast." *Ancient Mesoamerica*. 4, no. 1 (1993): 67-84. http://www.jstor.org/stable/26307326.

Kennedy, Alison Bailey. "Ecce Bufo: The Toad in Nature and in Olmec Iconography." *Current Anthropology* 23, no. 3 (1982): 273-90. http://www.jstor.org/stable/2742313.

Manzanilla, Linda R. "Cooperation and Tensions in Multi-ethnic Corporate Societies Using Teotihuacan, Central Mexico, as a Case Study." *Proceedings of the National Academy of Sciences*. 112, no.30 (March 2015): 9210-15. https://doi.org/10.1073/pnas.1419881112

Matthew, Laura E., and Michel R. Oudijk. *Indian Conquistadors: Indigenous Allies in the Conquest of Mesoamerica*. University of Oklahoma Press, October 22, 2012.

McVicker, Donald. "The 'Mayanized' Mexicans." *American Antiquity* 50, no. 1 (1985): 82-101. https://doi.org/10.2307/280635.

Miller, Mary Ellen. *The Art of Mesoamerica: From Olmec to Aztec (World of Art)*. Thames & Hudson, 2019.

Moran, Barbara. "Lessons from Teo." *The Brink: Boston University*, 2015. https://www.bu.edu/articles/2015/archaeology-teotihuacan-mexico/

Pasztory, Esther. *Teotihuacan: An Experiment in Living*. Norman: University of Oklahoma Press, 1997.

Pomar, Juan Bautista de. "Relación de Tezcoco," In *Relaciones de la Nueva España*, edited by Vázquez Chamorro. Madrid: Historia 16, 1991.

Powis T. G., A. Cyphers, N. W. Gaikwad, L. Grivetti, and K. Cheong. "Cacao Use and the San Lorenzo Olmec." *Proceedings of the National Academy of Sciences*, 108 (21) (2011): 8595-600, https://www.researchgate.net/publication/51110764_Cacao_Use_and_the_San_Lorenzo_Olmec

Pratt, John P. "Ixtlilxochitl's Toltec History," August 1, 2019, https://www.johnpratt.com/items/docs/2019/ixtlil.html

Recker, Jane. "Researchers Decipher the Glyphs on a 1,300-Year-Old Frieze in Mexico." *Smithsonian Magazine*, March 8, 2022. https://www.smithsonianmag.com/smart-news/researchers-decipher-the-glyphs-on-a-1300-year-old-frieze-in-mexico-180979691/

Robb, Matthew, ed. *Teotihuacan: City of Water, City of Fire*. Berkeley: University of California Press, 2017.

Sabloff, Jeremy A. "It Depends on How We Look at Things: New Perspectives on the Postclassic Period in the Northern Maya Lowlands." *Proceedings of the American Philosophical Society* 151, no. 1 (2007): 11-26. http://www.jstor.org/stable/4599041

Sahagún, Fray Bernardino de. *Historia General de las Cosas de Nueva España*. Edited by Francisco del Paso y Troncoso. Madrid: Fototipia de Hauser y Menet, 1905.

Schroeder, Susan, ed. *Chimalpahin's Conquest: A Nahua Historian's Rewriting of Francisco Lopez de Gomara's La conquista de Mexico*. Redwood City: Stanford University Press, 2010. https://doi.org/10.1515/9780804775069-184

Shook, Edwin M., and Alfred V. Kidder. "Mound E-III-3, K'aminaljuyu, Guatemala." In *Contributions to American Anthropology and History*, Vol. 9 (53) (1952): 33-127. Washington DC: Carnegie Institution of Washington.

Smith, Michael E., Abhishek Chatterjee, Angela C. Huster, Sierra Stewart, and Marion Forest. "Apartment Compounds, Households, and Population in the Ancient City of Teotihuacan, Mexico." *Ancient Mesoamerica* 30, no. 3 (2019): 399-418. doi:10.1017/S0956536118000573.

Smith, Michael E., and Kenneth G. Hirth. "The Development of Prehispanic Cotton-Spinning Technology in Western Morelos, Mexico." *Journal of Field Archaeology* 15 (1988): 349-358.

Spence, Lewis. *The Myths of Mexico and Peru*. London: George Harrap, 1913. https://www.sacred-texts.com/nam/mmp/index.htm

Sprajc, Ivan, Takeshi Inomata, and Anthony F. Aveni. "Origins of Mesoamerican Astronomy and Calendar: Evidence from the Olmec and Maya Regions." *Science Advances* 9, no. 1 (2023). doi:10.1126/sciadv.abq7675.

Sugiyama, Nawa, Saburo Sugiyama, and Alejandro Sarabia. "Inside the Sun Pyramid at Teotihuacan, Mexico: 2008–2011 Excavations and Preliminary Results." *Latin American Antiquity* 24, no. 4 (2013): 403-32. http://www.jstor.org/stable/23645621.

Taube, Karl A. "The Teotihuacan Cave of Origin: The Iconography and Architecture of Emergence Mythology in Mesoamerica and the American Southwest." RES: *Anthropology and Aesthetics*, no. 12 (1986): 51-82. http://www.jstor.org/stable/20166753.

Townsend, Richard F. *The Aztecs* (3rd, revised ed.). London: Thames & Hudson, 2009.

Printed in Great Britain
by Amazon